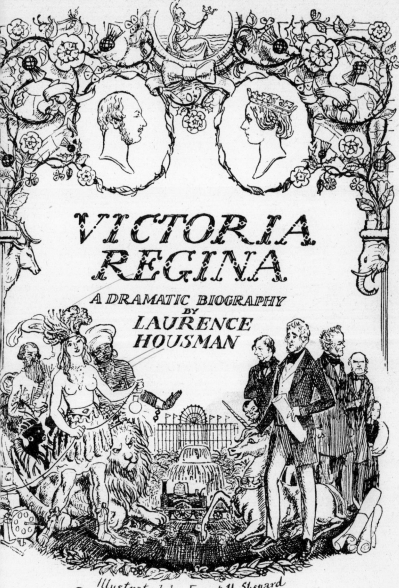

VICTORIA REGINA

A DRAMATIC BIOGRAPHY
BY
LAURENCE HOUSMAN

Illustrated by Ernest H. Shepard
Published by Charles Scribner's Sons, New York.

Printed in the United States of America

Contents

Preface

ENGLISH HISTORY has to its credit two Queens of great reputation—so great that each in turn gave her name to the age in which she lived. But there can be no doubt to-day which of the two mattered most to the life of the Nation, moulding it positively to her will in ways which, amid constant threat of danger, she knew to be wise. Elizabeth, more than anyone else during her reign, saved England. Even the defects and tortuosities of her character had their political value; for had she been more direct and forthright in her decisions, she might greatly have failed; and so uniquely indispensable was she during the most crucial period of her reign, that her downfall would, in all likelihood, have involved also the downfall of the Nation.

Can it be claimed for Queen Victoria that she, to any comparable extent, moulded history? In any positive sense, certainly not; but negatively she had a power, and a 'way with her,' the formidable weight of which has become more apparent since she resumed at Frogmore, under an effigy set back to date, association with that part and partnership of her reign to which she more naturally belonged.

As successive volumes of her letters and diaries are made public, with a frankness hitherto unexampled in the official editing of Royal remains, it becomes more and more evident that she was the mourning widow, not only

II

of a beloved and worthy Consort, but of a whole set of cherished notions, which in the 'sixties and 'seventies were already moribund, and are now finally dead and disposed of. Some of them may have been quite good notions in their day: but the moving spirit of the age decided against them; and the mind of Victoria was sedentary, and did not move. In the last two-thirds of her long reign, no reform of major importance was proposed, or carried by her Ministers, which did not rouse her suspicion or her hostility; and when the measure embodying those reforms became the subject of long and acrimonious debate, and of successive general elections, the Queen, behind the scenes, was putting her spoke into the wheel, hampering their advocates by her steady disapproval, and favouring their opponents. Her resistance to Gladstone's Home Rule policy took shady forms; and her favour of his Conservative opponents was so notorious that, when the result of the Election of 1895 became known, she received the effusive congratulations of her grandson, the Kaiser—an impropriety which she did not resent as much as her admirers might now wish.

My own memory of Victoria's reign does not go back farther than to the time when, emerging from the strict retirement which, in the 'sixties and early 'seventies, had threatened her popularity, she became the figure-head, or symbol, of that spectacular Imperialism which, with the Congress of Berlin and the Occupation of Egypt as its stepping-stones, culminated in the Boer War. But her attainment of that eminence was not due to any initiative of her own. It was not she who 'took occasion by the hand' —occasion took hers, and pushed her into a position which satisfied, more than it had ever been satisfied before, her sense of what Monarchy should look like. The rising

12

religion of Nationalism required a tutelary deity to crown its edifice; and the Queen, from the commanding position she already occupied, passed upwards by easy stages; and—the date falling fortunately during a period of national prosperity—in the year of her first Jubilee she became sacred. From that time on, she was regarded by the vast mass of her subjects as a divine institution, without flaw; and at the very time when she was behaving more unconstitutionally than ever before, intriguing against her Prime Minister behind his back, she acquired a reputation for constitutional correctness which was wholly undeserved. And her wrong-doing, so far as it was known, was not only condoned by her worshippers, it was approved. Though she was supposed to take no sides in politics, they were pleased with her for doing so; and her victims themselves conspired to conceal misdeeds and manœuvres which, if practised by herself a few decades earlier, or by any of her successors since, might have caused a vacancy upon the Throne. The loyalty and self-immolation of her sorely-tried Ministers was heroic; and they never got the credit for it till both her day and theirs were over. But to those who knew then, as much as we know now, of those ministerial difficulties, the complaint of her son and heir that though the compulsory day of mourning once a year made him accustomed to an everlasting Father, an everlasting Mother in addition was too much of a good thing—that complaint must have seemed to them less of a witticism than the statement of an unfortunate truth.

Queen Victoria, in her capacity of a reigning sovereign, lived too long; but until recent years it would have been blasphemy to say so. And yet, though she outstayed posterity's welcome from the political point of view, from the human she remains extraordinarily interesting and attractive; and her encumbering prejudices matter so little to-day that one can afford to enjoy them and see, through their intellectual limitations, what a remarkable and forceful character she was up to the last. Fuller knowledge, though it has destroyed a legendary figure, has given us a far more interesting personality. In the thirty-three years which have passed since her death, she has become a much more real character than the one which was fictitiously made known during her lifetime; and it is her own diary, with its accompaniment of letters and memoranda, which (like the diary of Pepys) has made the portrait so life-like. All those dottings of the 'i's,' those crossings of the 't's,' of which she was so profuse an exponent, indicate more than mere words could do the workings of an impetuous yet obstinate mind, ever busily setting its mark— three or four times in a single sentence—against the thing she reprobated, or would not allow! And though we are told that she knew when to yield to advice of which she disapproved, her mind was of the kind that could not change; and her imperious underlinings of quite unimportant words in her letters and diaries, were symptomatic of her social and political underlinings of things which to her mattered tremendously, but to the coming generation were going to matter very little.

But though a wise liberality over documents, dealing with the official side of her reign, has allowed her real character to become public property, her personality is still reckoned too sacred for the Censor to allow of its stage-representation. And since the theatre is denied to them, I have, in the writing of these plays, constructed the dialogue rather more on literary than on theatrical lines. I have also, for the most part, drawn my material from side-incidents, which have not as yet found their way into

14

history. But it will be well for readers not to assume too hastily that certain things, which seem rather unlikely, did not actually occur. 'Morning Glory' was a true incident, and took place on the date named. The question of Jonah and the Whale did really arise to cause spiritual disturbance to the Queen's mind. The Mahdi's head *was* made into an inkpot, and probably remains one to this day, since Lord Kitchener's skilful marshalling of the facts induced Her Majesty to condone the outrage.

Whether first-hand proof of these things any longer exists, has become doubtful. The Society for the Preservation of Ancient Monuments has not, unfortunately, been granted the custody of Queen Victoria's Diaries.

L. H.

Coming Events

Coming Events

1837

*The chamber is lofty but not large; its proportions, win-
dows, doors, furniture, all suggest that it has larger
connections than its floorspace alone would indicate.
This often happens to the smaller apartments of great
houses; proportionate breadth denied, height is thrust
upon them by the architectural design of the main building. The result here is a spindly pretentiousness,
modified by age; for the hangings, once splendid, are
faded and shabby; the crimson carpet is worn, and the
red of the curtains has had its day. In the centre of this
too aspiring chamber sits a young maiden, fair and of
fresh complexion; submissive in attitude, diminutive in
stature, she seems nevertheless a figure of more importance than the large lady her companion, who, defer-
entially strict, sits directing her studies — for this is the*
PRINCESS VICTORIA, *so soon to become* QUEEN. *The*
GOVERNESS *has at her side a small table; on it lie books
and needlework. Her pupil occupies an upright chair
with gilt legs, too high to be comfortable; upright as the
chair she sits, straight and symmetrical, holding a book
in both hands.*

GOVERNESS You have read enough for to-day, Princess.
Begin your recitation.

*(She takes a book from the table, opens it at a
marked page; and the* PRINCESS, *who has
watched her with waiting eye, receives the
signal to begin.)*

PRINCESS 'Hope deferred maketh the heart sick: but
when the desire cometh it is a tree of life.

'Whoso despiseth the word shall be destroyed: but he
that feareth the commandments shall be rewarded.

'The law of the wise is a fountain of life to depart
from . . .'

GOVERNESS No, Princess, no! After the word 'life'
there is a pause. Say it again!

PRINCESS 'The law of the wise is a fountain of life. . . .
To depart from the snares of death.'

GOVERNESS You see—it makes a difference!

PRINCESS 'A wicked messenger falleth into mischief:
but a faithful ambassador is health.

'Poverty and shame shall be to him that refuseth instruction: but he that regardeth reproof shall be honoured.'

(The door opens; a lady of stiff dignity enters. GOV-
ERNESS *and pupil rise and curtsy; for this is
H.R.H. the* DUCHESS OF KENT; *and though a
widow of restricted means, she holds her narrow
court with a rigour of decorum that requires
everything. The* DUCHESS *seats herself, and by
a gesture indicates that the others may sit also.
She and the* GOVERNESS *both speak with a
foreign accent.)*

DUCHESS What are you doing?

GOVERNESS The Princess was reciting her Scripture, Madam.

DUCHESS Continue.

PRINCESS 'He that walketh with wise men shall be wise: but a companion of fools shall be destroyed.

'A good man leaveth an inheritance to his children's children: and the wealth of the sinner is laid up for the just.'

DUCHESS My dear, sit up, and sit straight!

PRINCESS I *was* sitting straight, Mama!

DUCHESS Never answer your Mother, my dear!

(*The* PRINCESS *struggles with her emotions. Habit is powerful: she controls herself.*)

GOVERNESS Go on, Princess.

PRINCESS 'He that spareth the rod spoileth the child: but he that loveth him chasteneth him betimes.

'The righteous eateth to the satisfying of his soul: but the belly of the wicked shall want.'

DUCHESS Lehzen! The Princess should not have been permitted to learn *that*!

GOVERNESS It's in the Bible, Madam.

DUCHESS There are things *in* the Bible, as well as out of it, which are not seemly on the lips of a young girl. . . . I hope you do not allow the Princess to read *all* the Bible?

GOVERNESS There are parts of it I do not read myself, Madam.

DUCHESS Very proper of you, I'm sure. Victoria, bring me your diary.

(*The* PRINCESS *does so; her Mother turns the pages.*)

DUCHESS When did you write in it last?

PRINCESS This morning, Mama.

DUCHESS You have not put the date. Nor have you entered the fault for which I corrected you yesterday. Go and do it at once.

PRINCESS Which fault, Mama?

DUCHESS *Which!*

PRINCESS There were so many!

DUCHESS My dear, that is almost like answering me again! Do you pretend not to remember how, when I questioned you about certain things, you lost your temper? . . . Do not lose it again *now!*

PRINCESS No, Mama.

DUCHESS There, take it to the table. . . . Mind! Do not leave anything out!

PRINCESS No, Mama.

> (*The* PRINCESS *goes to a table near the window and begins writing.*)

DUCHESS Lehzen!

GOVERNESS Madam?

> (*By a gesture the* DUCHESS *draws her toward her for a confidential exchange of words.*)

DUCHESS You have the history lesson prepared, as I told you?

GOVERNESS Yes, Madam.

DUCHESS You have marked the passage? You have put in it—the—?

GOVERNESS Yes, Madam.

DUCHESS You are sure that you have made it *quite plain*?

GOVERNESS Yes, Madam. I have numbered the names of all heirs to the succession in order, and have underlined them in red ink. Under the Princess's name I have made *three* underlinings.

DUCHESS That is as I wished it. . . . Have you heard how the King is to-day?

GOVERNESS No, Madam.

DUCHESS They never let *me* know anything—that they can help.

GOVERNESS I heard yesterday that he was a little better. He had taken a good turn, they said.

DUCHESS They told *me* that yesterday—to annoy me. It was not true.

GOVERNESS Indeed, Madam? Then your Royal Highness has had news?

DUCHESS I have means of information about which *they* know nothing.

GOVERNESS That is very fortunate, Madam.

DUCHESS It is not a question of *fortune*. It is the respect that is due to me. They seem to forget that some day *I* shall be the Queen-Mother.

GOVERNESS They will soon find themselves reminded, Madam.

DUCHESS They will. Victoria, have you done?

PRINCESS Yes, Mama.

DUCHESS Read it!

PRINCESS Yesterday, at breakfast, after the Chaplain had read prayers, Mama said to me, 'Victoria, did you fold up your night-gown?' 'Yes, Mama,' I said. 'Did you clean your teeth?' Mama then inquired. 'Yes, Mama,' I said. Her next inquiry—

DUCHESS '*Mama's* next inquiry.' Alter it!

(*The* PRINCESS *makes the alteration.*)

PRINCESS Mama's next inquiry was whether, I had said my prayers. I answered, 'You know quite well that I said them, Mama; for you were there!' My dear Mama told me not to answer like that; and I lost my temper. This was wrong of me. Mama then kindly explained that she asked all these questions—not because *she* wanted to know, but in order to get me into the habit of asking them of myself, which I always do.

DUCHESS Those last three words had better be erased. If true, it is unnecessary to say so. If not true, they sound a little like defiance.

PRINCESS They *are* true! Why mayn't I write the truth?

DUCHESS The truth, when it means answering your Mother defiantly, is not a suitable weapon in the mouth of a young girl. . . . Not another word, Victoria! You will now do your history lesson.

(SIR JOHN CONROY, *the* DUCHESS'S *major-domo, enters and comes confidentially towards her. He brings her a letter.*)

24

Ah, my good Sir John, so you have returned. You have news for me?

CONROY A letter, Madam. It has just come.

(*He hands it.*)

DUCHESS Ah! I will see you again, when the Princess has finished her lessons—alone.

(*In the last word there is an implied intimacy of understanding.* SIR JOHN *goes: he looks back; she is looking at him. Their eyes meet. Yes, there is an understanding between them. Meanwhile, the* GOVERNESS *has begun the history lesson.*)

GOVERNESS We were reading yesterday, you will remember, Princess, about the House of Hanover. Why was it so called?

PRINCESS It was so called because my three-times great-grandfather came over to conquer England for the Protestant faith.

GOVERNESS Not exactly to *conquer* it, Princess. He was called constitutionally, to establish the Protestant succession, and keep out all Papist pretenders.

PRINCESS Are *all* Papists pretenders?

GOVERNESS Yes, Princess. No Papist can sit on the throne of Great Britain.

PRINCESS Or Ireland?

GOVERNESS Or Ireland.

PRINCESS The Irish are pretenders too, aren't they?

25

GOVERNESS 'Are they not'—not 'aren't they. . . .' They are Papists and rebellious—a very troublesome and disagreeable people.

PRINCESS Then I need not like the Irish, need I?

GOVERNESS Only those who live in the north, in Ulster. They are industrious, and loyal, and deserving. For the rest you can have only pity.

PRINCESS And try to convert them?

GOVERNESS *Pray* for their conversion, Princess. That is all you can do.

PRINCESS I will do so to-night.

DUCHESS The dear King is worse, much worse, they tell me. Victoria, you must remember to pray to-night that his precious life may be spared. That is far more important than the conversion of the Irish. I do not think they would ever make good Protestants.

PRINCESS Very well, Mama.

GOVERNESS Begin your reading, Princess: page 273.

PRINCESS (*opening the book*) Oh, what is this?

GOVERNESS That is a chronological table, Princess, showing the succession to the crown at the present day.

PRINCESS Oh, how interesting! I have never seen this before. Am I in it?

GOVERNESS Your Royal Highness's name is there—with others.

PRINCESS What is the red ink for?

26

GOVERNESS That is to show, Princess, the order of inheritance, in the last—and in the present generation.

PRINCESS I see my Father's name.

GOVERNESS Yes, Princess. Had your Royal Father lived, he would now have been heir-presumptive to the throne.

PRINCESS Why 'presumptive'?

GOVERNESS On the presumption that His Majesty the King has no children.

PRINCESS Oh, but Cousin George told me the other day that he's had lots.

(*There is a moment of painful embarrassment. Then the* DUCHESS *speaks.*)

DUCHESS They have all died, or have passed from the succession in other ways.

PRINCESS (*a little puzzled*) Oh? . . . Then it would have been my Father?

GOVERNESS Undoubtedly.

DUCHESS (*consequentially*) Of course it would have been your Father, my dear! And *I* should have been Queen.

PRINCESS (*genuinely astonished*) La! Mama! How you surprise me! . . . Then now it is one of my uncles?

DUCHESS (*with asperity*) *None* of your uncles, Victoria. They do not come in, I'm thankful to say.

PRINCESS Then . . . do *I*?

DUCHESS You have the table there, my dear. Study it.

27

PRINCESS (*after further examination*) Oh! Oh! I didn't know . . . I never thought I was quite—quite—so near as that. Oh, Mama, Mama!

DUCHESS What is it, my dear? It is nothing to be upset about.

PRINCESS Oh, now I know why you have always been—so—so— Oh, I will be good! I will be good!

DUCHESS Indeed I hope so! For that a great deal depends on *both of us*. It has been *my* care hitherto. In the future it will have to be yours.

PRINCESS Oh, Mama, forgive me if I have ever—ever seemed—ungrateful! I am so young for it!

DUCHESS I shall always be there, my love. You will be Queen. But I am your Mother. I shall not go away and leave you.

PRINCESS Oh? . . . No, of course not.

(*Disappointed, she weeps.*)

DUCHESS (*soothingly*) Of course not.

GOVERNESS Why, of course not, Princess. There, there! Don't cry!

DUCHESS Let her cry, Lehzen! It will be good for her. After all it's only natural; a great shock. It was time she had it.

PRINCESS It's so sudden!

DUCHESS Not as sudden as it might have been. Considering his age, the King must have a very strong constitution. It is wonderful how it has lasted. So now I must go

28

and see after my black, to be ready in case anything happens.

GOVERNESS Is the last news very alarming, Madam?

DUCHESS Everyone had given up hope yesterday, they tell me. And now he has given it up himself.

PRINCESS Is he conscious, Mama?

DUCHESS No, not conscious, my dear. He has given that up too. Perhaps that is as well. I fear he did not lead a good life.

PRINCESS But he was *married*, Mama!

(*This causes shock.*)

DUCHESS My dear! All married people do not lead a good life—not all.

PRINCESS Oh, I thought they did!

DUCHESS Victoria, you shock me! Who has been talking to you?

PRINCESS Talking to me?

DUCHESS Yes, about marriage, and—and things of *that* sort.

PRINCESS No one . . . only Cousin George. The other day he asked me to marry him. He said it would make him good.

DUCHESS Your Cousin George!

PRINCESS Yes; he said that all my uncles wished it, and the King wished it too. So that was why he asked me.

DUCHESS Yes. I daresay they do . . . I daresay they do! But I can tell them *this*—and I tell you too—you are

29

not going to marry your Cousin *George*. *He* is not going to be King.

PRINCESS No, Mama, not if I am to be Queen.

DUCHESS Kiss me, my dear! Ah, you do not know the dangers from which I have protected you. I hope that you will never have to know. . . . That will do, Lehzen, for the present. You may go. The Princess will finish her lessons later.

(LEHZEN *curties and retires.*)

My child, listen to me! It's time that you knew—*this* at least. Ever since you were born, I have been fighting a battle to save you from the hands of *wicked men*.

PRINCESS Oh, Mama!

DUCHESS Yes. They wanted to get hold of you; but I would not let them. They wanted to choose a husband for you—your Cousin George, and then to make *him* King instead of you. But I saw what they were after. I saved you from *that*. That is why I never left you alone— never let you go out of my sight, except sometimes when we were at Windsor, and it could not be helped. That is when your Cousin George spoke to you, I suppose? . . . What did you say to him?

PRINCESS Of course, I said he must first ask Mama!

DUCHESS My own darling child!

PRINCESS And that didn't seem to please him.

DUCHESS No, I daresay not!

PRINCESS He said that in that case it was 'all up'!

30

DUCHESS That is the sort of language I should expect from him!—'All up!' He has been learning English from his uncles—and other things as well, I'll be bound! So marrying you was going to make him *good*, was it? ... Oh, my darling, now that you see from what I have saved you, I only ask you to remember, and be a little grateful. You are so young, so inexperienced—and such a child! But I know, oh, I know *things*! ... But Mama is still with you, my child; always will be with you. Trust Mama! Come to Mama about *everything*!

> (*The* PRINCESS *stands dutifully attentive, wistful, interested, a little alarmed, and yet self-possessed; and when the* DUCHESS *at last pauses for her to speak, it is a portent of coming events that she does not say, 'Yes, Mama,' as perhaps she was expected to do; but stands looking out—into the future. The door opens.* SIR JOHN CONROY *enters, and stands looking at mother and daughter.*)

DUCHESS Go, now, for your walk with Lehzen.

> (*The* PRINCESS *curtsies and retires.* SIR JOHN *holds opens the door, shuts it, and advances toward the* DUCHESS. *Oh, yes, there is an understanding between them. She puts out her hand, and he takes it.*)

The Six O'clock Call

The Six O'clock Call

1837

*It is still dark; for in the entrance hall of Kensington
Palace the shutters have not yet been unclosed. Behind
a wide archway at centre burns a dim light: there is the
staircase lobby. To the left of the archway one sees the
foot of the stairs.*

*In the dark emptiness goes the clanging of a bell, followed
by knocks. A* FOOTMAN, *not quite dressed as he should
be, enters carrying a light. He crosses from left to right,
and passes out of view. You hear unchaining and un-
bolting of a door; then, indistinctly, voices, which grow
louder as the visitors enter and become visible. Heavily
cloaked,* LORD CONYNGHAM *comes in, followed by the*
ARCHBISHOP OF CANTERBURY.

CONYNGHAM Tell them to take the message at once!
Say the matter is urgent.

FOOTMAN Yes, my Lord. But Her Royal Highness isn't
up yet, my Lord.

CONYNGHAM 'Up?' Of course she's not up at this hour!
Send Her Royal Highness's maid to call her.

> (The FOOTMAN, *having the only candle, is busy now
> lighting others. But the urgency of his lordship
> stops the business half-way; and only one set
> of candles gets lighted before he goes.*)

35

FOOTMAN Yes, my Lord.

CONYNGHAM And say His Grace the Archbishop of Canterbury, and Lord Conyngham are here to see Her Royal Highness on important business.

FOOTMAN Yes, my Lord.

CONYNGHAM Hurry, man! Hurry!

FOOTMAN Yes, my Lord; but I'll have to call the maid first.

CONYNGHAM Well, call her!

FOOTMAN Yes, my Lord; but the maids sleep where I'm not supposed to go; and the door up to it is locked. I shall have to throw up at the window.

CONYNGHAM Isn't there a bell?

FOOTMAN Yes, my Lord; in her Royal Highness the Duchess's room there is a bell.

CONYNGHAM Well go and ask that it may be rung!

FOOTMAN (*aghast*) I daren't go to Her Royal Highness the Duchess's room, my Lord: not now. Her Royal Highness the Princess is there too.

CONYNGHAM Well, go and do the best you can. But say Her Royal Highness *must* come—

FOOTMAN Yes, my Lord.

(*Exit* FOOTMAN.)

CONYNGHAM (*finishing his sentence*)—at once! . . . Good Lord! What a house! Sleeps with the old Cat, does she?

ARCHBISHOP (*corrective, but suave*) I beg your pardon?

CONYNGHAM I—I beg yours! Yes; I suppose one oughtn't to say that now. But your Grace knows that the Duchess has been a difficulty all along.

ARCHBISHOP The Duchess is a determined character.

CONYNGHAM Yes.

ARCHBISHOP It has had its advantages.

CONYNGHAM They have escaped my observation, I'm afraid.

ARCHBISHOP The Princess has not seen a great deal of her uncles. Her education has been—safeguarded.

CONYNGHAM (*extenuatingly*) Well, of course, I know— I know—I know.

ARCHBISHOP (*less extenuatingly*) Yes, my Lord, we *know.*

CONYNGHAM Had we not better sit down? We may have to wait. If that man's stone-throwing is not good—we may have to wait a long time. . . . So this is how history gets written!

ARCHBISHOP *This* won't get into history, my Lord.

CONYNGHAM No . . . Your Grace?—may I? . . .

(*He offers a flask-cup, after filling it.*)

ARCHBISHOP Ah, no. I thank you.

CONYNGHAM It's a chilly hour to be up. I never go about, late at night, or early—without *something.*

(*Drinks.*)

ARCHBISHOP For you, my Lord, very wise, I've no doubt. But I never go out at night, you see; at least, not late.

37

CONYNGHAM Ah! I often wish I didn't, when the night is over.

ARCHBISHOP That is—understandable.

CONYNGHAM (*missing the note of sympathy*) It's only human nature, your Grace.

ARCHBISHOP Yes, I suppose so. I don't know . . . My office . . . There is a good deal of human nature that I have to avoid.

CONYNGHAM Rather difficult to avoid at the Court of the Regency, wasn't it?

ARCHBISHOP Oh, of course, sometimes I had to—well—look the other way. Still, I attended so seldom; only when called on officially.

CONYNGHAM Your Grace has officiated on a similar painful though auspicious occasion, I believe?

ARCHBISHOP Yes. Yes. I announced his accession to His late Majesty King William. But he was only in the next room waiting.

CONYNGHAM Ah! How did he take it?

ARCHBISHOP With alacrity . . . 'Bless my soul! you don't say so!' were his first words. And then—'Well, well, though I'm less of a figure-head, I shall make a better King than poor George.'

CONYNGHAM But he didn't, you know.

ARCHBISHOP No; a better character, but not a better King. That sometimes happens, I'm afraid.

38

CONYNGHAM Yes, kings often manage to do quite well without morals. Brain is more important.

ARCHBISHOP Not too much of that either, I should have thought. Don't those with brain give much more trouble to their ministers?

CONYNGHAM Oh, they manage to do that without any! His late Majesty was a conspicuous example of it. You wouldn't believe—no, you wouldn't believe the trouble we sometimes had with him. They say you can make a donkey go by tying a carrot in front of its nose. Well, he was like a donkey with a carrot tied to its tail.

ARCHBISHOP Really?

CONYNGHAM Just like that. Over the Reform Bill, you know, we almost had a Revolution—almost. Not *his* fault that we didn't.

ARCHBISHOP (*discreetly*) Was he just a little—like his Father, you know?

CONYNGHAM Mad, eh? No, not mad. It was the shape of his head, I think. It was pear-shaped, you know—just like a pear. 'The weakest fruit drops earliest to the ground,' says Shakespeare. Well, his head was weak fruit distinctly—amazing how it *hung on*: one can't exactly say 'lasted.'

(*The* FOOTMAN *re-enters.*)

Well? What have you done?

FOOTMAN I've called the maid, my Lord. Would your Lordship like more light?

39

CONYNGHAM Oh yes; a little more light would, I suppose, be better. (*Then to the* ARCHBISHOP) For so auspicious an occasion.

FOOTMAN The windows, my Lord?

CONYNGHAM No, no, not the windows, I think. *The blinds—the blinds* must stay down at any rate.

(*The* FOOTMAN *lights more candles.*)

ARCHBISHOP (*confidentially*) Very sad, very sad, you know! Good old King George—such a large family—so many sons, and not one of them what he should be.

(*Exit* FOOTMAN.)

CONYNGHAM (*grimly*) And she—the daughter of one of them.

ARCHBISHOP Ah, but women are different—so different, you know. Let's hope! Let's hope!

CONYNGHAM Well, we must get her married, and then —married to the right man—the difference won't so much matter—her Cousin, Prince George of Cambridge, would be very suitable—same age, and can talk English now, so I'm told, like a native.

ARCHBISHOP Over that you will have difficulty with the Duchess.

CONYNGHAM Oh, yes; the Duchess is going to be difficult whatever's proposed. She will regard this as her own succession almost.

ARCHBISHOP (*wisely*) It almost will be.

CONYNGHAM That is what we must *prevent*.

ARCHBISHOP The Duchess has privately planned a marriage more to her own liking, I'm told.

CONYNGHAM Eh? Who?

ARCHBISHOP She has two nephews—through her brother the Duke of Saxe-Coburg—Prince Ernest, and Prince Albert.

CONYNGHAM But that won't do! Tainted blood! Tainted blood!

ARCHBISHOP Indeed!

CONYNGHAM (*disgustedly*) Ye-es: bleeding skins—haemophilia. It's in the family. Cousins. No; it won't *do*.

ARCHBISHOP But Prince George is her cousin, also.

CONYNGHAM Ah, but it's not on that side. It's on the mother's—the Coburgs. And, you know, it comes through the women. The males have it: the women don't; but they pass it on. Do you know her brother, the Duke, once nearly bled to death?

ARCHBISHOP Dear me! Is that so?

CONYNGHAM Marrying her daughter to *his* son would be fatal! You know, it's all very well, in one way, Royalty to make itself a class all by itself. But it's a German notion: 'tisn't English. And when it leads to so much inbreeding, it gets dangerous. English kings have married commoners in the past; they'd better do it again—or into the peerage. Do you know—if the Duke of Wellington had been—well, twenty years younger, I'd have married her to him.

41

ARCHBISHOP You don't mean it!

CONYNGHAM I do. 'Twould have been very popular; and a foreign marriage won't be. (*He looks at his watch.*) Tut, tut! That girl's a very long time coming!

ARCHBISHOP (*correctively*) The Queen?

CONYNGHAM (*plausibly covering his mistake*) No, no; I mean the maid. I'm wondering whether she has called her . . . It's a pity you know, a pity! I don't know what to think of it!

ARCHBISHOP 'It' meaning what?

CONYNGHAM A female on the throne; a King would have been so much better.

ARCHBISHOP I don't know, my Lord. Heirs male of the last generation have not been a conspicuous success.[1]

CONYNGHAM No English King has been a conspicuous success since Edward I.

ARCHBISHOP Yet the monarchy has—gone on.

(*Enter* MAID-SERVANT.)

CONYNGHAM Yes; but it's gone off.

MAID I beg your pardon, my Lord.

CONYNGHAM Yes? Well?

MAID Her Royal Highness, my Lord. I went in, but Her Royal Highness was asleep.

CONYNGHAM Well, you must wake Her Royal Highness up, then.

[1] This remark having been ruled out of one of my plays by the Lord Chamberlain, now goes into another.

MAID Such a beautiful sleep, my Lord: I didn't like to.

CONYNGHAM Even the most beautiful sleep must give way to affairs of State. You know who I am?

MAID Yes, my Lord.

CONYNGHAM You know His Grace?

MAID Yes, my Lord.

CONYNGHAM Then go at once: wake Her Royal Highness, and tell her that we are here, waiting—for an audience.

> (*Awestruck and submissive, the* MAID *goes. A clock strikes.*)

Six o'clock. There is to be a Council at ten.

ARCHBISHOP Where? Here?

CONYNGHAM At St. James's, I imagine. No, perhaps it will have to be here. She mustn't appear in public yet. 'Twouldn't be quite decent. People might cheer.

> (*Enter the* DUCHESS OF KENT: *she is robed rather than dressed; but her heavy négligée has a certain dignity about it. She enters, a conscious 'Presence.' They rise and bow.*)

DUCHESS Your Grace, my Lord Conyngham, you have news for us?

CONYNGHAM For her Royal Highness the Princess, we have news, Madam.

DUCHESS Ah! The King then—?

CONYNGHAM Is dead.

DUCHESS Then my daughter is now—?

43

CONYNGHAM Queen.

DUCHESS It has come, then—at last! And I—I am the Queen Mother!

CONYNGHAM No, Madam: your Royal Highness is not the Queen Mother.

DUCHESS (*affronted*) Not?

CONYNGHAM Your Royal Highness is the Queen's Mother; that is the distinction. Only had your Royal Highness been Queen in the first place, would that other title now follow.

DUCHESS Then, if it is not mine by your laws, she shall give it me.

CONYNGHAM That, Madam, I fear, will be impossible.

DUCHESS Ah! I will go myself and speak to her at once. That shall settle it!

CONYNGHAM Madam, we are here to see Her Majesty the Queen on urgent business; and we must not be delayed. Your presence at the interview, Madam, will not be required, unless Her Majesty sends for you.

DUCHESS Ah! This is not to be borne!

ARCHBISHOP (*conciliatory*) Madam, this is a very historic occasion. We are here officially only. Etiquette and immemorial tradition prescribe certain rules which have to be observed. Your Royal Highness would not wish to break them.

CONYNGHAM (*at centre*) Your Grace, she's coming!

44

ARCHBISHOP Then, Madam, for a moment—for a moment only!

> (*He opens a side-door and bows the* DUCHESS *through it. She goes, compelled, but reluctant. The shadow of* QUEEN VICTORIA *is projected upon the wall of the lobby as she descends. She enters: the* ARCHBISHOP *and the* LORD CHAMBERLAIN *kneel and kiss her hand. The side-door opens again; the* DUCHESS *thrusts in her head; she watches spell-bound.*)

CONYNGHAM Your Majesty, it is our painful duty to announce to your Majesty—

DUCHESS (*not waiting for the sentence to finish*) Ah! my daughter, she is Queen—Queen!

> (*The curtain slowly descends; after a few seconds it rises again.* VICTORIA *stands alone at the foot of the stairs. Away to the right, ceremoniously backing from the Presence, the* ARCHBISHOP *and the* LORD CHAMBERLAIN *make their last bow and go. Into this solemn scene no* FOOTMAN *intrudes; they let themselves out. At the sound of the shutting door, the side-door opens fully: the* DUCHESS *enters, and advances rapturously to claim her daughter's homage.*)

VICTORIA (*still a little mazed at the wonder of it all*) Mama!

DUCHESS (*embracing her*) My child! My child! Oh, my child!

VICTORIA They came to tell me that I am Queen.

45

DUCHESS Yes: you are Queen at last!

VICTORIA But really Queen—*now*: before I have been crowned?

DUCHESS Yes: now, at once! The King is dead: you are Queen!

VICTORIA Then my reign has already begun? I can do—as I like?

DUCHESS Yes; as you like! Do not mind what anyone says. If you want to do it—do it!

VICTORIA Oh! . . . Then . . . Mama. There is something I would like.

DUCHESS Ah, yes! Say it! It shall be done.

VICTORIA How strange that it should have all come—so suddenly!

DUCHESS Yes, so suddenly—after we have waited so long. But now, my love—do not stay here to catch cold. Come back to your own Mother's bed!

VICTORIA No, Mama dear. As I may now do as I like, I wish in future to have a bed, and a room of my own!

DUCHESS (*stupent*) *Of your own?*

VICTORIA Yes—please, Mama.

DUCHESS Oh! so you have been waiting—for *that*!

VICTORIA I should be glad, if you don't mind—now that I am my own mistress. Yes, I would rather be alone.

(*She does not wait to hear more.*)

46

DUCHESS   Mind! . . . Glad! . . . Alone! . . . O   God!
What is going to become of me?

> (*She stands and watches, while* VICTORIA, *mistress
> henceforth of her own destiny, turns and goes
> quietly upstairs again, having imposed, even
> now, her wish to be alone for a while.*)

'Poor Mamma!'

'Poor Mamma!'

20th June 1837

The clock at Kensington Palace is about to strike ten. And in the ante-room to the Council Chamber there are signs of ceremony. Before a closed double-door stand two Attendants. From another door THE QUEEN *enters, robed in black, toweringly followed by the* DUCHESS OF KENT, *in black also. After her come two Ladies-in-Waiting and* SIR JOHN CONROY, *who halt within the door of their entry. An Attendant opens one half of the closed door just sufficiently to admit a* COURT OFFICIAL, *then closes it again. The* COURT OFFICIAL *bows, advances toward* THE QUEEN, *and bows again.*

COURT OFFICIAL If it please your Majesty, your Majesty's Privy Council is now in attendance.

THE QUEEN It is already the time?

COURT OFFICIAL The hour is now striking, your Majesty.

THE QUEEN Very well. Will the ceremony, my lord, take long?

COURT OFFICIAL Oh, no, your Majesty. A matter of a few minutes only. Your Majesty makes the statutory declaration, and signs the Oath. That is all.

51

THE QUEEN Thank you.

> (*The* COURT OFFICIAL *bows her toward the door.* THE QUEEN *turns.*)

THE QUEEN Good-bye, Mamma.

DUCHESS Am I not to come with you?

THE QUEEN Not now, Mamma. To meet my Privy Council I must go alone.

DUCHESS (*icily*) Very well.

> (THE QUEEN *moves toward the doors, which the Attendants throw wide. 'Her Majesty the Queen' is announced. There is a sound of rising. The doors close again.*)

DUCHESS (*turning to* SIR JOHN CONROY) You see?

> (*He comes towards her.*)

SIR JOHN Does your Highness intend to wait?

DUCHESS Yes. I must wait. That is my duty. Tell those two women that they can go outside.

> (SIR JOHN, *with courteous movement and gesture, fulfils the order. The two Ladies curtsy and retire.* SIR JOHN *and the* DUCHESS *are alone, except for the two Door-keepers—automata, who cannot be removed. The* DUCHESS *comes down the room, followed by* SIR JOHN, *and sinks to a settee.*)

DUCHESS Sir John! See how she has changed already! She is no longer the same person.

SIR JOHN (*extenuatingly*) At that one can hardly wonder, your Highness. It is a great change for her.

DUCHESS Yes; but why should she change to *me*?

SIR JOHN Just at first, perhaps, she feels strange to everybody. Presently she will come back to you, and be natural again.

DUCHESS No. My little Vicky has gone—for ever! I feel it. I am sure. Now I shall be alone always.

SIR JOHN But, Madam, to preside at the Council it was necessary that she should go without you.

DUCHESS (*clutching at hope*) Was that so? You say? You are sure? You are not deceiving me?

SIR JOHN I am quite sure, Madam. A State function: it would have been impossible—against all rules for it to have been otherwise.

DUCHESS (*returning to her grievance*) And she knew *that*, and did not tell me till she came—to the door!

SIR JOHN Perhaps she assumed that your Highness knew already.

DUCHESS Oh, Sir John, you are now trying to comfort me with words—inventions. But my own heart tells me! In there my Daughter is getting rid of me.

SIR JOHN Her Majesty is taking the Oath, Madam, before the members of the Council, and is receiving theirs of allegiance in return. It is all a formality—but necessary.

DUCHESS Are her Uncles in there—too?

SIR JOHN Undoubtedly, Madam. Everybody must be there who possibly can be. Their Royal Highnesses—the Lord Chancellor—the Prime Minister—and all others who hold office under the Crown.

DUCHESS The Prime Minister? Ah! He hates me. So do her Uncles—all of them. Everyone there is my enemy. They are going to take her from me.

SIR JOHN I think they will not succeed, Madam. Her Majesty, though young, has a will of her own.

DUCHESS Oh! So *you* have found that out too?

SIR JOHN Dear Madam, was it not always apparent?

DUCHESS No! She concealed it from me—until to-day. I did not know that she ever wished to think differently from what *I* wished. Oh, and I have tried so hard to make her all that she should be! But now, there she is—without me—in the hands of my enemies, of those who all her life have been trying to steal her from me. You know how always I have defeated them, even when it was the King—yes, even the King!—because I had Parliament and the law behind me. I was her Guardian by law, and they could not take her from me. But now that is over; she is her own mistress; and if she goes from me herself, I can do nothing—nothing—nothing!

SIR JOHN Do not distress yourself, dear Lady, unnecessarily. What you fear may never happen. The change will not be so great as you now make yourself imagine. Certain changes under the new circumstances —in things ceremonial and official—there will have to be; they are unavoidable. But whatever happens, Madam, you

54

have a great position; and it is still yours. . . . Also, dear Lady, your life is now your own; with many years yet to come, in which you will have leisure—and freedom. You will be less tied than you have been. Is that not something that *we* can look forward to?

DUCHESS Oh, dear Sir John, you are very kind to me; and I will try to believe what you say. . . .

(*She breaks off, and sits listening.*)

Why does she not come back? Why have they not done with her? They are keeping her from me, her own mother!

SIR JOHN Ah, no, Madam. It is all over; for I can hear. The Council has risen. She will be with you again in a moment.

(*There is a pause. The* DUCHESS *rises in agitation, and moves away.*)

DUCHESS Ah! What is going to happen to me? Sir John, let me see her alone. And tell the women not to come back—just yet.

(*The stroke of an Official's wand from within gives the signal. The Attendants open the doors.* SIR JOHN *goes out.* THE QUEEN *enters and advances quietly towards the* DUCHESS.)

THE QUEEN Mamma, dear, how good of you to wait for me!

DUCHESS I could not go away! I could not! I was so anxious for you, my dear! Did all go well? Was everything done properly?

THE QUEEN Oh, quite, Mamma. Everyone has been very nice to me. They made things so easy—when I did not quite know what to do.

DUCHESS And what do you think of it all, now that you are Queen?

THE QUEEN Of course, at first, it was a little strange, Mamma. But I am sure that presently I shall get used to it. Taking the Crown Oath and receiving the formal homage of so many whom I already knew—including one of my Uncles—made it all very solemn and impressive. I wish you could have seen it, Mamma.

DUCHESS (*whom this speech has mollified*) Yes, if that had been possible. . . . Well, I shall see you crowned, my dear. I shall be allowed to see that, shall I not?

THE QUEEN Why, yes, Mamma, of course!

DUCHESS But in there I was not allowed. No! Why?

> (*Before* THE QUEEN *can answer, the* COURT OFFICIAL *has come through the door and again stands before her, waiting permission to speak. By a gesture it is accorded.*)

COURT OFFICIAL If it please your Majesty, His Majesty the King of Hanover and His Royal Highness the Duke of Sussex request permission for a short audience of your Majesty.

THE QUEEN Oh, yes. Ask them to come in. And tell the Attendants to go.

DUCHESS (*significantly*) Your Uncles! What do they want with you now?

56

(The folding doors are fully opened to admit Royalty. As they close them again the Attendants retire within. The two Dukes enter, side by side. They are dressed in black, but, for the occasion of State which has brought them, they are wearing their Orders. Of all the Royal Dukes the KING OF HANOVER *is the least well-favoured; beside him his quite plain brother, the* DUKE OF SUSSEX, *looks almost handsome. But they are both said to have 'the Royal manner,' and are now on good behaviour. Whatever else may be said against them, they do not pull long faces, or pretend a grief they do not feel.)*

SUSSEX *(coming cordially to the point)* Very good, my dear, very good! Couldn't have done it better! Not if you'd been born to it!

THE QUEEN But, my dear Uncle, I was born to it, as you know.

SUSSEX Ah, yes; but a good many years to wait for it, hadn't you? Well, well!—made your old Uncle proud of you. Here's His Majesty, your Uncle Ernest, come to say the same thing.

THE QUEEN How very kind!

HANOVER Yes, Niece, it's going to be all right. You've got the trick of it. You came in just as if—well, just as if you were *me*! Of course, you haven't your poor Uncle George's style—a wonder he was!—but you don't need it, your own way's better. Stick to your own way, my dear, in all things. Don't let anyone—

THE QUEEN Uncle Ernest, Uncle Augustus, here is
Mamma.

THE UNCLES (*in mixed greetings*) Ah, yes, to be sure.
How do you do, Duchess? Good morning. Hope we see
you well.

> (*In response to their greetings, the* DUCHESS *curtsies
> silently. And the two Dukes, having been
> forced to recognise her presence, waste no more
> time on her.*)

SUSSEX Well, Victoria, my dear, circumstances have
prevented me from seeing much of you till now. Hardly
know each other, do we? Never kissed your Uncle yet,
have you? Never! Circumstances—call 'em that—have
prevented. Almost strangers, you and I. Not my fault,
my dear, not my fault; nor my wish either. Now I hope
we shall see more of each other—you being now your own
mistress.

THE QUEEN I am sure, Uncle Augustus, I shall always
be pleased to see you—at any time.

HANOVER I suppose you know, my dear—you heard
your Uncle call me 'His Majesty' just now—that I have
become King of Hanover—reigning sovereign, like yourself. 'Sire, my brother,' you've got to call your old Uncle
now, when we meet on ceremony. That's why I had to
keep out of it just now; couldn't take the oath of allegiance
to you, you know—being a reigning sovereign myself.
'Twouldn't have done. Well, you and I have divided the
inheritance between us, and we shan't quarrel about it:
kingdom's divided—honours equal. Your poor Uncle,
King William, was the last to hold both. Perhaps it's

58

better as it is now. What does England want with Hanover? Or Hanover with England, for that matter? I only came over to say good-bye to him. You didn't see him, did you? No. But he spoke of you—more than once. He was fond of you, my dear: said he hoped you'd know how to be your own mistress—without interference from anyone. And I hope you do.

THE QUEEN It's very kind of you, Uncle, to say so. But quite unnecessary. I hope that some day I may be able to come and visit you—in Hanover. And now, my dear Uncles, if you will excuse me; for I have much to do. But, please, before you go, there is just something I want to say to you as now representing the Family. I want, in your presence, to thank my dear Mamma for all that she has done for me in the past. I want to say that no one could have done more. I wish you both to know how very much I owe to her, and how grateful I feel.

> (*This testimonial to the woman they detest puts the Uncles somewhat out of countenance. But between them they manage to say what, under the circumstances, they are obliged to say, since* THE QUEEN, *in her quiet mastery of the situation, has made it impossible for them to say otherwise.*)

HANOVER Ah, yes, yes! Very right and proper of you, I'm sure, and like a dutiful daughter. And I hope Her Royal Highness, your Mamma, appreciates it, as I am sure she ought to do.

SUSSEX Very handsome of you, my dear, very! You couldn't have said more, could you? Well, Ernest, now I think we'd better be going. And I hope you'll have a happy reign, my dear, and everything in the proper time to make the succession safe for others after you.

HANOVER Yes, Niece, you'll have to marry, and the sooner the better. Choose well! Good-bye.

(They go together to the door. Then the DUKE OF SUSSEX *returns, and says a last kind word.)*

SUSSEX Don't worry about the funeral, my dear. We shall be there: but you won't be expected to go. 'Twouldn't be the thing. Ah, your poor Uncle! Now he's gone, only three of us are left. But there, there! Life doesn't last for ever: never did, never will! Good-bye.

THE QUEEN Good-bye, dear Uncle. Thank you so much for coming to-day.

SUSSEX Thank *you*, my dear. Thank you. It was a pleasure to see you do it. Good-bye, Duchess.

(And, with a grunt at having to say good-bye to 'that woman,' off he goes.)

DUCHESS Those are your Uncles—two of them. Now you have *seen* them.

THE QUEEN Yes, Mamma.

DUCHESS What do you think of them?

THE QUEEN They were both very kind, Mamma.

DUCHESS Kind! Kind! Oh, take care of yourself, my child! Take care of yourself! Kiss me, Vicky! Kiss me! Do not ever forget what I have done for you!

THE QUEEN Mamma, dear, you are tired: you were up so early. Go and lie down!

60

DUCHESS And what are you going to do?

THE QUEEN. I am going to write letters, Mamma.

DUCHESS Who to?

THE QUEEN To so many people. To my Uncle, King Leopold, for one.

DUCHESS Ah, yes! Write to *him*: tell him *everything*!

THE QUEEN I must also write to the poor Queen— Queen Adelaide, I mean. I am going to tell her that she must not leave Windsor till—till she wishes.

DUCHESS Then when do you mean going to Windsor yourself?

THE QUEEN Not for some time, Mamma. I have not yet decided. I shall first consult the Prime Minister.

DUCHESS It seems to me that, in your mind, you have arranged everything.

THE QUEEN Almost, Mamma; not quite. Now go and lie down and rest.

DUCHESS That is the first time, Victoria, that you have given an order to *me*.

THE QUEEN Mamma dear, you know that I only do it for your good.

DUCHESS (*turning away*) Oh, yes; it is for my good, I suppose. Oh, I am so tired—so tired of everything.

> (*She goes out, leaving the door open. Tentatively, one of the Ladies-in-Waiting enters and, after curtsying, stands to attention.*)

THE QUEEN Ah, Lady Charlotte, will you, please, open those doors?

> (LADY CHARLOTTE *goes and throws wide the doors leading into the Council Chamber.*)

Thank you. That will do. You may leave me.

> (LADY CHARLOTTE *curtsies and retires.* THE QUEEN *remains alone. She goes slowly toward the doors, enters, stands within the doorway, and looks round on the large empty chamber in which the first ceremonial event of her reign has taken place. She turns back and, recrossing the threshold, halts, and speaks.*)

THE QUEEN So. Now I am Queen. And my reign has really begun. . . . Poor Mamma!

Suitable Suitors

Suitable Suitors

1838

THE QUEEN *is still in mourning but she does not mourn. Animated and happy, she sits listening to what, in earlier youth, she was never allowed to hear—the conversation of a gentleman of breeding, worldly, witty, and to a certain extent wise. This she thoroughly enjoys. And* LORD MELBOURNE, *her Prime Minister, enjoys talking to her. She is not clever; she cannot say clever things; but the mingled strain of artlessness and self-possession, of dignity and simplicity, which he finds in his Royal Mistress's character—a character which he is artfully moulding, not so much to his own ends as his own convenience—attracts and delights him. They are now on such intimate terms that* THE QUEEN, *when he comes for an audience, does not keep him long standing. They are seated now; and as an indication of their pleasant relations,* THE QUEEN *is going on with her wool-work.*

VICTORIA How do you begin the day, Lord Melbourne?

MELBOURNE Begin it, Ma'am?

VICTORIA Yes. What do you do first—you, who have so many things to do in the day? I find it difficult to know myself where to begin.

MELBOURNE Well, starting at the very beginning, Ma'am, I breakfast—if I may be allowed to say so—in bed.

VICTORIA Oh! I should never have thought of that!

MELBOURNE Try it, Ma'am, try it! It makes an invaluable break between sleeping and waking. Sleeping is one thing: it takes time. Waking is another: it takes more time. Working is another: and takes more time than all the others put together.

VICTORIA. And after breakfast, what then?

MELBOURNE Well, let me think! . . . First, I rise, Ma'am. Over that I need not go into details.

VICTORIA No?

MELBOURNE Or—would you like me to, Ma'am?

VICTORIA (*a little disappointed*) No, oh, no. You rise?

MELBOURNE I rise from my bed. Then I ride in the Park; when I come home I write. So I begin with the three R's.

VICTORIA But 'write' begins with a W.

MELBOURNE I am corrected, Ma'am. 'Write' *does* begin with a W. Your Majesty is right, as usual.

VICTORIA (*laughing*) Oh! you are funny, Lord Melbourne.

MELBOURNE Funny?

VICTORIA So witty, I mean. You always say something amusing. Yes; please go on!

MELBOURNE That, Ma'am, is all the beginning of my day. When that is done, the day is half over.

66

VICTORIA   And when do you say your prayers, Lord Melbourne?

MELBOURNE   My prayers? Oh, I say them whenever I have time for them.

VICTORIA (*a little shocked*)   But—Lord Melbourne!

MELBOURNE   As often, and as long as possible.

VICTORIA   That seems to me a little irregular.

MELBOURNE   Did your Majesty never hear the story of the holy monk who had a Vision vouchsafed to him: a Vision of—well, of a very high character? And just as the Vision appeared, the chapel-bell began ringing. Duty—discipline—required the monk to leave the seraphic Vision and go into chapel with the rest: a function which, in these circumstances, was so like praying to the Vision behind its back, that it seemed almost foolish. It was a hard thing to do; but the monk did it. In great anguish of spirit, he left the Vision to itself, and went and did his duty. The service seemed intolerably long; he was dying to get back to his Vision. At last he was able to do so. The Vision was still there; and as he fell down before it in renewed adoration, the Vision made this remark: 'If you had not answered that bell, I should not have stayed'—or words to that effect. Ma'am, my position as Prime Minister is very similar to that of the pious monk. I am constantly having to leave the vision to answer the *bell*.

VICTORIA   I thought, Lord Melbourne, that visions were rather superstitious things.

MELBOURNE   They are, Ma'am. In these days they are! Do your best to avoid them. They savour too much of

Roman Catholicism. And so, Ma'am, with your Majesty's permission, let me, for the moment, leave visions and come down to facts, and the affairs of State. There are certain things which will have soon to be decided, and one or two in which delay—delay of preparation at all events—is inadvisable.

VICTORIA Oh, yes; there are many, I'm sure.

MELBOURNE There is one especially, which your Majesty graciously deigned to mention the other day. You then said, Ma'am—with a courage which I thought remarkable in one so young—'Some day we must marry' ... Has your Majesty given that matter any further thought?

VICTORIA Oh, yes, Lord Melbourne, I have thought of it a great deal.

MELBOURNE Is your Majesty prepared yet to take me into your Majesty's gracious confidence?

VICTORIA You mean?

MELBOURNE As to the possible recipient of so over-whelming an honour.

VICTORIA Oh, I have not thought of any person—in particular. I mean, I have made no decision.

MELBOURNE I am relieved to hear it, Ma'am. Then your Majesty has still an open mind!

VICTORIA An open mind? Oh, *of course*, I shall make my own choice, Lord Melbourne.

MELBOURNE Why, of course, Ma'am. I would not suggest otherwise, for a moment.

68

VICTORIA But there are certain things as to which I am quite resolved.

MELBOURNE As for instance?

VICTORIA My marriage, Lord Melbourne, must be a marriage of affection.

MELBOURNE That, I am sure, Ma'am, can be arranged without difficulty.

VICTORIA Someone, I mean, whose character I can respect: one whom I can love and look up to.

MELBOURNE Look up to?

VICTORIA Yes, Lord Melbourne, it may sound strange to you; but I must have as my husband one whom I can eventually look up to—when I have trained him for the position he will have to occupy.

MELBOURNE Oh, quite so, quite so. I trust that such a person will be found. And as your Majesty has owned to an open mind on the subject, I have here with me a list of—of possibles.

VICTORIA Oh, Lord Melbourne, how interesting! . . . How many?

MELBOURNE Well, at present, Ma'am, only five. But more are coming.

VICTORIA Coming?

MELBOURNE That is, I am making inquiries about them.

VICTORIA What kind of inquiries?

MELBOURNE All kinds of inquiries, Ma'am: my bounden duty. I would not wish to present your Majesty with one to whom there could be any possible objection.

69

VICTORIA And you have already found *five*! Lord Melbourne, how clever of you!

MELBOURNE 'Possibles,' I said. The inquiry is still going on; I am making it now. After inquiry of your Majesty, possibly there will be only one left.

VICTORIA I would like to see your list, Lord Melbourne.

MELBOURNE If your Majesty will pardon me a moment. When I have fully explained the considerations which guided me in my selection, I will submit my list for your Majesty's judgment, and (as I hope) approval.

VICTORIA I cannot approve all five!

MELBOURNE Just as a preliminary, Ma'am, why not? From five in the running select your favourite—the winner.

VICTORIA Perhaps I shall not choose one for a long time. But go on; I am quite interested and excited.

MELBOURNE The conditions, Ma'am, for a suitable consort to your Majesty's throne are necessarily special and particular—I might even say, peculiar. He must, of course, be of Royal blood; on the other hand, he must not be the direct or likely heir of any foreign king or reigning prince.

VICTORIA But why not, Lord Melbourne?

MELBOURNE Political complication might arise, Ma'am. The crown of Hanover has passed from your Majesty to another, because of the law which limits the succession to males only: a circumstance which I regard as fortunate. We want no more crowns of Hanover; the country is better without them. To proceed, then: he must be a

70

Prince of some Royal House, not too petty, not too important. We must avoid entangling alliances. He must also be of the Protestant faith.

VICTORIA Oh, yes, *I couldn't* marry a Papist.

MELBOURNE You could not, Ma'am. The Act of Settlement forbids it. He must be sufficiently young to be a suitable life-partner to your Majesty. He must know, or be capable of learning the English language; capable also of adapting himself to English customs, habits, and prejudices. The last is the most difficult of all, since the English have a prejudice against foreigners.

VICTORIA But, Lord Melbourne, that makes it impossible!

MELBOURNE No, Ma'am. It only rather restricts the choice. Someone must be found who, once naturalised, is able to share the prejudice. I've known it done. Your Majesty's cousin, Prince George of Cambridge, for instance, is rapidly acquiring a thoroughly British outlook. In another five years or so he will have learned to dislike foreigners as much as we do.

VICTORIA But do *you* dislike foreigners, Lord Melbourne?

MELBOURNE No, Ma'am, no: of course not! But sometimes, for political reasons, one has to pretend to.

VICTORIA Well, and what more?

MELBOURNE It would be well, Ma'am, if he had some means of his own; though they need not be large. Parliament will provide whatever addition is necessary. He must have presence suited to his station; also a certain

71

amount of brain, but not too much. He must not expect to interfere in politics.

VICTORIA Indeed, no! I should never allow it.

MELBOURNE Finally he must have health, and a sound constitution; he must—that is to say—come of good stock. And that, Ma'am, has been our main difficulty. Good stock, in the Royal Families of Europe, is rare.

VICTORIA Please explain, for I don't quite understand. 'Good stock'—I thought that meant cattle.

MELBOURNE It does, Ma'am, in certain connections. But it also means—what comes from father to son. You find it referred to in the Second Commandment where we are told that the sins of the fathers are visited on the children: also their virtues. In certain Royal lines the sins and the virtues have been mixed; and one has to be careful that they shall not be more mixed. For that reason the marriage of Royal cousins is generally inadvisable.

VICTORIA Oh.

MELBOURNE Generally, I say. In the case of a certain branch of your Majesty's family connections it is unfortunately true in a rather special degree. For that reason, in the list I am about to submit, I have not included— though it was suggested to me—two of your Majesty's cousins, who might otherwise have been desirable candidates—their Serene Highnesses Prince Ernest and Prince Albert of Saxe-Coburg Gotha.

VICTORIA But they both looked quite strong and healthy when I last saw them two years ago.

MELBOURNE Apparently, Ma'am. But appearances are sometimes deceptive. It is, of course, a delicate—

even a painful subject. But, acting under medical advice, and with a due sense of my responsibility, I have not included either of those young Princes in the list which I have now the honour to present to your Majesty.

(*He rises, and puts the list into her hand: hurriedly she glances down the names.*)

VICTORIA Oh, but do I know any of them?

MELBOURNE Your Majesty knows one of them very well.

VICTORIA Oh—I didn't see. But Prince George is my cousin too.

MELBOURNE By another branch, your Majesty. There is not there the same objection.

VICTORIA Oh, but I couldn't marry my Cousin George! He is so—so—

MELBOURNE Nobody wishes to decide your Majesty's choice. There are others.

VICTORIA But, as I say, I don't know any of them.

MELBOURNE That, Ma'am, can easily be remedied. You ask them to your Court in turn, saying nothing. And you let them go away again—saying nothing; or you *do* say something; and then—either they stay, or they come again.

VICTORIA But it is for me to decide, is it not?

MELBOURNE It is for your Majesty to decide. Your Majesty need not marry at all.

VICTORIA Oh, but I must marry. Mama always said so.

73

MELBOURNE So I have been told. But in so important a matter, even devoted filial affection should not be allowed to influence your *choice*. I have merely indicated, Ma'am, that were any attempt to be made to influence your choice in a certain direction, that choice—for reasons already given, I should have to oppose.

VICTORIA Lord Melbourne, I should not allow any opposition in a matter of that kind. It would not influence me for a moment.

MELBOURNE No?

VICTORIA Indeed, rather the other way.

MELBOURNE I see. I understand, Ma'am. I sympathise. I shall say no more. I will only commend the matter to your Majesty's good sense—and conscience.

VICTORIA Oh, how kind you always are to me, Lord Melbourne! What a lot you are teaching me!

MELBOURNE What a lot you are teaching *me*. I have served under older sovereigns—under two. But I have never served under one who listened to advice so wisely or so well.

VICTORIA (*rising*) Good-bye, Lord Melbourne. Will you keep the list, or shall I?

MELBOURNE By your leave, Ma'am; let what I have said be either remembered or forgotten. (*He tears the list and throws it into the fireplace.*) The choice must be your own.

VICTORIA Yes; but you haven't yet shown me—any portraits.

74

MELBOURNE Portraits, Ma'am? Why portraits?

VICTORIA I can't decide about anyone—till I know what they are like. It wouldn't be fair to them—or to me.

MELBOURNE But your Majesty can send for them, and see.

VICTORIA Oh, no. I'm not going to send for any, if I don't like the look of them.

MELBOURNE Portraits are sometimes deceptive, Ma'am.

VICTORIA Yes; I saw a portrait of my Cousin George of Cambridge the other day: quite handsome he looked.

MELBOURNE I can get their portraits, Ma'am, if you wish. But Court Painters, like Prime Ministers, know their duty; and they only do what is expected of them. If they can't do that, they have to go.

VICTORIA (*going toward a table, on which stands a framed portrait*) Here is a portrait that was sent to Mama, the other day—of my Cousin, Prince Albert.

MELBOURNE (*who has followed to the table*) Oh! Ah! Yes. H'm.

VICTORIA Surely *he must* have grown very handsome! It would not be possible for a Court Painter to imagine anyone like that.

MELBOURNE. You never know, Ma'am, you never know. Imagination sometimes goes a long way. Well, the list having gone, am I now to make a collection of portraits for your Majesty?

VICTORIA Oh, no, Lord Melbourne. I wasn't speaking seriously when I said that.

75

MELBOURNE No more was I, Ma'am. But I do ask your Majesty to *think* seriously. The future welfare of this country is now in this little hand.

(*He stoops and kisses it.*)

VICTORIA Indeed, Lord Melbourne, I pay great attention to everything that you say. And I shall continue to take your advice, whenever I find it—possible. Good-bye.

(LORD MELBOURNE *bows himself out. She goes and takes up the portrait and kisses it.*)

Albert . . . Albert . . . Albert . . . will you marry me?

A State Secret

A State Secret

1838

LORD MELBOURNE, *the Prime Minister, sits in his writ-ing-room at Downing Street. With him is* MR. TUDOR, *British Minister at the Court of Saxe-Coburg Gotha, now on home leave. The Prime Minister lolls indolently at ease; so far the official report has not much interested him.* MR. TUDOR *sits upright in his chair, precise and respectful. He is much the younger man; but already he has been taken into the confidence of persons of importance; and is not without a certain sense of his own.*

MELBOURNE Yes? Well? What also have you to report?

TUDOR The Court of Saxe-Coburg is a little anxious, my Lord, because nothing has been said lately about the possible arrangement—of a marriage.

MELBOURNE *(his interest awakened)* Ah?

TUDOR The Court is anxious, my Lord, because the Princes are now of marriageable age; and it doesn't want to let good chances slip.

MELBOURNE Are any other brides in the market then?

TUDOR For His Serene Highness Prince Ernest there is the prospect of a very eligible offer. But a rumour of

79

this other possibility has got about; and they won't make the offer if it is going to be refused.

MELBOURNE So they want the coast cleared for Prince Ernest, eh? What about Prince Albert?

TUDOR I have reason to believe that they would prefer it should be Prince Ernest.

MELBOURNE And I have reason—very grave reason—to prefer that it should be neither. Anyway, let Prince Ernest go. Tell 'em to give him away to anybody as quick as they like. That'll be one off my mind, at any rate.

TUDOR Your Lordship does not now favour the proposal, then?

MELBOURNE I never did. It was the Duchess with her damned interference. She seems to think this country was invented entirely for the benefit of her own family. 'Twas she made the match, as far as it could be made.

TUDOR Is Her Majesty greatly under the influence of Her Royal Highness the Duchess, my Lord?

MELBOURNE Not now; no, not now. But she is greatly under the influence of her own feelings. And it so happens that—before I could be there to prevent—the thing was done. She has seen both of them. Oh, yes; she'd have liked Prince Ernest well enough, if Prince Albert hadn't been there also.

TUDOR At Saxe-Coburg they do not wish it to be Prince Albert, my Lord.

MELBOURNE What they don't wish is not going to count. I'm afraid, I'm very much afraid she will go her own way in this matter. She's in love with him. She kisses

80

his portrait, I'm told. And it's very serious—very serious indeed. Cousins of that stock marrying may be *fatal*.

TUDOR If your Lordship wishes to prevent the marriage with Prince Albert, it can be done quite easily.

MELBOURNE I've been trying all I know how. And it's God damn difficult. She shut me down—as if I were nobody. I've tried more than once.

TUDOR It need not be difficult, my Lord. You have merely to state certain facts, and—the match will be off.

MELBOURNE Well, now you do interest me exceedingly! Already morganatically married to some German wench, eh?

TUDOR Oh, no, no. Nothing of that sort. The Prince has a blameless character. The same cannot be said about his late mother, the Duchess.

MELBOURNE No, so I . . . His parents separated over something, I believe.

TUDOR They separated when the Prince was five years old. She went to live in Paris; he never saw her again. The *cause* of the separation was of *more* than five years' standing, my Lord. (*This is said with meaning.*)

MELBOURNE (*rising, with sharp interest*) Heh? . . . You don't say so!

TUDOR After five years the parties forgot to be prudent: the thing got about.

MELBOURNE (*sitting down*) Who was—the *other* party?

81

TUDOR One of the Court Chamberlains: a very charming and accomplished person; but a commoner, and of Jewish extraction.

MELBOURNE (*pondering deeply*) Dear me! Dear me! . . . *Healthy?*

TUDOR Oh, quite. . . . You have only to tell Her Majesty that her cousin, Prince Albert, is not quite so much her cousin as she imagines, and I apprehend that you will have no further difficulty.

MELBOURNE (*following his own line of thought*) The *Mother* was healthy, was she not?

TUDOR Well, she produced two fine boys. But *Prince Albert is the finer*.

MELBOURNE Then only Prince Ernest is really related?

TUDOR That is so.

MELBOURNE And the Duke can't be the father of Prince Albert?

TUDOR Unfortunately, no.

MELBOURNE You are sure?

TUDOR I have confidentially been shown documents which put the matter beyond dispute. In the deed of separation the facts were fully admitted.

MELBOURNE Why were you shown them?

TUDOR I imagine, my Lord, because at Saxe-Coburg there is a wish that Prince Ernest should be Her Majesty's choice—not Prince Albert.

MELBOURNE (*rising, in a tone of deep satisfaction*) Ah! . . . Mr. Tudor, I am enormously obliged to you—*enormously* obliged to you. Your information is a godsend! And—if my term of office holds for a while, as I think it will, I can promise you promotion. The next suitable vacancy will be yours. Understand: you have done your country a great service.

TUDOR (*who has risen at the same time as his chief*) My Lord, I thank you.

MELBOURNE I thank *you*! Good-bye.

> (MR. TUDOR *bows over his hand with deep respect, and goes.* MELBOURNE *rings, and walks about excitedly. A* SECRETARY *enters.*)

MELBOURNE Has Lord Conyngham waited?

SECRETARY Yes, my Lord.

MELBOURNE Then ask his Lordship to be good enough to come in.

> (*The* SECRETARY *goes.* MELBOURNE *sits down, writes, gets up again, rubs his hands. He is as happy as a schoolboy. Enter* LORD CON-YNGHAM.)

MELBOURNE Conyngham, we've done the trick! We are going to marry her to Prince Albert.

CONYNGHAM (*aghast*) Good Heavens! You don't say so! . . . But—

MELBOURNE (*going up to him, and speaking with an intensity of significance which at last has its effect*) It's all right! . . . It's all right! . . . *It's all right!*

83

CONYNGHAM But, my dear Mel, what has made it—
'all right,' as you say?

MELBOURNE *Human nature.*

(*And at last the* LORD CHAMBERLAIN *comprehends.*)

CONYNGHAM Well! It seems almost like—Divine
Intervention.

MELBOURNE It was, Conyngham, it was! It isn't only
marriages that are made in Heaven. Liaisons are made
there too. Thank God! .

Strained Relations

Strained Relations

1838

The DUCHESS OF KENT *sits in her old apartment in Kensington Palace, to which new splendours have recently been added. Before her stands* LADY CHARLOTTE—*one of her Maids of Honour.*

DUCHESS So; she said you were to go? What did you say?

LADY CHARLOTTE Madam, I only said that my appointment was to the Household of your Royal Highness.

DUCHESS Ah! You said that! Good! And she—what?

LADY CHARLOTTE She said that, when your Royal Highness had a separate household of your own, there would be no further objection.

DUCHESS 'Separate!' . . . 'Separate!' She has not yet said that to *me*; but she has meant it. It has been coming, from the first day: her own bed, her own room—now it is her own house. Presently it will be her own country that I am not to share! (*Enter* VICTORIA.) So! You are sending me away!

VICTORIA Mama!

DUCHESS You are turning your own Mother out of doors.

VICTORIA Lady Charlotte, go, please!

87

DUCHESS Why is she to go? She is mine: she is not yours.

> (*But without further word, the look of direct authority has been sufficient.* LADY CHARLOTTE *disappears.*)

VICTORIA Mama, I wish you would not speak to me like that before—servants.

DUCHESS Servants? Lady Charlotte is my friend, one of the few I have left.

VICTORIA You pay her for her service.

DUCHESS *You* are paid for *your service* too—the country pays you. Does that give it the right to dismiss you at a week's notice?

VICTORIA Mama dear, don't be foolish.

DUCHESS Oh, what has happened to you? You are no longer the same!

VICTORIA How can you expect me to be? I belong now to myself. I find that a great change.

DUCHESS And who made you be—yourself? What had you done *for yourself*, till you got rid of me?

VICTORIA Very little, almost nothing. For eighteen years I was not even allowed to go downstairs without somebody to hold my hand. But I did it sometimes, when no one was looking.

DUCHESS Behind my back?

VICTORIA Yes. I would look out from the room. If there was a servant-in-waiting, I would send them on an errand. Then—when I was quite sure that no one could

88

see—I would run down—down and up again, as fast as I could go. That was about my only chance of doing anything, *for* myself, by myself.

DUCHESS Then you were deceitful.

VICTORIA Had you asked me, I should have told you. I have never told you an untruth, Mama; and I am not going to begin now.

DUCHESS Then now tell me the truth—quick! Do you any longer love me?

VICTORIA Of course I love you, Mama.

DUCHESS Though you take from me everything that is mine.

VICTORIA On the contrary, dear Mama. I am going to give you something more than you have ever had before. Often now I have to leave you alone.

DUCHESS Yes.

VICTORIA But not so much alone, in one sense, as you would like to be. You and Lehzen do not get on well together.

DUCHESS We do *not*. Why do you keep her? She was only your governess. Send Lehzen away.

VICTORIA No, Mama.

DUCHESS 'No, Mama!' 'No, Mama!' It is always 'No, Mama,' now to everything I ask you.

VICTORIA When you said you did not wish to go to Windsor last week, did I make you go?

DUCHESS No, but you only put it off. I do not like

Windsor. It reminds me of your Uncle too much. It was there that he insulted me before everybody.

VICTORIA You need not go to Windsor now, unless you like, Mama.

DUCHESS Need not go? If you go to Windsor, I must.

VICTORIA No, Mama. It is not necessary now. Should I need you, I can send for you.

DUCHESS But—you are not going to Windsor without *me*! It would be in all the papers.

VICTORIA I want you to have a change, Mama. It will do you good; and I am sure that, when you have tried it, you will like it. I have given directions that in future you are to have your own suite of apartments at Buckingham Palace, with a separate service of your own. Next week, when I go to Windsor, it will be ready for you.

DUCHESS I do not like Buckingham Palace. I am not going there . . . I say that I am not going there . . . Do you hear me? I am not going to Buckingham Palace, I am going to Windsor.

VICTORIA You are mistaken, Mama dear. You are not going to Windsor, for I do not invite you. I will do so later. When Ernest and Albert pay their promised visit, it will, of course, be necessary that you should be there.

DUCHESS Then I will not come!

VICTORIA I don't think we need discuss the matter any further: the date is not yet fixed. And now, Mama, about Lady Charlotte; for I see that she has been speaking to
90

you. When you have a Household of your own, I shall not interfere. If you wish then to have Lady Charlotte as one of your Maids of Honour, she can come back to you again. Here, for reasons with which I need not trouble you, I do not wish her to remain.

DUCHESS So!

VICTORIA And if you stayed with me, Mama, there would have to be *other* changes.

DUCHESS What do you mean?

VICTORIA I would rather not say. I hope that, in the short time you are still with me, it may not be necessary.

DUCHESS Oh, why is there always now this—this opposition? This *battle*? It never happened before.

VICTORIA Often, Mama. But *then* you always got your way. If it is painful to you now when I decide things for myself, think how painful it used to be to me, when I was never allowed to.

DUCHESS You throw my training of you back into my teeth, eh? You would have liked better to be with those wicked Uncles of yours, with their wine, and their women, and all!

VICTORIA Mama, don't forget yourself.

DUCHESS Forget myself!

(*Enter* LEHZEN.)

VICTORIA Ah, Lehzen dear, is it already time for me to come?

DUCHESS Let that woman go! I have not said yet all that I want to say!

VICTORIA Good-bye, Mama.

DUCHESS Victoria, I am your Mother, and I command you to stay!

> (*But* VICTORIA *and* LEHZEN *have gone. The* DUCHESS *sits down to weep.*)

DUCHESS To think that this should have happened to me, of all people!

> (*Enter* SIR JOHN CONROY.)

CONROY Dear Lady, what is the matter?

DUCHESS My daughter is the matter.

CONROY I met Her Majesty just now, with the Baroness.

DUCHESS Did she say nothing?

CONROY Nothing.

DUCHESS Did she look at you?

CONROY Yes: she looked at me.

DUCHESS You bowed: did she return it?

CONROY Hardly.

DUCHESS You are going to be the next—if she can manage it. But I shall not let it be. No; she shall not send you away—my friend.

CONROY What has happened?

DUCHESS To-day she takes from me one of my friends. Lady Charlotte is to go. Yesterday I was not to dress myself as I liked.

CONROY Not dress?

DUCHESS No! . . . I had my dressmaker there. I was going to leave off some of all this stuff and nonsense which

I am wearing for a man that hated and insulted me. She said the dates for change of mourning were all in the Court circular, and must be obeyed. And when I asked her if I was expected to consult the Court circular, she said yes, as long as I stayed at the Court; which was almost like telling me to go away. And when I asked was she still in deep mourning for having become Queen, she said, 'Don't talk nonsense, Mama dear!' That—to *me*! Whenever she has anything unkind to say to me now, she puts 'Mama dear' at the end of it. I always made her say it when I punished her for anything. Now she says it to punish *me*.

CONROY Why do you still stay with her? Aren't you free now to go where you like?

DUCHESS Oh, how can I go away from my own life? She was everything to me. And now to her I am nothing! There is only one thing now left me to work and hope for. When that is done I shall just go away to my own country —and die.

CONROY What is that, dear Lady?

DUCHESS Just to see her married to Albert or Ernest. I planned it from the day she was born. But I'm beginning to be afraid even that won't happen now. Oh, what a miserable woman I am! And I thought I was going to be so happy!

CONROY Dear Lady, don't make me feel that I am useless.

DUCHESS. You? What can you do? She won't take advice from *anybody* now, except that wicked Melbourne. And he hates me. It is all *his* doing. She could not have changed to me like that, unless someone had come between.

93

CONROY (*embracing her*) My dear Lady, and mistress!

DUCHESS Oh, my friend! I am so utterly alone!

CONROY Alone? No: not while you have *me*.

DUCHESS Oh, yes, I have *you*. But if she knew—or even guessed—it would be all over. She has not pity for anyone. Human nature means nothing to her—nothing!

CONROY (*renewing his embrace*) While to us it means so much! Everything.

(*Enter* VICTORIA. *They break apart.*)

DUCHESS I thought you were going out with Lehzen.

VICTORIA (*coldly*) Have I returned sooner than you expected, Mama?

DUCHESS Oh, it does not matter.

VICTORIA No? (SIR JOHN, *meanwhile, is making for the door.*) Do not go, Sir John. I have something I wish to say. I am making certain alterations in the arrangements of my Household. You have been told of them, perhaps, and were taking your leave of Her Royal Highness when I came in. As I do not wish that there should be any delay in the matter, let it be so. You will see the Comptroller before you go. I have given directions that a solatium shall be paid to you in recognition of your past services. You will leave to-day.

DUCHESS You are sending away my friend?

VICTORIA I did not know he was your friend, Mama.

DUCHESS You shall not! This is unheard-of. It is monstrous!

VICTORIA No, Mama; not monstrous, only wise.

DUCHESS I will not allow it! I will not allow it! If he goes, you kill me.

VICTORIA Mama! Sir John Conroy, will you retire?

DUCHESS Do not! Do not move! (*She rushes to the central door and stands barring it.*) He shall not go!

> (*Undiverted, the* QUEEN *points quietly to another door, which has no tragic figure standing before it.*)

VICTORIA *That* door, Sir John.

> (*Such perfect common-sense commands the situation. Without hesitation he goes.*)

DUCHESS (*coming away from the door, her defence of it now useless*) Oh, you—you—you, that was once my little daughter! That I taught to be so good!

VICTORIA You, my Mother, that I was taught to think so good.

DUCHESS What do you mean? What do you say?

VICTORIA Nothing—that needs repeating.

DUCHESS Oh, you have no heart in you! You are harder than a stone wall. If you can no longer respect me—have you no pity?

VICTORIA Pity?

DUCHESS Yes, what is my life without you? What has my life been for? Why did your Father and I marry? For you to be born. He did not love me: I did not love him. It was for *you*. No, *he* did not do it for *you*. *He* wanted a son. When you came, he was disappointed. But I—I was not. He died, and you were everything to me.

95

And ever since, I have been alone—*except for you*. Then you became Queen, and you are mine no longer; all at once you are your own, and I am *nothing*! And I am to live without love, and to have no friend? You see a little love offered to me—nothing wrong—just friendship, kindness, and you take it away from me, you drive him away. But he shall come back to me—he shall come back!

VICTORIA Mama dear, when you have a Household of your own, you will have in it whoever you like. I said so before; if it will be any comfort to you, I say it again. I have had to send Sir John Conroy away because here, it seems to me, he does not know his place. What his place is likely to be in the future, when the matter is in your own hands, I see only too clearly.

DUCHESS Victoria, you forget yourself!

VICTORIA No, Mama; the forgetfulness is yours.

DUCHESS I forget *nothing*!

VICTORIA Then, please to remember, Mama dear, that you are now my subject.

DUCHESS (*hardly believing her ears*) Your *what*?

VICTORIA If you wish me to repeat the word, I will. All my duty of obedience to you is over. It is now rather the other way.

DUCHESS Oh! Oh! This is too much!—This to be the end of all my care of you! Have I become the mother of a revolting daughter?

VICTORIA Of a reigning Queen, Mama.

(*She seats herself at the writing-table.*)

96

I am going to write some letters now, Mama; and I would prefer to be alone. I am going to invite Ernest and Albert to come and stay at Windsor early next month; and I shall want you to be there, so please make no other engagements.

DUCHESS (*to herself*) Ernest! Albert! Ah, then I am not quite dead yet. So you are writing to them? Very well. My love to both of them—especially to Albert.

(*She goes out. A* FOOTMAN *enters.*)

FOOTMAN If it please your Majesty, Lord Melbourne asks if he may see your Majesty.

VICTORIA Ask Lord Melbourne to come in.

(*She continues writing, till* MELBOURNE *enters. Then goes to meet him.*)

Dear Lord Melbourne, I am so pleased to see you.

MELBOURNE That is kind of you, Ma'am: but your Majesty is always kind. I also am pleased—more pleased even than usual—to see your Majesty; for I have come to inform your Majesty of a happy circumstance.

VICTORIA Yes?

MELBOURNE In a matter where I feared we were going to differ somewhat seriously, we now see eye to eye.

VICTORIA About what, Lord Melbourne?

MELBOURNE As regards your Majesty's proposed marriage—

VICTORIA But, Lord Melbourne, I have not proposed marriage to anyone.

MELBOURNE Matrimonial intentions, then, let me say—
(*Very respectfully he takes up the portrait of* PRINCE ALBERT
and looks at it.) I now withdraw all opposition. In fact I
cordially agree. I think your Majesty's choice is excellent.
In your hands the future welfare of the country is
safe.

VICTORIA Oh, that is very kind of you, Lord Melbourne; and I am glad to hear it. But I feel bound to tell
you that, even had you *not* agreed, it would have made no
difference at all.

MELBOURNE No, Ma'am. The facts being what they are,
it *would* have made no difference at all. Not the least!

VICTORIA I wanted you to know that, Lord Melbourne

MELBOURNE (*bowing acknowledgment*) And the Prince
comes—when, Ma'am?

VICTORIA Next month, I hope.

MELBOURNE Next month, let us all hope! And what,
Ma'am, does Her Royal Highness the Duchess think
about it?

VICTORIA Mama will be pleased, I'm sure.

> (*She takes the portrait from his hand and kisses it.
> But—she does not know—the facts!*)

MELBOURNE 'Mama' ought to be very pleased, indeed—
with such a daughter! So they married and lived happily
ever after. And the world said—

VICTORIA Oh, Lord Melbourne, you are funny!

MELBOURNE Your Majesty is right as usual. The
world said 'Oh, Lord Melbourne, you are funny!'

Woman Proposes

Woman Proposes

15th October 1839

In a sitting-room at Windsor Castle PRINCE ALBERT *of Saxe-Coburg Gotha stands looking rather sadly out of the window. The outside prospect is beautiful; but some other prospect seems to depress him. Still very young, he has already a full-grown conscience, which at times becomes too much for him.*

The door opens, his brother, PRINCE ERNEST, *enters, shuts the door, and stands looking at him. After a pause he speaks: his English is good, but he has a foreign accent.*

ERNEST Well, Albert?

ALBERT (*not turning*) Jawohl, mein Bruder?

ERNEST We must speak English.

ALBERT (*turning*) Why?

ERNEST For practice. One of us—you or I—will have to always.

ALBERT (*sighing*) I suppose!

ERNEST (*guardedly*) Which of us, do you 'suppose,' it is going to be?

ALBERT That is not for me to say. The decision will not be ours.

ERNEST. But we shall have to say *something*—one of us—presently.

ALBERT Yes, presently. And only one answer will be possible.

ERNEST You mean it must be 'yes'?

ALBERT Since it cannot possibly be 'no.'

ERNEST Then—you do not wish—?

ALBERT I have given up 'wishing,' Brother. Wishes might hinder.

ERNEST You don't seem very happy about it. . . . No?

ALBERT This foreign land terrifies me. Look!

(*He indicates the landscape.*)

ERNEST Rather beautiful, don't you think?

ALBERT Beautiful? Yes, but all the same it means exile—to live in it.

ERNEST But then—to be almost a King!

ALBERT No! The English people will never allow a foreigner—you or me—to be King: nor anything like one.

ERNEST We are hardly more foreigners than are some of their own Royalty. We speak as good English.

ALBERT But we were not *born* in England.

ERNEST What real difference does that make to a man—where he was born?

ALBERT Real? None. But—to the English—*all* the difference. Has it never struck you, Ernest, that the English are a very romantic nation?

ERNEST Rather materialistic, I should say.

ALBERT Yes, but very romantic over their material—some of it. Their history—their wars—their royal successions—their revolutions. I have been reading English history lately. It is all a romance. Their lost battles? Where are they? Except for one or two—they do not exist.

ERNEST What about their lost countries—France, and America?

ALBERT They don't know they have lost them—till it is such old history that it means to them—nothing. For three hundred years after they had been driven out, their Kings still called themselves Kings of France. That is true, Ernest. Don't laugh!

ERNEST. Of France? Yet don't like foreigners, you say?

ALBERT Oh, they like *ruling* them. They do that as a favour. Here you or I will only be—a puppet, kept to breed by. If it is *you*, are you going to resign yourself to that—willingly?

ERNEST If it is to be *me*, you say? It is time that I speak, Albert. It *must* be me. Did not Papa tell you?

ALBERT Tell me? No! What?

ERNEST Oh, well: perhaps he found it more difficult to tell—you. I do not know. But this is quite sure. He wishes it shall be *me*.

ALBERT *You?*

ERNEST Are you sorry?

ALBERT (*resentfully*) Then—why did he make me come?

ERNEST (*with a touch of sarcasm*) Oh, she has to choose, she has to choose! But she has to choose—*me*.

ALBERT Why?

ERNEST It is Papa's wish. He says—that there are family reasons.

ALBERT Why did he not tell *me* so?

ERNEST I do not know, Albert; I do not know. But you were always our Mamma's favourite. So, perhaps, that is why I am his.

> (*Some new thought seems to have come to* ERNEST. *He looks at* ALBERT *curiously.*)

ALBERT What was their quarrel about, Ernest?

ERNEST It was more than a quarrel. I am thinking. (*Evidently he is.*) . . . Do you remember our Mamma at all, Albert?

ALBERT Oh, yes. I remember her, just once, very well. She was crying. She took me into her arms and cried, and cried, till I cried too.

ERNEST You were very young when she—went away from us. . . . I wonder . . . (*ponderingly*).

ALBERT She used to write me letters.

ERNEST Ah! She never wrote one to me!

104

ALBERT They came secretly, by hand. I was to let nobody know.

ERNEST Did you answer those letters?

ALBERT Yes.

ERNEST Secretly?

ALBERT Yes.

ERNEST So you never told *me*.

ALBERT I was not to do so, lest it should be found out.

ERNEST Though I was your Brother? Oh, yes! You were always more to her than I. She wanted to take you with her—did you know? *Me*—she did not want.

ALBERT When she went to live in Paris—alone, you mean?

ERNEST (*scoffingly*) Oh! not alone. . . . (*Suddenly a thought strikes him.*) Ah! So *that* is it? Now I understand! . . . Yes. . . . Listen, Albert. . . . *It has got to be me!* You are my Brother, but you are not the son of my Father. I have just come to be sure of it.

ALBERT I am not—?

(*He stands dumbfounded.*)

ERNEST (*with more emphasis*) *You are not the son of my Father*. And *that* is why he says now it must be *me*. . . . Forgive me, Albert! You are very dear to me. But you must obey my Father.

ALBERT If what you tell me is true, why should I obey—*your* Father?

ERNEST Oh, well, Albert, because—whatever you are *not*—he is still your Reigning Prince. You owe him loyal duty and obedience, like all the rest.

ALBERT No!

ERNEST No?

ALBERT (*touched in his pride*) He did not tell *me*! Had he wished for my obedience, he should have told *me*, not *you*.

ERNEST The explanation would have been rather difficult.

ALBERT No doubt. That he did not choose to explain— removes the difficulty—so far as it concerns *me*.

ERNEST (*startled*) What, then, do you mean to do, Albert?

ALBERT If she asks me, I shall accept.

ERNEST Then she shall *not* ask you! Albert, we have the same Mother, and your honour is mine, and this shall never be known. But I must see that my Father's wishes are obeyed. I shall have you sent home.

ALBERT Sent home!

ERNEST Yes, at once. You shall be ordered to return. I shall send word to-day.

ALBERT And what if I refuse to go?

ERNEST My dear Albert, we are not English, we are German. If the Duke, my Father, your Sovereign Prince, sends for you to return, you *will* return. You know that perfectly well.

(ALBERT *looks at him in silence for a while; then turns
slowly away.*)

I am not taking away from your happiness, Albert. You
will be happier than I.

ALBERT Happiness is not everything.

ERNEST Almost.

ALBERT Live for it, and you lose it! To be happy has
never been my thought—about life. I have not aimed for
that.

ERNEST No? What, then?

ALBERT To do something that shall be worth doing.

ERNEST Just now you said—to be a 'puppet.' I save
you from *that*.

ALBERT (*coldly*) I would rather save myself.

ERNEST Ah! So you have ambition?

ALBERT Ambition? . . . I wonder. . . . Is it ambitious
to give oneself—up?

ERNEST No, Brother; but you will not have to give up
yourself. Only, in this, do as you are told.

ALBERT As *you* tell me?

ERNEST As your Reigning Prince tells you. As you will
be told—very soon.

ALBERT Well, about that—we shall see!

ERNEST *Yes*, Albert.

(Hearing a step, they turn. VICTORIA *has entered. She has already taken in something of a situation which she is not to understand. And since she is to be denied its explanation, she intends to terminate it.)*

VICTORIA What are you two looking so serious about?

ERNEST The rain.

VICTORIA Oh, but it will clear presently; then we will go for a ride in the Park.

ERNEST Oh, that will be very nice, to be sure!

VICTORIA I hope you are going to enjoy your stay, Cousin.

ERNEST Very much. I shall find it most delightful.

VICTORIA And you too, Albert?

ALBERT You are very kind, dear Cousin. How could I help enjoying myself while I am with you?

VICTORIA Albert, that is the first pretty speech you have ever made me!

ALBERT I am sorry, Cousin.

VICTORIA Oh, but I like it!

ALBERT I mean—that it should be only the first.

VICTORIA Well, so long as it's not the last, I don't mind.

ERNEST The rain is clearing. It has stopped. Shall we go out now?

VICTORIA *(correctively)* Cousin Ernest, I have made all necessary arrangements. We shall go out when we do go

108

out—and not before. Besides—have you practised your music yet? At home, I was told, you practise every day.

ERNEST But here one cannot find the time.

VICTORIA Go, and do it now; and there will be time.

ERNEST I tried one of the pianos the day we arrived, Cousin. It was not in very good tune.

VICTORIA But that doesn't matter. You will be alone. No one will hear you.

ERNEST Generally, when we practise, Albert and I practise together.

VICTORIA Duets, you mean? Oh, but if the piano is out of tune, duets would be dreadful. Go and practise by yourself, Ernest; and Albert shall practise by *him*self, another time.

ERNEST Is it a command, Cousin?

VICTORIA My dear Ernest, I wouldn't think of commanding you. But I do want you to be quite at home here; and as you *always* practise at home, I want you to practise here, and now. We shall not start our ride for an hour. That gives you just time; so do go—now.

(COUSIN ERNEST *is not pleased; but the little creature is so born to rule that she gets her way.*)

ERNEST Very well, Cousin . . . Albert, *remember!*

(*He goes out, with a jerk of the head toward* ALBERT, *which conveys a meaning.*)

VICTORIA How strangely Ernest spoke to you, then! Is anything the matter?

109

ALBERT (*with reserve*) Oh, no; nothing serious.

VICTORIA You haven't been quarrelling, I hope?

ALBERT We never quarrel.

VICTORIA I think it would be very hard to quarrel with *you*, Albert. *I* couldn't.

ALBERT Please, don't ever try!

VICTORIA Some people are able to quarrel without trying.

ALBERT Yes.

(*A pause.*)

VICTORIA I suppose they like it.

ALBERT Yes, I suppose so.

(*A pause.*)

VICTORIA Won't you sit down, Albert?

(*He takes a distant seat.*)

Why don't you sit nearer? Talking then is so much easier.

(*He comes towards her.*)

ALBERT You are very kind, Cousin, ever since we came: to both of us, I mean.

VICTORIA I am very fond of—Ernest.

ALBERT Yes, so am I.

(*He sits down.*)

VICTORIA You've always been together, haven't you?

ALBERT We've never been apart yet.

VICTORIA How very nice that has been—for both.

(*A pause.*)

Would it be a great trial to you, if you had to live away from him?

ALBERT Of course, the parting would be a trial. But one would get used to it—as to other things—if it had to be.

VICTORIA My life has been so different from yours. I have never had anyone always with me like that—one of my own age. All my life I have been so much alone, except, of course, with Mamma. I don't know what it can be like—to have a brother.

ALBERT One gets very fond of a brother.

VICTORIA Yes; but one can get fonder of someone else—can one not?

ALBERT It happens, sometimes.

(*A pause.*)

VICTORIA Albert! What are you doing?

ALBERT I was listening to Ernest, practising. I can just hear him; it is Beethoven.

VICTORIA Don't listen to Ernest! You must listen to me!

ALBERT I beg your pardon, Cousin; I was listening. Please don't think I am inattentive.

VICTORIA (*after a long pause*) Albert . . . I have something to say to you.

ALBERT Yes . . . what is it, Cousin?

III

VICTORIA In my position, it is I who have to say it—unfortunately. Ordinarily it is not what a woman would wish to say herself. She would rather—*he* said it.

ALBERT Is there anything you wish me to say—that I can say?

VICTORIA (*tremulously*) To hear you say you *can* love me, is all I can hope—yet. If you could say that you already *do* love me, that would be—almost like Heaven.

ALBERT I do . . . love you, Cousin.

VICTORIA Enough to marry me?

ALBERT More than enough to marry you. For people in our position often marry without any love at all.

VICTORIA I couldn't do that—Albert.

ALBERT Nor could I—Victoria.

VICTORIA Then you will marry me?

ALBERT If it is still your wish—when you know me— I will, very gratefully and humbly, accept this dear hand that you offer me.

VICTORIA When I know you?

ALBERT Yes; for I, too, have something to say. A few minutes ago, I did not know about myself what I know now. Even now I have no proof. Yet something tells me that it is true.

VICTORIA Don't tell me—if it is anything I shouldn't wish to know, Albert.

ALBERT But I must. My brother Ernest and I had the same mother; but not the same father.

112

VICTORIA I don't understand.

ALBERT I am sorry you should have to. . . . My Mother and my Father (Ernest's Father) separated—after I was born. They did not love each other. . . . My Mother must have loved someone else.

VICTORIA While she was married? (*His head makes silent assent.*) Before you were born—or after?

ALBERT Before.

VICTORIA. Who?

ALBERT I don't know. So neither do I know who *I* am. Perhaps I shall never know. Yet there must still be someone who could tell me—more than I have been able to tell you. . . . Shall I—? Do you wish me to go now? I had to tell you this.

VICTORIA Yes . . . of course.

ALBERT Then now—you wish me to go?

VICTORIA No. . . . No. . . . I wish you to stay. It makes no difference to *me*. . . . And besides, who knows?

ALBERT Somebody must know. Ernest knows.

VICTORIA Ernest?

ALBERT It was he who told me. And his Father knows.

VICTORIA But his Father sent you here—let you come.

ALBERT Yes. But he hoped it would be Ernest.

VICTORIA How very silly of him!

ALBERT Why?

113

VICTORIA How could it possibly be Ernest, after I had seen you? . . . Oh, Albert! Albert! What does it matter? It is not your Father that I shall marry: it is you!

> (*And as she speaks they are in each other's arms. Her passionate abandonment awakens response, though of a more restrained nature.*)

ALBERT My very dear Cousin! My sweet Wife that is to be.

VICTORIA Aren't you going to kiss me?

ALBERT If I may. (*The kiss is given.*)

VICTORIA Again, please! . . . Again!

ALBERT I pray God you do not ever have to repent of this.

VICTORIA Repent? How could I repent! It is not in my nature, Albert. Besides, there isn't going to be time. We must be married quite soon. Everybody expects it.

ALBERT Expects it? They don't know!

VICTORIA Expects me to marry, I mean. I had to choose *some*body. But I wasn't going to choose *any*body.

ALBERT Not even Ernest?

VICTORIA Oh, I liked Ernest very much, from the first. . . . I do still.

ALBERT (*with a touch of humour*) Is that why you sent him to practise? . . . He *knew*.

VICTORIA That this was going to happen?

ALBERT No; he did not know *that*.

VICTORIA What, then?

ALBERT That you were going to ask me.

VICTORIA Well, then, what else could he suppose *would* happen?

ALBERT He expected me to say no.

VICTORIA (*almost affronted*) But you couldn't have said 'No' to a Queen—could you, Albert?

ALBERT No, dear; one couldn't say 'No' to a Queen.

VICTORIA But did you want to?

ALBERT No, Dearest One. All it means is that Ernest will be disappointed.

VICTORIA Oh, I see. Poor Ernest! . . . Well, we must both try to be very nice and kind to him. . . . And now it is quite time that we went for our ride.

ALBERT Isn't Ernest to come, too?

VICTORIA Why, yes, of course!

ALBERT Then won't you send and say he may stop practising? This hasn't taken an hour, you know.

(*Enter* ERNEST.)

VICTORIA Nor has he, either; for here he is. Are you ready to come riding, Ernest?

ERNEST Quite, if you are, Cousin.

VICTORIA Oh, yes, we are quite ready *now*. Everything has been settled. Tell him, Albert.

ALBERT Ernest. . . . You told me to remember. . . . I forgot.

> (ERNEST *has only to look at them, and the awful
> situation is explained. It will also have to be
> explained elsewhere. For when* VICTORIA *says
> that a thing is settled, it* is *settled—for good.*)

115

Enter Prince

Enter Prince

1840

In the same room in which she made her proposal of marriage, THE QUEEN *sits waiting, radiantly happy, and expectant; and when one of her* GENTLEMEN *opens the door to announce,* 'HIS ROYAL HIGHNESS, PRINCE ALBERT OF SAXE-COBURG GOTHA,' *she springs eagerly to her feet.* THE PRINCE *enters; the door closes; and—for her, at any rate—ceremony is over. But* THE PRINCE *remains a little stiff.*

VICTORIA Good morning, Albert!

ALBERT Good morning, Victoria.

VICTORIA A kiss, please!

ALBERT (*conscientiously*) Three, if you prefer.

VICTORIA (*as she kisses him*) I would prefer so many—more than we have time for, Dearest! . . . But now we have to talk business.

ALBERT (*stiffly*) Oh, yes; business.

VICTORIA The time being now so short for getting everything settled—as it must be settled.

ALBERT (*coldly*) I thought that you had settled everything for me already—before I came.

VICTORIA Almost; not quite. You see, Albert, you were not altogether pleased·with what I wrote to you in my letters. Talking things over is so much better and easier; because then I can explain. And I do so want you to be quite satisfied with everything I have arranged for you, and to understand that I was right.

ALBERT I will do my best, Victoria, to be satisfied with all that you say is necessary.

VICTORIA I am quite sure you will, Albert dear, now that we are together, so that I can make everything plain. . . . Here is the list of all the things I want to speak about.

(*She seats herself.*)

ALBERT Oh, yes.

VICTORIA Please sit down, Albert! I can't have you standing before me, when we are *alone*.

ALBERT Not even when I am receiving orders?

VICTORIA You mustn't call explanations 'orders,' Dearest! The only Order I have given you is my Order of the Garter, which I sent to you on the day when our betrothal was made public.

ALBERT That was a great honour—very gratifying.

VICTORIA What is the matter, Albert?

ALBERT Nothing. You give me everything that it is right for me to have.

VICTORIA Yes; I *like* giving it.

ALBERT I am sure you do.

VICTORIA Of course there are some things which must wait; and others which—for you—would not be suitable. Uncle Leopold wanted you to be made a Peer. But Lord

120

Melbourne and I don't think it will do. A Peer, being a member of the House of Lords, has a voice in the government of the Country; and of course, in your case, that will be quite out of the question.

ALBERT So? I see.

VICTORIA It is so important for everyone to realise that, though you are my Consort, you will have nothing to do with politics.

ALBERT Am I not to take an interest in your politics?

VICTORIA Oh, yes; you may take an interest, Albert— I would like you to. But I shall not discuss them with you, as I do with my Ministers, or ask your opinion about them. That would not be right.

ALBERT I see.

VICTORIA It is the duty of my Ministers to advise me on all affairs of State; and then—when I have heard them —either I give my consent, or I advise them differently. But they must never think that the advice I give them comes from anyone but myself.

ALBERT But you read, Victoria, books and newspapers; and you get some ideas from them, which help you to decide.

VICTORIA Oh, yes, sometimes. But books and newspapers are different; they are quite impersonal.

ALBERT They are all written by persons.

VICTORIA Yes; but, in reading, one forgets that.

ALBERT Then some day I will write a book for you, Victoria; so that you may forget it is *me*.

VICTORIA Indeed, no, Albert! You couldn't write a book, and put your name to it. That would *never* do!

ALBERT Anonymously, my Dear; so that you need not know.

VICTORIA I hope, Albert, you will *never* do anything that I am not to *know*!

ALBERT But you are going to do many things that *I* am not to know.

VICTORIA Yes; but that is quite different. I am the reigning sovereign . . . but you will be only—

ALBERT Yes? Only what?

VICTORIA My own dear darling Husband: the only person I shall ever love more than I have loved anyone yet!

ALBERT That is just between ourselves, Victoria—we two alone. But what am I to be in public? Where do I find myself then?

VICTORIA *That* I was going to explain, Albert. Though I have quite decided that you cannot be a Peer, I shall make an Order in Council that you are to take precedence of all other members of my Family. To that my two Uncles—the Duke of Cambridge, and the Duke of Sussex—have quite agreed; for, of course, I had to ask them first.

ALBERT Of course.

VICTORIA To make it quite pleasant, I mean. But I should have done it in any case; since you are my first consideration; and *that* everybody will have to understand—even my Uncle Ernest, who may be a little difficult about it.

ALBERT Being himself a King, you mean?

VICTORIA Yes. But, when he comes here, the King of Hanover is not to think himself more important than the

122

Prince, my Consort. I shall not allow it! If he means to, he must stay away.

ALBERT Decide that as you like, Victoria.

VICTORIA I have quite decided. . . . And now for the next thing that I have here on my list. . . . It is about our Honeymoon. Of course, it was very natural and dear of you, Albert, to wish that we should remain alone together for a longer time; but that is impossible. Two or three days are all that I can spare. When Parliament is sitting, I have to be consulted every day by my Ministers. Also I must have my Court about me: I cannot be alone.

ALBERT But for a Bride to appear in public after only the second day—will not that be rather embarrassing?

VICTORIA Oh, no, Albert; for a Queen, not at all. We have to accustom ourselves to living in public. It is expected of us: people like it.

ALBERT And you like it, also?

VICTORIA (*feeling that she is being criticised*) I like to do what is *right*, Albert; when I am sure—as I am now.

ALBERT (*nerving himself to speak*) Are you sure, Victoria, that you are 'right' to marry me?

VICTORIA Albert!

ALBERT It is going to be difficult to be—all that you wish.

VICTORIA But you are that already, Dearest! How can you think of such a thing? I have not told you before, how many others were offered me to choose from. But I could only choose *you*.

ALBERT That was very kind of you.

VICTORIA Though there was one whom all my Uncles would have much preferred.

ALBERT Indeed? Who was that?

VICTORIA My cousin, George of Cambridge. They thought that would be so much better than what they call a 'foreign marriage.' But I didn't wish it: nor, I think, did he. He came to see me again the other day—for the first time since the announcement: very kind and civil, but not at all embellished in his appearance, and evidently quite happy to be clear of me.

ALBERT A foreign marriage, they call it?

VICTORIA Yes; though already you speak English as well as he does. It is only your moustache that makes you look different.

ALBERT To cut *that* off will be quite easy—if you wish me to.

VICTORIA Oh, no! I couldn't bear for you to do that!

ALBERT But if it would make me more popular. . . . Have you read this?

(*He puts a printed leaflet into her hand.*)

VICTORIA (*as she begins reading it*) How did you get this, Albert?[1]

ALBERT Quite a number of it was kindly sent to me by the post.

[1] The verses which the Prince has given her to read are from a broadsheet, hawked in the streets of London at the time of the Royal Marriage, and run as follows:

> " His Royal Mistress, mournful and depressed,
> Pined in his absence, whom she valued best—
> Missed the hoarse whispers of his German tongue
> And the moustache above his lip that hung:
> That dear moustache which caused her first to *feel*,
> And filled her bosom with pre-nuptial zeal."

VICTORIA But how abominable! How dare anybody write about you and *Me* like that?

ALBERT Your English public, that you so like, is just a little difficult to please, that is all . . . it does not like foreigners.

VICTORIA No; but they will not go on thinking of you as a foreigner, after I have married you.

ALBERT No?

VICTORIA That would be impossible!

ALBERT It is not going to be easy for me to become English all at once—just by marrying you, Victoria.

VICTORIA No; but all the arrangements I am making for you will help, I am sure. For instance, about the Gentlemen of your Household, whom I have chosen for you—you said you wished to choose them yourself. But that is impossible, Albert.

ALBERT Why?

VICTORIA How can you choose them for yourself, when you know nobody? At present they are all strangers.

ALBERT Yes. So I would like to have for my Secretary someone that I know, and can trust.

VICTORIA But he *must* be an Englishman, Albert. You cannot possibly have a foreigner for your Private Secretary.

ALBERT Why not? Is not your own Private Secretary, the Baroness Lehzen, a foreigner?

VICTORIA Oh, but that's different. Lehzen was my Governess. She has been with me all my life.

ALBERT That was before you became Queen.

125

VICTORIA Yes; but I could never let that prevent me from choosing my own Private Secretary.

ALBERT No? But it is to prevent me now, when I become your Husband.

VICTORIA Yes, Albert; that is quite different.

ALBERT I am to be given to strangers.

VICTORIA They won't remain strangers. I shall take the greatest care to find for you someone whom you will really like and trust.

ALBERT I would prefer to do that for myself.

VICTORIA I have already told you that is impossible, Albert. Please do not say it again!

> (THE PRINCE *rises quickly; then, restraining himself,*
> *he moves slowly to the window.* THE QUEEN
> *consults her list.*)

Now, I wonder, is that all?

ALBERT (*turning*) Is there anything else that I am to learn this morning?

VICTORIA (*anxiously*) Has all this talking tired you?

ALBERT Oh, no! I am not 'tired.' I am feeling too much alive! I would like to open this window. May I?

VICTORIA Oh, Albert, on such a cold day: do you think it wise?

ALBERT I do not know, Victoria. I only know that I would like to open it, for a little breath of fresh air.

> (*Before* THE QUEEN *can answer, one of her* GENTLE-
> MEN *enters to make announcement.*)

GENTLEMAN If it please—your Majesty's Ministers are in attendance.

126

VICTORIA Oh, Albert dear, now I must go, then. I do hope you will be able to amuse yourself. There is the Library, you know.

ALBERT I think that my friend, Baron Stockmar, will be waiting to see me.

VICTORIA Oh, yes. Then see him at once; and when I come back, we will go out together.

> (*The* GENTLEMAN *has gone; but as she moves to the door it opens and closes again behind her.* THE PRINCE *sinks down into a seat in deep dejection, and is so sitting, when the door is discreetly opened, and* BARON STOCKMAR *enters. He stands for a moment looking at* THE PRINCE *with kindly understanding, then speaks.*)

STOCKMAR Does your Highness's servant intrude?

ALBERT Come in, Baron.

> (*He rises, and moves despondently away.*)

STOCKMAR They informed me that your Highness was now ready to receive me.

ALBERT I am at liberty for a short time, Baron. Yes? Was there something you wished to speak to me about?

STOCKMAR A good many things, if there is time. But —pardon!—your Royal Highness does not seem in very good spirit to-day.

ALBERT Indeed, I have been merrier!

STOCKMAR Shakespeare.

ALBERT Yes; I have been reading Shakespeare a good deal lately—in English.

STOCKMAR And how does your Highness find him?

ALBERT I find him—like the English people—rather hard to understand.

STOCKMAR Your Highness has not been in the country very long. Just at first, the people—like their language—are a little difficult. And so—your position also.

ALBERT Difficult! Impossible! Baron, it is now a question whether I can—go on!

STOCKMAR (*in consternation*) Oh! Your Highness! but that is incredible! You cannot break off from marriage with a Queen!

ALBERT What does he become, who marries a Queen?

STOCKMAR That—depends.

ALBERT On what?

STOCKMAR On who means to be master.

ALBERT There you have it! She is that already; her great position gives it her.

STOCKMAR No doubt . . . till she gives it to *you*.

ALBERT She will never do that—willingly!

STOCKMAR Oh, yes: . . . she will . . . she will.

ALBERT But how is it possible? Why should she?

STOCKMAR She loves you—very much.

ALBERT Too much! but not as I would wish to be loved. I am not to belong to myself any more.

STOCKMAR Patience, patience! It will come in time.

ALBERT And what—meanwhile? Have you thought enough about that?

STOCKMAR Yes . . . yes. . . . For my beloved Prince there is going to be a hard time. . . . But he will win.

128

ALBERT But, Baron, how can I—fight for myself against one who—so loving, and so generous—is giving me *every*thing, as the world sees it?

STOCKMAR Will your Highness listen to one who, in his life, has had much experience: not indeed just alone with himself, but from watching others? . . . This little Queen—still so young, so pleased, and proud of herself, as she is now: of her position, her importance, her power— as she thinks. It will not go on. Her Ministers flatter her, making things easy for her—and for themselves. Presently she will have to change her Ministers for others whom she does not so much like, or so much trust. Then it will be *your* turn. She will come to you—for help. . . . And, besides (THE BARON *is now smiling*)—have you ever looked at yourself, enough to know how handsome you are? No, do not laugh! Look at yourself, my Prince! look! (*He leads* THE PRINCE *up to a mirror*.) Some day—it may be quite soon—she will become a mother—of *your* children. Then, my Prince, if she still loves you, you will not be her Puppet, nor her Plaything any more. You will be *King*.

ALBERT King?

STOCKMAR Oh! The title does not matter; that is nothing! You have a head of your own, my Prince, that you know and can use—well. And if you keep your head *now*, you are not going to have it cut off—not by her, nor by anybody. No! . . . By your Highness's leave, now I go. . . . I have said what I came to say.

> (*Whereupon, he bows himself out.* THE PRINCE *returns to the mirror, and stands looking at himself. And if he does not see there a full prophecy of what is to be, at least he sees nothing to make him despair.*)

Morning Glory

Morning Glory

11th February 1840

A bell has just sounded. Into THE PRINCE'S *dressing-room at Windsor, where two candles are already burning, comes an elderly Valet. With deft movement, and the utmost correctitude of deportment, he places hot water, razors, soap, shaving-brush, and towel. He then proceeds to lay out in orderly sequence* THE PRINCE'S *clothing for the day; then goes to the window, draws back the curtains, raises the blind, and puts out the candles. The sun is already well up, for the hour is late. Having done all, he stands to attention, and waits. A door opens;* PRINCE ALBERT *enters, in a fine brocaded dressing-gown, and a silk night-cap of rather Eastern design, in which he looks well.*

ALBERT That will do. I will shave myself this morning. When I want you, I will ring.

> (*The Valet makes a short bow, and retires.* THE PRINCE *goes to the glass, throws off his night-cap, and, taking up a comb, passes it through the long locks of his rather disordered hair. He then uncords his dressing-gown, sits down, and removing his fur-edged slippers, draws on a pair of pantaloons. He rises, resumes his*

*slippers, and advances to the dressing-table.
Opening the collar of his night-shirt, he prepares
to shave himself, and is already applying the
lather, when there comes a light tabbering on
the door by which he has just entered. He turns
a little surprised; the door opens: it is* THE
QUEEN. *At first we only see her head, in a
pretty frilled night-cap, with the strings hang-
ing loose; but presently she is all there, wearing
a rose-coloured dressing-gown, and over it a
white Cashmere shawl with long fringes. She
looks very happy and charming.*

THE QUEEN Albert, may I come in?

ALBERT Yes, Dearest, if you wish to.

> (*She gazes in pleased astonishment at a spectacle she
> has never seen before: the solid foam of shaving-
> soap on a human countenance is something quite
> new to her.*)

THE QUEEN What *are* you doing?

ALBERT Shaving.

THE QUEEN Oh! How exciting! May I stay, and watch
you?

ALBERT If it would interest you, Weibchen.

THE QUEEN But, of course! to see you shaving is
wonderful! Something I never thought of.

ALBERT Oh? Did you think one did not have to shave
at all?

THE QUEEN I never thought about it—till now. . . .
You see, Albert, I have never seen a man shave himself
before.

134

ALBERT No, I suppose not.

THE QUEEN How often do you have to do it? Once a week?

ALBERT Every day.

THE QUEEN Every day! But how absurd! It can't grow as fast as all that.

ALBERT Oh, yes, it does.

THE QUEEN How very troublesome! Why, I only cut my *nails* once a week.

ALBERT Nails can wait longer; beards won't.

THE QUEEN I wouldn't like you to have a beard, Albert!

ALBERT Nor would I. That's why I am taking it off now.

> (*Having sufficiently lathered, he now begins to shave.*)

THE QUEEN How strange it looks! . . . and how interesting!—fascinating! . . . Is it dangerous?

ALBERT Not if you don't talk to me—

THE QUEEN (*a little startled*) Oh!

ALBERT —not just while I am stroking myself.

THE QUEEN Stroking yourself! Oh, Albert, you are funny!

ALBERT Is that not the right word? Ought I to have said 'wiping myself'—or what?

THE QUEEN Really, I'm not sure, Albert. It's a part of the English language, which—from not having to know—I've not been taught.

ALBERT Ah, Vicky! It is nice to hear you say that! Then you, too, do not know the English language quite

135

like a native. For that—if it were not for the soup—I would kiss you.

THE QUEEN The soup?

ALBERT This, I mean.

THE QUEEN Oh! not 'soup,' Albert darling. *Soap!*

ALBERT Ah! Soap, then.

THE QUEEN But I don't mind the soap, Albert—*your* soap—if you would like to.

ALBERT Very well; then; now I will.

> (*Having wiped his lips, he kisses her, and then goes on with his shaving.*)

THE QUEEN Let me see what you do it with.

> (*He gives her a razor; she takes it, and examines the edge.*)

Oh! how sharp it is!

ALBERT Yes, it does have to be sharp—always.

THE QUEEN Does it hurt?

ALBERT No.

THE QUEEN Do you ever cut yourself?

ALBERT No; not when I am alone. I had a valet once, that used to shave me, before I knew how for myself. One day, he cut me, rather badly. After that, I had to learn; and for a long time, shaved only myself.

THE QUEEN And what happened to him?

ALBERT Oh, he had his head cut off, I suppose. . . . I did not inquire. I sent him out of the room, and told him never to come back. And oh, how he ran!

> (*He laughs.*)

THE QUEEN And then?

ALBERT Then the Court Physician came running in a terrible fright, for the man having told him. He thought to find me bleeding to death.

THE QUEEN To death? Why?

ALBERT Because, my Dear, my brother Ernest—and his father—once so nearly did. But that did not happen to *me*. . . . I am not that way, you see. What I told you makes the difference.

THE QUEEN Oh, Albert! Then that 'difference' has, perhaps, saved your life?

ALBERT Possibly.

THE QUEEN Then, how thankful I really ought to be.

ALBERT To my Mother, and my Father, you mean?

THE QUEEN Yes. . . . Albert, suppose you had died before we got married, *could* I have married anyone else?

ALBERT Of course, Dearest. You had to marry someone. You could not disappoint your people by not giving them an heir to the Throne.

THE QUEEN Oh, Albert! Shall I? Will that really happen?

ALBERT We will hope so, Dearest—in time.

THE QUEEN In time? I hope it will be very soon. Oh, isn't it wonderful? We really are—married now, aren't we?

ALBERT (*covertly amused*) Yes, Weibchen, I think so.

THE QUEEN Yesterday seems almost like another world —so different. All the crowds, and the cheering, and the firing, and the bells: and thousands and thousands of people all looking at us, as if we belonged to them: as, of course, in a way, we do. . . . And now we are all by ourselves—all alone—just we two.

ALBERT Yes, all alone—just we two. Shall I be able to make you happy,—you think? . . . You *are* happy?

THE QUEEN Happy? So happy, I can't—I can't tell you, Albert! . . . And to think that this will go on, and on, for years and years . . . It's like Heaven!

ALBERT No, Vicky, not just like this—that is not possible . . . That is not human nature.

THE QUEEN But I shall never love you less than I do now, Albert.

ALBERT No, Dearest, perhaps not. But you will be less excited about it—less romantic, perhaps. I shall have become less strange to you. We love each other, but we are still both rather strangers. We have to learn each other's characters—and ways. That will take time. . . .

(She shakes her head fondly, confident that she knows him already—by heart.)

ALBERT Oh, yes. . . . You have come to see me shave to-day—for the first time. That pleases—that excites you. But it will not always excite you as much as to-day. You will not come, I think, to see me shave every day—for the next twenty years.

THE QUEEN Why not?

ALBERT Because, Dearest, you will have too much else to do. Also you will know so well what it looks like, which to-day you see only the first time. So, that it should become less of a spectacle, is only reasonable.

138

THE QUEEN I don't want to be reasonable with *you*, Albert!

ALBERT But you *will* want—in time, I hope, Vicky. So shall I. You have a great life of duties to perform, in which I am to share. Is that not so?

THE QUEEN We can't share everything, Albert. Some things I shall have to do alone—affairs of State, in which it would not be right for you to concern yourself.

ALBERT (*a little sharply*) So?

THE QUEEN Yes. You must take great care, Dearest. The English are jealous; and to them you are still a foreigner.

ALBERT And—to *you*?

THE QUEEN To me you are everything—life, happiness, peace, and comfort! When I am with you, I shall want to forget everything—except our love.

> (*It is a prospect over which, as she flings herself into his arms, she looks more happy than he does. All at once, from the Terrace outside, comes a burst of music. With the happy excitement of a child, she draws him to the window, and points.*)

Hark! Look! That is the Band of my Royal Life Guards. I gave orders for it to be here this morning an hour earlier—so that we might hear it before we came down. . . . I thought you would like it.

ALBERT Oh, yes; it is very good music.

THE QUEEN What is it they are playing?

ALBERT You do not know?

139

THE QUEEN No. I only said that some suitable pieces were to be chosen—it being such a special occasion. What is it?

ALBERT That, my Vicky, is Mendelssohn's *Wedding March*, from his new setting to Shakespeare.

THE QUEEN Mendelssohn! Oh, I'm glad. He is one of the world's greatest composers, is he not?... No, I have never heard it before. But now it is going to be my favourite piece.

ALBERT. You could not choose better. But you will not want to hear it every day, Weibchen.

THE QUEEN Perhaps not quite every day.

ALBERT Any more than you will want to see me shave— every day.

THE QUEEN Now you are laughing at me.

ALBERT Just a little, Dearest; because you—and I, are both to-day so young.

THE QUEEN And so happy! Look how the sun is shining!

(She goes and stands in the window.)

ALBERT Ah, do not stand so near to that window, Vicky!

THE QUEEN Why not?

ALBERT The people might see you.

THE QUEEN Well, but why shouldn't they? It would please them.

ALBERT (*uncomfortably*) Yes: too much. .... That is why I say—*don't!*

140

THE QUEEN Albert, darling, we have got to appear in public again almost at once. It's no use being shy. And why should we, when I'm so proud of having got you?

ALBERT (*rescuing modesty with common sense*) I want my breakfast, Vicky! Please to go and get yourself ready— quick. I am going to ring now for my dresser to come.

THE QUEEN (*revelling in wifely submission*) Order me to go, Albert! . . . *Order* me!

ALBERT (*playing up*) *Go*, woman! He says to you, *Go!*

(*Gazing at him adoringly, she drops a deep mocking curtsy, and retires. He stands looking fondly after her: then, with a sigh, turns, and rings the bell. His Valet enters. The Band plays on.* THE PRINCE *proceeds to dress himself with formal correctness for the very difficult new life which now awaits him.*)

Leading-Strings

Leading-Strings

1841

THE QUEEN (*it is still in the early days of her marriage*) *sits writing in one of the private apartments at Windsor. She looks at the clock which has just struck, and speaks to a Lady-in-Waiting, who stands at attention in the background.*

THE QUEEN Will you, please, go and send the Prince to me? It is ten o'clock; he ought to be here.

> (*The Lady curtsies and goes.* THE QUEEN *takes up a small framed portrait, gazes upon it fondly, and resumes her writing. A stage-minute later* (*that is to say, ten seconds*) PRINCE ALBERT *enters: he carries a small nosegay, which he deposits with courtly grace in front of her. She lays down her pen, and, taking up the flowers to smell, says, correctively but not severely.*)

Ah! I was wondering when these would come.

ALBERT (*still very foreign in his pronunciation*) You did not think that I had forgotten?

THE QUEEN No, I only thought you were a little late; as you *are*.

ALBERT Just one minute. I do not yet quite know, to realise, how long at Windsor, it shall take to get from one place to another.

THE QUEEN It is all very grand and large, is it not? But that is what we—in our position—have to put up with.

ALBERT Would it not be rather nice to make one corner of it our own?

THE QUEEN How do you mean—our own? It is *all* ours.

ALBERT More private: where no one can come but ourselves. I mean—during the day.

THE QUEEN But we are quite private enough here, are we not?

ALBERT No. At any moment someone comes and knocks; one of your Ladies, or Secretaries. I mean a room—a suite all private to itself—where, when you have seen your Ministers, and all the rest, we can go in together, and not be disturbed by anyone: where it is known that—except on something emergent—no one shall come.

THE QUEEN Yes. Ah! yes.

ALBERT Where, by ourselves, you could sing to me, and I could play to you, and read to you.

THE QUEEN Yes, Albert, that is just what I should love. I will have it all arranged for.

ALBERT Will you not let me do it—my own way?

THE QUEEN You think I shall not do it as you wish, Albert?

146

ALBERT Not so at all. But this I would just like to do—myself. At present it seems there is so little I *may* do.

THE QUEEN But you do a great deal, Dearest, everything that I *want* you to do.

ALBERT (*sadly*) Yes. And that is all.

THE QUEEN Is that not enough? . . . What is the matter?

ALBERT I could wish that you wanted me to do a little more, Vicky—in my own way.

THE QUEEN But what else *can* you do?

ALBERT Who knows—till you have let me try? There are so many things here that want doing badly.

THE QUEEN What sort of things?

ALBERT Almost everything. The service—the ménage here is more than one hundred years old. We are still in the Middle Ages—almost.

THE QUEEN But that is so interesting!

ALBERT And so wasteful.

THE QUEEN Wasteful? Why?

ALBERT I will give you just an instance. The other day, for curiosity, I asked to be told the scale on which things for the commissariat are ordered—daily, weekly, monthly; the meat, the wine, and all the rest of it. My Dear, it is more like the provisioning of an army than of a single establishment.

THE QUEEN But this is Windsor.

ALBERT It is a dozen Windsors—the Windsors of four Reigns at least all rolled into one. One of the things I discovered was that anything once ordered always goes on being ordered. The thing is sent in and paid for, but it is not used.

THE QUEEN Then where does it go?

ALBERT Where? You may well ask.

THE QUEEN Then I shall look into it at once, and have it altered.

ALBERT Why not let *me* do it?

THE QUEEN You, Albert? But you do not understand our English ways.

ALBERT But it is I who have discovered it.

THE QUEEN Yes. How did you? Did you go into the kitchens, Albert?

ALBERT No; and I did not disguise myself either. I went to the Controller's office, to the desk of the Head Accountant, and asked if I might see the books. I was told no, impossible. I went and took them down from the shelf, and looked at them myself. I have been doing that now for a week.

THE QUEEN Behind my back; without asking me?

ALBERT Behind your back, Weibchen. And now, to your face, I tell it. Here you are, the Queen of England, and being cheated by your own servants. Let me give you just one or two instances. You have in your stables twice so many horses than you can use. Who uses them? They have become the perquisite of your head-stableman. He hires them out.

THE QUEEN My horses hired! How improper! How abominable!

ALBERT Yes.

THE QUEEN And how dishonest!

ALBERT They do not think so. Custom has sanctioned it. They are quite open about it, when it is found out; and when you alter it, as it should be altered, they will consider themselves defrauded.

THE QUEEN Then they shall! But how extraordinary that such a thing should ever have been allowed!

ALBERT I will give you one other instance—very funny. I found there was in the provision list, every month, forty pounds' weight of tallow candles. It surprised me to find that tallow candles were used here at all. I inquired; they were not. The tallow candles just come in to be looked at, and go out again. They are one of the kitchen perquisites.

THE QUEEN (*scandalised*) Really!

ALBERT And how did they come in the first place? Thirty years ago, old King George, your Grandpapa, had a cold in his nose; and tallows were ordered for it. In those days that was the cure. So the tallow has been on order ever since, though the nose that it was ordered to soothe has been twenty-one years in the grave.

THE QUEEN But forty pounds, Albert!

ALBERT Yes, my Dear, for the nose of a King—forty pounds; anything less than that would not have looked well in the accounts.

THE QUEEN And you have found all this out, Albert, by yourself?

ALBERT Yes. With a lot of black faces looking on— while I did so.

THE QUEEN I think you should have come to me first, before doing so.

ALBERT Why?

THE QUEEN For permission; that you might have my authority.

ALBERT No, Vicky, I am not going to ask your permission for everything.

THE QUEEN Do you mean that?

ALBERT Very much so, I mean it.

THE QUEEN Albert, is this going to be the first time that you disobey me?

ALBERT Perhaps it should have come earlier. It will not be the last.

THE QUEEN Albert! You forget yourself!

ALBERT I think, sometimes, that *you* forget *me*: that I am not your lover only, for you to play with and fondle. I am your husband too.

THE QUEEN And am not I—a good wife?

ALBERT You are all that is kind; and I am grateful. But am I always to be a stranger in this country of yours?

THE QUEEN Oh, do not say that; you hurt me! But it takes time. You see, Albert, Dear, you are so good—so serious about things—that you find it difficult to understand people—*other* people, I mean, who are different.

150

ALBERT Goodness should not prevent understanding, Vicky.

THE QUEEN But it does, Dearest! It makes you judge people too strictly.

ALBERT But do I?

THE QUEEN Of course you do! And in a way, I like it—because it shows me *you*. But sometimes it is rather inconvenient, you know.

ALBERT For instance?

THE QUEEN Well, don't you remember, the other night, when Uncle Augustus came in after dinner, having dined elsewhere. And of course, he *had* dined as *usual*; and so—almost at once—you sent one of your gentlemen, with your compliments, to tell him that his carriage was waiting.

ALBERT How did you know?

THE QUEEN He wrote to me the next day: such an explosive letter, saying such things about you, that I couldn't possibly let you read it. . . . So you see, Dear—

ALBERT Do you wish that I had let him stay?

THE QUEEN I wish that you had left it to me, Albert; for I had already decided what to do.

ALBERT And what had you decided?

THE QUEEN I was going to bring the Court to an end by retiring early. Then all would have gone off quite naturally, and no one would have noticed. It would have been better, Dearest.

ALBERT And suppose the incident had been repeated?

THE QUEEN Well, Albert, after all he is an old man; and we can't expect to alter him now.

ALBERT But we do expect your Court to alter, from what it has been, do we not? From what I have heard, there is already a great difference.

THE QUEEN Oh, yes; and it is nearly all your doing, Albert. And I would not have it otherwise, except for my Uncle, for whom we must make allowance.

ALBERT Even your Uncles should be made to respect you.

THE QUEEN But they do, I am sure.

ALBERT It was not respectful for him to come as he came the other night.

THE QUEEN It would not have been, had he quite realised—had he known—

ALBERT How drunk he was?

THE QUEEN Albert, he *is* my Uncle. Please don't use such a common expression about one of *us*.

ALBERT Is it too common—that word—said in English? Forgive me; I will say it in German.

THE QUEEN No, Albert. I wish you to talk English still, till you are more used to it.

>   (*He moves away from her, controlling himself by an effort. She goes after him.*)

Of course, Dearest, I love to hear you speak your own language, *sometimes*. It is so much more yourself. But till you know it better, you must, please, still speak English. And it is the same about English ways and customs—you

152

must get to know them better, and be more like the rest of us.

ALBERT You wish me to become English?

THE QUEEN Why, of course. *I* am English; so my Husband must be English, too.

ALBERT For that one should have begun earlier.

THE QUEEN I married you as soon as ever I could, Albert.

ALBERT Ah! Weibchen! So long as you do not repent of it.

THE QUEEN You are happy, Albert?

ALBERT I will be more than happy, so long as—serving you—I am able to make a life worth living. But you must let me serve you—not feel myself useless.

THE QUEEN Useless!

ALBERT Sometimes I feel that I am put—not quite in the corner, but on the shelf, just a little.

THE QUEEN Who does that?

ALBERT You, my Dear.

THE QUEEN But I— I worship you, Albert.

ALBERT Too much! Let me come down to earth a little, now and then. Give my hands and brain something to do, so that I may be able to respect myself. Am I only your plaything? Your—

THE QUEEN Albert!

ALBERT All day you work for hours with Ministers and Secretaries. And while they are with you, I may

153

not come in. At the end of it I see you worn out from doing it all alone; but I may not help you. You do not even speak! Sometimes there are things that are still doubtful—how to decide; and I may not advise you. You do not ask me, or tell me anything!

THE QUEEN But Albert! Albert! You do not understand! The English are so jealous; they don't know you as I know you. They still look upon you as a foreigner, and are suspicious, for fear I should let you—advise me.

ALBERT Am I *never* to help, or advise you—never? From your life's work am I always to be shut out?

THE QUEEN But you do help me—so much!

ALBERT Let me help you *now*.

THE QUEEN How?

ALBERT Let me see some of those papers that you spend so long over. I could read them for you, and make a few notes. That would save you time.

THE QUEEN Oh, but I must see everything *myself*. That is what I am here for.

ALBERT Do you suppose your Ministers show you everything?

THE QUEEN Why, of course!

ALBERT Impossible. Government is not as simple as all that. They themselves have to rely upon others for much that has to be done; even in things for which they are responsible. Cannot you rely upon me . . . a little?

THE QUEEN Albert, Dearest, you distress me! In every way that is possible, I do already rely on you; and always,

154

in everything that I have had to decide *for* you, I have only done it for your good

ALBERT Yes, you even chose my secretary for me.

THE QUEEN Why of course, Albert! How could *you* know—coming here a stranger—who would be the best?

ALBERT (*continuing*) Who reports to you—regularly, I believe.

THE QUEEN Surely you don't mind my knowing?

ALBERT I would prefer to tell you myself what I do. In future I mean to.

THE QUEEN Why, of course. I always wish to hear everything.

ALBERT Yes. The other day I made an engagement. You cancelled it.

THE QUEEN Yes, Albert. I had very good reason for doing so

ALBERT No doubt. You did not speak to me about it.

THE QUEEN But that was to spare your feelings.

ALBERT But my secretary knew. When I questioned him why one engagement entered into my diary for this week had been struck out, he said he had done so under instruction.

THE QUEEN Yes, Albert.

ALBERT From *you*.

THE QUEEN You were going to dine, he told me, with a foreign Minister. It would have been in the papers. My Government did not wish that, just now, any member of the Royal Family should pay him such a compliment.

155

ALBERT You see, I am told nothing of your relations with foreign countries. I see only what appears in the newspapers. . . . Not only do you not give me your confidence, but you have me watched. To-morrow I am going to choose another secretary—for myself.

THE QUEEN Albert, you are making a great mistake!

ALBERT Repairing one. I ought to have done this before.

THE QUEEN You are not to do it, Albert. . . . I say you are not to.

ALBERT Then, for the present, I leave you.

(*He turns to go.*)

THE QUEEN Where are you going?

ALBERT In here, to my own room, to write my letters—alone.

(*He goes in, and closes the door. We hear the key turn in the lock.* THE QUEEN *also hears it, and starts to her feet. Very angry, but a little frightened, she pauses, then advances resolutely to the door, and tries it. The door does not yield. She beats upon it violently with her hand, pauses, then beats again.*)

THE QUEEN Open the door! Albert, open the door!

ALBERT (*from within*) Who is that speaking?

THE QUEEN Her Majesty, the Queen!

ALBERT Her Majesty, the Queen, must wait.

(THE QUEEN *stands, hardly believing her ears. She stands for a long time. Her eyes turn to the*

156

*door questioning it about this unbelievable
situation, which (for such a thing has never
happened before) she cannot yet understand.
For a moment, foolish, fiery resolution takes
hold of her: she crosses the room and lays her
hand upon the bell-rope. Ye Gods! What is
her little Majesty going to do now? But
fundamental common sense comes to her rescue;
and with common sense comes, also, understanding. Timidly now, biting her lips, trying
to keep back the tears, she crosses again, and
stands irresolutely at the door. In a very
different way now, her hand advances, she
knocks softly, pauses, and knocks again. And as
she listens the beloved voice speaks again from
within.)*

ALBERT Who is there?

*(There is a pause. The tears come rushing; her voice
trembles as she speaks.)*

THE QUEEN Your Wife, Albert! Your poor, unhappy
little Wife!

*(The door opens. ALBERT appears. She flings herself
into his arms.)*

Oh, Albert! Albert! Albert!

ALBERT Hush, hush, Weibchen! Don't cry! Don't
cry! It's all right.

*(But she does cry. How long does not matter, for it is
doing her good.)*

'A Good Lesson!'

'A Good Lesson!'

1842

It is ten o'clock, and a bright morning. In THE PRINCE'S *writing-room at Buckingham Palace,* MR. ANSON, *his Private Secretary, stands by the table, sorting correspondence; opened letters he places in one heap, unopened in another. The door opens; one of* THE QUEEN'S GENTLEMEN *enters.*

GENTLEMAN Her Majesty wishes to know whether the Prince has yet returned?

ANSON (*in a quiet, matter-of-fact tone*) No.... At least, so far as I know, he has not.

GENTLEMAN (*hesitating*) Oh?... Do you know, Mr. Anson, where the Prince *is*?

ANSON (*with studied nonchalance*) Now?... No, I don't.

GENTLEMAN (*with embarrassment*) You know, I suppose, that His Highness did not return to the Palace, last night?

ANSON (*as before*) From the Royal Academy Dinner? Oh, indeed... didn't he?

GENTLEMAN (*making a plunge*) Did he *go*, Mr. Anson?

ANSON Oh, yes, I think so. The papers *say* that he did. Here is his speech, fully reported, in this morning's *Times*; and a very good one, too.

GENTLEMAN Very strange, Mr. Anson!

ANSON Not at all. His speeches generally are.

GENTLEMAN I meant—his not returning.

ANSON (*coldly*) Hadn't you better report to Her Majesty that His Highness has *not* yet returned? That, I believe, was all you were sent to find out.

GENTLEMAN (*stiffly*) Certainly. I will.

> (*He goes.* ANSON *continues sorting the letters. There comes a knock at the door; and permission given —in comes* THE PRINCE'S *Valet,* MR. RICHARDS.)

RICHARDS I beg pardon, Sir. I heard you were alone: so I came to see you, Sir.

ANSON Yes? What is it, Richards?

RICHARDS His Royal Highness, Sir. . . . He hasn't sent for me this morning, Sir: and didn't last night, either. He doesn't seem to have been in his dressing-room at all, Sir: not since I dressed him last night, for the Dinner.

ANSON Oh, it's all right, Richards. His Royal Highness was unexpectedly called elsewhere, at a late hour last night, so did not return.

RICHARDS (*re-assured*) Oh, very good, Sir.

ANSON I expect His Royal Highness to be back before long. So you be ready for him.

RICHARDS Yes, Sir. Very good, Sir.

> (*He goes.* ANSON, *left to himself, can no longer conceal his anxiety.*)

ANSON But is it 'all right,' I wonder? . . . God!

(*Nervously he snatches up the paper, then throws it
down again. He moves restlessly to the window,
and back again. The door opens; in comes*
PRINCE ALBERT, *looking very calm and collected.*)

ALBERT (*quietly*) Good morning, Anson.

ANSON Good morning, Sir.

ALBERT Is there any news this morning?—anything
special?

ANSON In the papers, Sir? A full report of the Academy
Banquet. (*He takes up* The Times, *and offers it.*) Did that
go off well, Sir?

ALBERT (*not taking it*) Very well.

ANSON I was just reading your Highness's speech.

ALBERT Yes, Anson; of which you wrote for me the
notes.

ANSON At your Highness's dictation.

ALBERT Well, I did not make it too long, I hope?

ANSON It reads very well, Sir. And it seems to have been
well received.

ALBERT Yes; it was altogether a very well managed
affair. And I found the company quite interesting. We
were talking of the decorations for the walls of the new
Houses of Parliament; and I was proposing that there
should be a Competition and a Fine Arts Commission to
decide it. They thought it was a good idea.

ANSON Well, Sir, if a Competition will produce the
right artists, it certainly will be. But we have not had much

163

practice of mural art in this country, Sir, I'm afraid; we don't run to it.

ALBERT We must begin, then, and try.

ANSON Yes, Sir.

ALBERT That was Sir Francis Chantrey's objection. But when I said to him—'How would it do, then, to employ foreign Artists?' he said that if they came, their heads would be broken; and that—old as he was—he would himself lend a hand for the purpose.

ANSON Indeed, Sir?

ALBERT Yes, indeed! So you see! . . .

(THE PRINCE *seats himself at his writing-table.*)

ALBERT Letters?

ANSON (*handing some*) These, Sir, I think, are all that your Highness need see for the present.

ALBERT Thank you.

(THE QUEEN'S GENTLEMAN *again enters.*)

GENTLEMAN Her Majesty sent me to inquire if your Royal Highness was disengaged?

ALBERT Oh, yes. Tell Her Majesty I am quite free, if she wishes to see me.

(*The* GENTLEMAN *bows, and retires.* THE PRINCE *continues to look over his correspondence.*)

Now you may go, Anson. Take all those other letters, and leave me these.

(ANSON *retires.* THE PRINCE *goes on opening his correspondence. A minute passes; suddenly the door is flung open, and* THE QUEEN *makes a flamboyant entry.*)

THE QUEEN Albert! Where have you been?

ALBERT To Windsor, Victoria.

THE QUEEN Windsor? Impossible! Why did you not come back, last night?

ALBERT I did not come back last night, Victoria, because of the way in which you sent for me.

THE QUEEN I told you before you went, that I wished you to be back by half-past ten at the latest.

ALBERT Yes.

THE QUEEN At half-past ten you had not come; so I sent for you.

ALBERT Yes, I received from you this note. (*He produces it.*) . . . 'Albert, it is quite time you were back. Please to come at once!'

THE QUEEN Yes; I wrote it; I sent it; and my orders were that it should be put into your hand by the Messenger to whom I gave it.

ALBERT It was put into my hand. I sent back word to say that I had received it.

THE QUEEN Yes; but you did not come!

ALBERT I did not come, because I was not then ready to come.

THE QUEEN Albert! when you go anywhere without *me* (as you *had* to do on this occasion), I do not expect you to be late.

ALBERT No. But when I do go without you, you must leave it for me to decide, myself, when I shall return.

165

THE QUEEN But this time I had already told you my wishes, and had decided *for* you. . . . I sent again.

ALBERT Yes. At eleven o'clock, I received this. (*He produces it.*) 'Albert, I order you to return at once! V. R.'

THE QUEEN And still you did not!

ALBERT I did not.

THE QUEEN So you disobeyed your Queen!

ALBERT (*serenely*) Yes, my Dear; I disobeyed my Queen. Send me to the Tower for it, and cut off my head.

THE QUEEN I do not regard this as a subject for amusement and jest, Albert.

ALBERT No? Then it is lucky that *I* do. For if neither of us thought it amusing, we might have quite a serious quarrel about it. But now—as it is only you who do not think it amusing—the quarrel will not be so serious.

THE QUEEN Albert, what did you do, after I had ordered you to return? Where did you spend the night?

ALBERT At Windsor, as I have told you.

THE QUEEN I don't believe it!

ALBERT Don't you?

(*Quietly he turns back to his letters.*)

THE QUEEN Albert, I will not be treated like this! Please to remember that, though I am your Wife, I am also your Queen.

ALBERT (*kindly*) Sit down, my Dear, sit down! there is nothing to stand up about. . . . Last night there was; so I had to. But now I am ready to sit here and talk it over,

166

quite reasonably and comfortably: just you and me, Weibchen—with the Queen left out. . . . Please! (*With a gesture he gets her seated.*) Listen to me, my Dear. When you married me, you made a promise that was strange for a Queen to make: but you made it. . . . To love, honour, and obey. And because it was so strange—so unlikely—I have never once told you to obey me—except for fun, when you wished it. Now, my Dear, as I have not expected *you* to obey *me* in anything—so there are some things in which you must not expect *me* to obey *you*.

THE QUEEN When you do things for me in public—officially, that is to say—then I *do* expect you to obey me.

ALBERT When I do things for you in public, my Dear, I obey you by doing them. But you must trust me to do them in my own way—

THE QUEEN No, Albert.

ALBERT —not to interfere with me, while I am doing them, as you did last night. That is why, when I started back—after having received your 'orders'—I told the Coachman to drive—not to Buckingham Palace, but to Windsor.

THE QUEEN The Coachman! You told him that! What must he have thought?

ALBERT I will tell you what he thought. . . . At first he thought it was very strange. But when we got to Windsor, he thought that he knew the reason.

THE QUEEN Why, only then?

ALBERT It was rather late: almost half-past one. But when we got there, there were lights, and music, and dancing.

167

THE QUEEN Music! . . . Dancing! . . . *In* the Castle?

ALBERT In the Castle. . . . Behind our backs—so sure that we should be away—the servants were having a fancy-dress ball.

THE QUEEN (*her anger quite diverted*) What an improper liberty! Most extraordinary! And how fortunate that you should have caught them!

ALBERT Yes; a curious coincidence, was it not? So, of course, the Coachman thought that I had got wind of the affair, and had come there to catch them at it.

THE QUEEN Where were they dancing, Albert?

ALBERT In the great Hall.

THE QUEEN And in fancy-dress, you say?

ALBERT Yes. Two of them had dressed up to look like you and me.

THE QUEEN Albert! Did you see who they were?

ALBERT No. They ran too quick! I went in, and stood. . . . They were all very much surprised to see me.

THE QUEEN Indeed, I should think so! . . . What happened then?

ALBERT First, the dancing all stopped; then all the music. . . . I stood there and looked at them. It was very funny: I tried not to laugh.

THE QUEEN I hope you did not, Albert!

ALBERT No; I composed myself to look as though I was very angry.

THE QUEEN I hope you did. And then, what did you do?

168

ALBERT I told them that they might go on for just five minutes more; but that it was not to happen again.

THE QUEEN No, indeed!

ALBERT And it will not, I am sure.

THE QUEEN Did you get any explanation, as to why they had *dared* to do such a thing?

ALBERT Oh, yes; it was explained. You see, they were to have had a ball soon after Christmas; but on the very date the Court had to go into mourning; so it was put off, and forgotten. And as they had got all the dresses, they were naturally disappointed.

THE QUEEN But, Albert, that such a thing *could* happen without our knowing—well, it means that such a lot of other things may be happening too.

ALBERT Yes; I am afraid so ... I think, my Dear, that you had better make me your Manager of Windsor—factotum, you call it? They will not like it, because I have too much of a head for business; but it will be good for them. And for you, a great saving of unnecessary expense.

THE QUEEN Yes; and if I do it at once, everybody will understand *why*.

ALBERT It was a good thing, Vicky, was it not, that I was brought up rather poor?

THE QUEEN So was I.

ALBERT Yes? But you had not to manage much for yourself, had you? What for are you smiling at?

THE QUEEN The Coachman, Albert! It *was* funny! I'm so glad you went; for now they will all be thinking how clever it was of you to find out! And what a good lesson it was for them, to be sure!

ALBERT Yes, my Dear, a good lesson. . . . But Weibchen, you have not kissed me 'Good Morning' yet. . . . Please!

> (*And he says it so simply and sweetly, that, quite forgetting now what she first came about, she kisses him with true wifely affection, very fondly and contentedly.*)

Under Fire

Under Fire

30th May 1842

In a room of Buckingham Palace overlooking the Park,
PRINCE ALBERT *moves impatiently to the window, and
back again. He looks at his watch: a slight sound of
annoyance escapes him. The door opens; his Private
Secretary enters.*

ALBERT (*stiffly*) Mr. Anson, you are late.

ANSON I am sorry, Sir. I was just coming, when the
Chief Inspector of Police sent word that he wished to see
me.

ALBERT (*sharply*) Has he news?

ANSON None, Sir. They can't trace the man. So he
very urgently begs that Her Majesty shall not drive out
to-day.

ALBERT But that is nonsense! If Her Majesty does not
drive in the Park as usual, the man will suspect that we
know. So we shall not catch him.

ANSON It is a great risk, Sir.

ALBERT It is a risk. It has to be taken. It will be a
greater risk if we leave him to choose his own time later,
when the Police will not be so ready for him as they are
to-day.

ANSON He will choose his own time in any case, Sir.

ALBERT Yes; but now it will be the earliest possible. Yesterday, when his pistol missed fire, he did not know that he was seen by anyone. Her Majesty herself was looking the other way.

ANSON That was very fortunate, Sir.

ALBERT Perhaps. . . . Why?

ANSON Had Her Majesty shown any alarm, it would have told him.

ALBERT Her Majesty would have shown no alarm. You may be quite sure of that. When I told Her Majesty afterwards, what had happened, she was not alarmed at all; only rather surprised that one of her subjects should have done anything so wicked and foolish.

ANSON Ah, yes, Sir; that is, indeed, how it might well—

ALBERT (*continuing*)—Nor is Her Majesty alarmed now. It was her own decision, not mine, that we should go out to-day. When I told her that the man was sure to make another attempt, she said that he had better make it at once then, and get it over.

ANSON That was very courageous of Her Majesty.

ALBERT And very sensible. Sense is sometimes more valuable than courage—and much rarer where Kings are concerned. It is so here. I have no doubt that this afternoon the man will try again. It is better that he should try again, when we expect it, than at some later time when we do not. And that, Mr. Anson, is why—if the Inspector is so stupid that he must have it explained—that

174

is why Her Majesty drives out again to-day, at her usual time. You will go and tell him that at once. (*He moves to the window.*) Out there are the people, waiting to see Her Majesty start. Tell him that we shall be punctual.

ANSON I will, your Highness. . . . I hope—

ALBERT (*cutting him short*) We *all* hope, Mr. Anson. It is the only sensible thing to do. Ah, here is Her Majesty.

> (THE QUEEN *enters in bonnet and shawl.* MR. ANSON *stands aside for her to pass, then bows himself out. A little nervous, but very self-controlled,* THE QUEEN *advances towards* THE PRINCE.)

ALBERT (*approvingly*) You are very punctual, my Dear.

THE QUEEN Yes; we mustn't be late to-day.

ALBERT You look very well—very charming! That bonnet suits you.

THE QUEEN Kiss me, Albert.

ALBERT (*as he does so*) You make a very good Queen, my Dear.

THE QUEEN With you to help me.

ALBERT Even by yourself, I think, you would not do so badly.

THE QUEEN That will never happen, Albert. I couldn't live without you.

ALBERT You can do very unexpected things, my Dear. You never expected that you would have to do anything like this. But you are going to. It is having to do it that makes it possible.

THE QUEEN Doing it with you, Dearest, I *like* doing it.

ALBERT So do I. It makes our life mean so much more to us. . . . Look at all those friendly people, waiting for you to smile on them. . . . Rather amusing, is it not?—that none of them knows in the least—what *we* know.

THE QUEEN (*tremulously*) Albert, this must be rather like going into battle.

ALBERT Just a little, my Dear. But we have to do it in cold blood, without any excitement. That makes it rather more difficult, perhaps.

THE QUEEN Oh, but it excites me very much, Albert. For this is really to be a Queen. And with you I feel quite safe that I can behave like one.

ALBERT Yes; so do I, Weibchen; so do I.

> (*The door opens; a* COURT USHER *enters to make formal announcement.*)

USHER May it please: your Majesty's Ladies are in attendance.

THE QUEEN Oh, yes. . . . Tell them to come in.

> (THE USHER *retires.* THE QUEEN *turns quickly to* THE PRINCE.)

Albert, I didn't say anything to them before; I thought it was better not. But *they* mustn't come with us to-day; it wouldn't be safe.

ALBERT You are quite right, my Dear. It would be, for them, an unnecessary risk. We must go alone.

> (*The two Ladies-in-Waiting enter, dressed for going out. They make their curtsies, and stand to receive orders.*)

THE QUEEN Lady Muriel, Lady Grace, I do not require either of you this afternoon. I and the Prince are going out alone.

> (*The two Ladies receive this information with perfect correctness; but there is a suspicion of offended coldness in* LADY MURIEL'S *tone as she speaks.*)

LADY MURIEL And your Majesty will not require us again—later?

THE QUEEN No; not this afternoon. You can wait till we have gone. And then I shall not require your further attendance till this evening. . . . And now, Albert, I am quite ready to start. . . . I wonder if it is going to rain?

ALBERT I think not. Just now it looked quite promising.

> (*And so, talking of the weather, they go out, to give Fate and its Fool their opportunity for ending the Victorian Era before it has earned its name.*
>
> *And now the two Ladies-in-Waiting are alone; and, defrauded of her afternoon ride with Royalty, before admiring crowds (for which, with bonnet and shawl, she has so elaborately prepared herself),* LADY MURIEL *breaks out.*)

LADY MURIEL Well! I do think that's too bad! Here have we been kept waiting all for nothing; and if I'd known, I could have got off for the whole afternoon, as I very much wanted to do. I do call that inconsiderate of her!

LADY GRACE It's what she is, my dear. I suppose she can't help it. It's being a Queen. When you are so important yourself, you can't think much about other people. Oh, it's happened before; and it'll happen again! It's what we are here for.

LADY MURIEL. Oh, there! I've torn my glove. Dear, dear! My own fault, I suppose, taking it off in a temper.

LADY GRACE (*at the window*) Now, they're off. There they go! . . . No cheering this afternoon; the crowd isn't big enough. It always takes a certain number to cheer; —haven't you noticed? . . . But we bow, all the same. Oh, how he does take his hat off!—So like a foreigner! He'll never learn to be English.

LADY MURIEL Which way are they going?

LADY GRACE Which way? Why, there's only one way to the Park that I know of, my dear: up Constitution Hill.

LADY MURIEL If they are only going to the Park, isn't it rather strange that they should choose to go alone? The Prince so insists on the Queen being properly attended. It's my belief they've been quarrelling about something; and she wants to have it out with him.

LADY GRACE But she can't do that in the Park, with people staring at them.

LADY MURIEL Oh, *can't* she? She can say anything she wants to say, without moving a muscle of her face! She can whip you with a word, while she's smiling to someone else across the room. It's happened to me; so I know. She'll be able to say *all* she intends to say while they are driving in the Park. Yes; he's going to catch it about something.

LADY GRACE But does he ever 'catch' it?

178

LADY MURIEL My dear! She adores him, as we all know; but she can be jealous. And when she *is* jealous, she lets him know—you may depend on it.

LADY GRACE Well, of course, he *is* dangerously handsome. It's a wonder we don't all fall in love with him: but we don't.

LADY MURIEL Oh, he could be much more dangerous, if he chose, my dear. But it isn't manners that makes the man with him—it's morals.

LADY GRACE I suppose that's why he's so stiff when he talks to us. Oh, I've seen her watching him. I've been told that once, in the very early days, he gave one of her Ladies a present. There was a frightful row. He never did it again!

LADY MURIEL Perhaps it was something more than a present.

LADY GRACE Oh, my dear, I don't think you ought to say that!

LADY MURIEL I know I oughtn't! And that's why it's such a relief to say it! He's so good, he irritates me. Everything so proper! Life here is just a row of 'oughts,' all standing to attention—rules, rules, rules! I wonder he puts up with it.

LADY GRACE I think it's just as much his doing as hers. It's the way he was brought up: he doesn't know how to be natural.

LADY MURIEL Just as well, perhaps. . . . I don't believe he loves her a little bit.

LADY GRACE But he *must*!

LADY MURIEL Why?

LADY GRACE Well, he's stiff; but he's got a heart. And not to love one who loves him so terribly well, would be heartless.

LADY MURIEL She only loves him selfishly.

LADY GRACE No, my dear, not selfishly—jealously, perhaps. But she knows how much he's her superior; and a selfish person wouldn't. . . . What's that?

LADY MURIEL I didn't hear anything.

LADY GRACE It sounded like a shot.

(*But to neither of them does a chance shot seem a matter of importance; so talk goes on.*)

LADY MURIEL Well, my dear, I suppose we've been wasting time in a very ignoble conversation—running down our betters, which, after all, we have to admit they are. . . . What are you going to do?

LADY GRACE I don't know: it's too late to go anywhere now. But I don't want to stay here and watch them come back.

LADY MURIEL Isn't it funny how people *do*? Look, there's the crowd still waiting. They've seen them once; but they want to see them again. And I believe that sometimes it's the same people who come day after day—day after day.

LADY GRACE Oh, well, Royalty are one of the sights of London. Country Cousins expect to see them; and if you read your Court Circular, they can always be seen *here* at the stated hours.

180

LADY MURIEL My dear! What are all those people running for? Look! Constitution Hill is full of them! What can have happened?

LADY GRACE Has there been an accident?

LADY MURIEL No, no! Not an accident. They are cheering, waving, shouting! And here come mounted police—such a lot of them.

LADY GRACE They are coming back! They are coming back!

LADY MURIEL Who?

LADY GRACE The Queen! Something exciting must have happened! Has there been a declaration of War?

LADY MURIEL There's no one just now to declare war against, that I know of.

LADY GRACE Well, they must have done something very popular, anyhow. Look! The crowd's quite crazy.

> (*And then in bursts another of the Ladies-in-Wait-ing, panting, and flapping her hands with excitement.*)

LADY-IN-WAITING She's been shot at! She's been shot at!

LADY MURIEL AND LADY GRACE Who?

LADY-IN-WAITING The Queen!

LADY MURIEL AND LADY GRACE Where? When?

LADY-IN-WAITING Just now; on Constitution Hill.

LADY GRACE (*highly excited*) I heard it!

LADY MURIEL ⎱ Was she hurt?
LADY GRACE ⎰ Who did it?

LADY-IN-WAITING No; not hurt. A man—a madman, they think.

LADY GRACE Caught? Was he caught?

LADY-IN-WAITING Yes; they were expecting it. He'd tried to do it before—yesterday.

LADY MURIEL How do you know?

LADY-IN-WAITING I don't know. It mayn't be true. But everybody says so.

LADY GRACE Look! now they're coming in. The police are pushing the crowd back—such a lot of them on duty, they *must* have known.

LADY MURIEL Oh! Then—*She* must have known too!

LADY-IN-WAITING Yes; I suppose so.

LADY MURIEL (*catching hold of* LADY GRACE) Then that was *why*! Oh, my dear! She *knew*!—went, knowing that she was going to be shot at—*so didn't take us!* Oh! what a worm I feel myself now!

LADY GRACE (*sharing the feeling*) Yes, dear.

LADY MURIEL I want to run away, and hide; I'm so ashamed of myself!

LADY GRACE You can't go! They are coming.

(*The door opens;* THE QUEEN *enters, followed by* PRINCE ALBERT. *The Ladies curtsy with an emotional reverence which makes the formality almost beautiful.*)

LADY MURIEL Oh! your Majesty!

THE QUEEN Lady Muriel, why are you here still? Didn't I tell you that I should not want you again till this evening? Now go at once.

LADY MURIEL Oh, your Majesty! before I go, may I—may I—kiss your Majesty's hand?

THE QUEEN Why, certainly, if you wish to. Now don't cry: don't be silly! It's all over.

LADY MURIEL Oh, I'm so sorry, Ma'am: so sorry! So ashamed of myself!

THE QUEEN Ashamed? Why?

LADY MURIEL When your Majesty said we were not to come out with you this afternoon, I was foolishly cross: I didn't understand.

THE QUEEN Of course not. It was not necessary that you should. But now you *do*. So that will help you to know better—another time.

ALBERT (*turning sharply*) Another time!

THE QUEEN Go, please, Lady Muriel. I don't want you any more now.

> (*And* LADY MURIEL *curtsies herself out after the others who have already gone.*)

Why, yes, Albert: there *may* come another time. Why not?

ALBERT (*taking her in his arms*) Oh, my Dear, my Dear! And you can say that *now*—as if you did not mind if it *should* come again! Is that really true?

THE QUEEN Yes, Albert: it was wonderful! For, with you, I felt—so safe. . . . Didn't you?

ALBERT No, Weibchen. I was afraid!

THE QUEEN Afraid?

ALBERT I was afraid that—if he missed *one* of us, it might be *me* that he missed. Ah, no, no, no! do not talk of another time! I could not bear it—another time!

THE QUEEN (*startled*) Oh, Albert, had I thought for a moment that it might be *you*—I *couldn't* have gone! But that *that* could happen I didn't think!

ALBERT What a very good thing it was, then, my Dear, that you did *not* think. Queens must not think too much about others—only about themselves!

> (*And having made that little joke, very much to his own satisfaction, he kisses her.*)

THE QUEEN Dearest! Have I pleased you?

ALBERT Very much. You have more than *pleased* me You have behaved—like a Queen!

THE QUEEN Then now I must go and take off my things. Oh, dear! what a lot of letters I shall have to write *now*! To Uncle Leopold, and to everybody!

> (*And with this added inconvenience of attempted assassination upon her mind, off she goes, for there is no time to lose.*)

A Fall from Power

A Fall from Power

1842

In her private room at Windsor, THE QUEEN *sits at her usual occupation when alone, writing her diary. The door opens, and in the manner of one demanding, rather than soliciting permission for an audience, the* BARONESS LEHZEN *enters, and speaks. Her accent is decidedly German.)*

LEHZEN Your Majesty?

THE QUEEN Yes?

LEHZEN May I come in?

THE QUEEN (*laying down her pen*) Of course.

LEHZEN Your Majesty is disengaged—not too occupied? The Prince is not with you?

THE QUEEN As you see, Lehzen dear, I am quite alone. What is the matter?

LEHZEN I have to tell your Majesty—this cannot go on!

THE QUEEN What cannot?

LEHZEN Either I am your Majesty's Private Secretary, or I am not. Which is it to be?

THE QUEEN But, of course, you are my Secretary. Who said you were not?

LEHZEN I have only the facts, your Majesty. They speak for themselves—though nothing has been *said*.

THE QUEEN Please, explain, Lehzen.

LEHZEN Yesterday I wrote five letters, for your Majesty—to sign. To-day they come back to me unsigned. I am told that the Prince has written them for you—instead of me.

THE QUEEN Not all of them.

LEHZEN *Three* of them. So what I have done is of no use; and I am put in the waste-paper basket—*so!*

(*She makes a descriptive gesture.*)

THE QUEEN I am sorry. Lehzen. It happened that after I told you to write them, the Prince and I talked them over together; and when we had decided what to say, and how it should be said, he proposed writing them himself.

LEHZEN *He!* Ha, yes! So it was his doing, not yours.

THE QUEEN (*composedly*) I ought to have told you: I forgot. I'm sorry.

LEHZEN (*still unappeased*) This is not the only time.

THE QUEEN No? . . . When?

LEHZEN Every day. You do not now send on to me all the letters you wish to be written.

THE QUEEN No: some I still write myself; some the Prince writes for me. Isn't that quite natural? Often it is so much more convenient.

188

LEHZEN It did not use to be so. Till two years ago I did *everything*.

THE QUEEN Two years ago I was not married, Lehzen, and had nobody but you to help me.

LEHZEN Did your Majesty marry just to have a new Secretary, and so—to get rid of me?

THE QUEEN Lehzen, you hurt me! How can you think such a thing? Haven't you always been with me?—all my life, almost.

LEHZEN Yes. You were to me as my own child! I taught you everything.

THE QUEEN Almost.

LEHZEN And when you became Queen, I was not to go. . . . You did not wish to lose me, you said—ever!

THE QUEEN I hope I never shall, Lehzen.

LEHZEN (*vehemently*) But this cannot go on! If I am not your Majesty's Private Secretary—if my work is interfered with, and done by another—what am I left to be?

> (LEHZEN *has so 'let herself go' that when, at this moment,* PRINCE ALBERT *enters, it is quite evident to his observant eye that something unusual is happening.*)

ALBERT What is the matter?

THE QUEEN It was my fault, Albert. I forgot, yesterday, that I had given directions to Lehzen about those letters which you wrote for me. And now—in consequence—

> (*She pauses.*)

189

ALBERT Yes?

THE QUEEN Well, Lehzen feels that what she wrote is not wanted—after all.

ALBERT Of course not.

THE QUEEN But you see, Dearest, I ought to have told her.

ALBERT Why? If, by mistake, the letters were not sent twice over—does it matter?

LEHZEN Your Highness, as I am Her Majesty's Private Secretary by appointment, I would wish not to have my duties interfered with!

ALBERT They will not be, I am quite sure, Baroness—certainly not by me. But your duties do not require you to undertake more of Her Majesty's private correspondence than Her Majesty chooses to entrust to you.

LEHZEN Her Majesty had given me those letters to answer *myself*.

THE QUEEN Yes, Lehzen; but I have already explained.

LEHZEN (*with humble dignity*) Your Majesty's explanation—permit me to say—does not quite satisfy me.

ALBERT I am afraid it will have to, Baroness. A small mistake was made, which is not likely to occur again. In future it will be arranged that before *any* private letters are passed on for you to answer, Her Majesty and I will look through them together, and will reserve those which we wish to deal with ourselves.

LEHZEN Do I understand that your Majesty approves of that arrangement?

THE QUEEN Yes, Lehzen; I think it will be quite a good thing. It will save you from a lot of unnecessary trouble. I fear that I often give you more to do than you can easily find time for.

LEHZEN (*with offended dignity*) I have not complained, your Majesty, of having too much to do.

THE QUEEN No, Lehzen; it's all the other way. You do too much, without complaining.

LEHZEN If your Majesty thinks I am no longer equal to the duties which I undertook—so willingly, I would be glad if your Majesty would inform me.

ALBERT Her Majesty will, I am sure. And I think, Baroness, that, for the present, that will do; if, as it seems, Her Majesty no longer requires you.

THE QUEEN No, that is all. . . . You may go, Lehzen.

LEHZEN Then your Majesty has nothing more to say to me? . . . And when, may it please your Majesty, am I to know whether I am still to be—

> (THE PRINCE *crosses to the door, and opens it with stiff politeness.*)

ALBERT Baroness.

> (*Rigid with rage,* THE BARONESS, *forgetting even to curtsy herself out, sweeps from the room.*)

THE QUEEN (*compunctious, and a little distressed*) Oh, Albert! It's so difficult!

ALBERT Not at all, my Dear. . . . That woman must go.

THE QUEEN Go? How can she? She has been with me so long—as long as I can remember.

ALBERT Yes: when you were a child, she was your Governess, was she not?

THE QUEEN Yes.

ALBERT You must not have a Governess now, my Dear; it does not do. And that is what she does not understand.

THE QUEEN But to send her away, Albert—so faithful and devoted as she has been, seems too cruel! She loves me.

ALBERT Yes; and because she loves *you* she hates *me*. I do not mind her hating me; she is only one of many. But she must not prevent me from being useful to you. And that is what she would like.

THE QUEEN Oh, Albert—twenty years she has been with me. If I send her away, what will she do with herself?

> (THE PRINCE *walks slowly to the window, and stands
> looking out. He turns, and comes towards her.*)

ALBERT Weibchen, there is something I want to say to you.

THE QUEEN Yes?

ALBERT Rather difficult.

THE QUEEN Why should it be difficult for you to tell me anything?

ALBERT Because, Dearest, when you make up your mind, you are then a little *hard*.

THE QUEEN 'Hard'? . . . But not to *you*.

192

ALBERT To change, I mean.

THE QUEEN Perhaps . . . sometimes.

ALBERT (*seating himself*) You know, Vicky, that my Mother was not true to her own husband—went away, and left him.

THE QUEEN Yes.

ALBERT But I have always loved her: nor, in my own mind, did I ever really blame her.

THE QUEEN I know. But why do you tell me this—again?

ALBERT Vicky . . . Have you yet forgiven your own Mother, for something much less than what mine did?

THE QUEEN Less? It was the same thing, Albert.

ALBERT Oh, no, Vicky: she was a widow; she had no friends; she was lonely. . . . *Have* you forgiven her?

THE QUEEN Why do you ask me this, Albert?

ALBERT Because she writes to me, and is lonely. She loves you still. . . . Do you not love her?

THE QUEEN Yes, Albert, of course I love her.

ALBERT But you see her so seldom: never alone. You have always one of your Ladies with you. I go to see her; and you do not. . . . Why not now? There may once have been a reason. But *he* is no longer there.

THE QUEEN Oh, Albert!

ALBERT Shall I tell you why you do not go?

THE QUEEN Why?

ALBERT Lehzen is why. . . . Lehzen! . . . It was she who was jealous of your Mamma, as she was also jealous of me. I am not afraid of Lehzen—for myself; but is it right, Weibchen, that she should have decided it for you— and be doing it still—how you should treat your own Mother?

THE QUEEN You think I have been—*hard*, Albert?

ALBERT A little: but also weak, to let anyone else make you be hard to *her*.

THE QUEEN Weak, you say? Oh, I don't know what to think!

ALBERT Oh, yes . . . you do . . . you *do*!

(THE QUEEN *sits for a moment undecided. But now, with the truth put before her, she is too honest to deceive herself.*)

THE QUEEN Yes . . . you are quite right. . . . It's true. . . . It *was* Lehzen.

ALBERT I was sure of it, my Dear. Your Mamma and the Baroness are too like each other; they love you too much in the same way—jealously. But your Mamma has accepted *me*, very kindly, very generously. Lehzen never will.

THE QUEEN And you don't like Lehzen.

ALBERT No. . . . But only because I think she is bad for you.

THE QUEEN Then that must settle it, Albert. Yes; she shall go. . . . Poor Lehzen! Poor Lehzen!

(*She bursts into tears.* THE PRINCE *rises, and laying his hand fondly on her head, strokes it.*)

194

ALBERT Poor Vicky! . . . Poor little Vicky! . . . And to have only *me* instead!

(*She flings herself into his arms.*)

THE QUEEN Oh, Albert, Albert, Dearest! Promise, promise never to leave me! Promise to let *me* die first!

ALBERT That is not for me to decide, Vicky. . . . But I do not think I shall live to be very old.

THE QUEEN But why not?

ALBERT I am not so fond of life as you, my Dear. . . . If I were ever very ill, I should not make a great fight for myself. No.

VICTORIA But that would be very wrong—very selfish of you, Dearest!

ALBERT So? . . . Yes? . . . Why?

VICTORIA Think of me! Think of *me*!

ALBERT Ah, yes, Weibchen! I will try always to think of you—only of you!

The Intruder

The Intruder

1845

From the brilliantly-lighted drawing-room (Buckingham Palace has three, and this is the smallest of them) the Royal Presence has just been withdrawn. Backs are bent to the disappearing train, which is all that we see. Then, as the door closes, the GENTLEMEN *straighten their backs, the* LADIES *rise from their curtsies. In obvious relief from the tension of Court etiquette, faces and limbs find relaxation, the* GENTLEMEN *cough, draw breath, heave sighs of relief; the* LADIES *yawn politely behind their fans. A* DOWAGER-LADY *totters to an arm-chair, and sinks into it, half-fainting.*

DOWAGER Oh! my poor legs! What has become of them?

LADY-IN-WAITING Don't say 'legs,' Mamma! The Gentlemen! (*She indicates that they are listening.*) Feet!

DOWAGER Feet? I haven't any left! All this standing! . . . and after dinner, too! To people of my age—it's cruel! Why does the Queen allow it?

LADY-IN-WAITING The Prince insists on it, Mamma.

DOWAGER (*sighing*) Yes, I know . . . I know!

LADY-IN-WAITING Come to bed, Mamma, dear!

(She raises her Mother, and leads her towards the door.)

DOWAGER *(drawing back)* Wait! Take care! We mustn't overtake them. The Queen doesn't like it.

LADY-IN-WAITING It's all right, Mamma. They are letting us out now.

(For now the doors are opening again, an indication that the way is clear, and that the Court is now free to go to bed, if it likes. The GENTLEMEN stand back, and bow for the LADIES to pass first, and the LADIES curtsy themselves out.)

FIRST GENTLEMAN Did you hear what happened to-night?

SECOND GENTLEMAN Happened?

FIRST GENTLEMAN To Lady Peel, I mean?

SECOND GENTLEMAN What about her?

FIRST GENTLEMAN Well, you know that she is—expecting, quite soon. The Queen told her that, when the Prince came in, she might remain seated; and that two of her ladies should stand in front of her, so that the Prince shouldn't see.

SECOND GENTLEMAN Very kind of her . . . very considerate.

FIRST GENTLEMAN Yes, but he did see her; and word went to her that she was to stand.

SECOND GENTLEMAN How very like him! What a drill-master he would have made!

FIRST GENTLEMAN Well, of course. . . . German, you know, German. It's the mediæval idea. He can't get rid of it.

SECOND GENTLEMAN And yet, in other things—so alive and up-to-date!

FIRST GENTLEMAN Yes. He looks into everything—cupboards, even, so I'm told.

SECOND GENTLEMAN Eh?

> (*A respectfully hovering Attendant catches his eye; he perceives that they are the last. He takes his companion's arm.*)

Come, we must be going. It's Buckingham Palace's bed-time.

FIRST GENTLEMAN It's early yet. Will you come down to my Club with me?

SECOND GENTLEMAN Thanks. Delighted.

> (*They go out.*)
>
> (*And, now, with due ceremony, a transformation-scene takes place. The* ATTENDANT *crosses to a side-door, opens it, and calls, 'All out.' Through it enter, first a* SERGEANT STEWARD *of the Palace service, then a troop of Attendants, carrying dust-sheets and extinguishers. They proceed to cover the sofas and chairs for the night, and to put out the wax-candles. On the sofa, where the* DOWAGER *has sat, an* ATTENDANT *finds a fallen bracelet.*)

FIRST ATTENDANT (*to* SECOND) Hey! Here's something been left.

SERGEANT STEWARD (*sharply*) No talking, there!

FIRST ATTENDANT No, Sir. But this, Sir. Somebody's left it behind them!

(*He brings the bracelet.*)

SERGEANT STEWARD (*taking it*) You could have found that without speaking. In future, remember!

FIRST ATTENDANT Yes, Sir.

(*The Attendants pass on into the next room. The last candles are put out. In the next room we see the same process beginning. The* SERGEANT STEWARD *takes a last look to see that all is right, and goes, closing the door. A clock is heard striking the hour. It finishes. A side-door opens, through it comes a dim light; dark against it, a queer figure creeps stealthily in. He halts, strikes a match, and stands looking vacantly round him. He has a youthful face, with a half-witted expression. The match burns on; he fumbles in his pocket, pulls out a candle-end, which he lights, then drops the burnt-out match on to the floor.*)

INTRUDER Here I am, then! And nobody's seen me. My! What a place to burn down! And won't it be in all the papers?

(*Roaming the room, he goes to the window, and takes hold of the curtain-cord; he pulls it; the curtains open, revealing moonlight through blind.*)

INTRUDER (*startled*) Lord! Look at that, now! And I hardly touched it!

(He crosses to the main door, opens it, peeps, and is about to pass through, but draws back, closing it again.)

INTRUDER Someone coming!

(He stoops, lifts a dust-sheet, and creeps under the sofa. Slowly the door opens, PRINCE ALBERT appears, carrying a candle. He enters, leaving the door wide, and begins to inspect the room. Behind him, secretively inquisitive, perhaps a little suspicious, enters THE QUEEN; her evening toilette covered by a large cream-white shawl with long fringes. She stands looking at him; he turns, and sees her.)

THE QUEEN Albert, Dearest, what are you doing here?

ALBERT What are *you* doing here, my Dear?

THE QUEEN *(with a touch of fond reproach)* You went . . . I missed you.

ALBERT I came, Weibchen, to see whether my orders had been carried out.

THE QUEEN Your orders?

ALBERT Yes.

THE QUEEN You did not tell me of them.

ALBERT It was not necessary.

THE QUEEN But I would like to know, Albert.

ALBERT Very well. I found that it was the custom here to leave all the candles burning, and nothing covered for the night.

THE QUEEN The candles—burning?

ALBERT Yes, till they were all burnt out.

THE QUEEN Most extraordinary!

ALBERT Not at all, my Dear. Just the sort of thing that I would now expect.

THE QUEEN How did you find out?

ALBERT As I find out everything, my Dear. First by personal inspection, then by inquiry.

THE QUEEN The candles left burning—every night? How wasteful!

ALBERT Yes. And the reason? What, do you suppose, the reason was?

THE QUEEN Just carelessness, I suppose.

ALBERT Oh, no! Quite the reverse. It was by strict orders. During the Regency of your Uncle George, orders had been given that no servants were to enter, or be seen anywhere near the royal apartments, after midnight.

THE QUEEN After midnight?

ALBERT The Regent's late hours—and what he did with them—were not to be disturbed by any intruder.

THE QUEEN I see.

ALBERT And so—leaving the candles to burn out has become a Palace tradition.

THE QUEEN And when did you find that out, Albert?

ALBERT A few days ago.

THE QUEEN How?

ALBERT After we had gone to bed, I came down again.

THE QUEEN How was it I didn't miss you?

ALBERT I came down, my Love, from my dressing-room . . . before coming to you.

THE QUEEN I see. And you said nothing.

ALBERT I never do say anything, my Dear, which might worry you, that I can avoid saying.

THE QUEEN How thoughtful you are, Albert, always!

ALBERT There is so much here that needs to be thought about. In the past, things have been much neglected.

THE QUEEN I hope all this care is not going to age you, Albert. You are so beautiful! But often I see you looking tired.

ALBERT No, no. I like it. It interests me.

THE QUEEN Because you are so good and conscientious in everything you do. You were born to rule, Albert!

ALBERT Ah! Weibchen, if I had not your love and your trust, I could do nothing. Everyone here is jealous of me.

THE QUEEN Yes, I know! And it makes me so angry, Albert! One day, I mean that you shall be made King.

ALBERT King?

THE QUEEN Yes. Not Prince, or Prince *Consort*: *King* Consort—as you really are.

ALBERT Why cause trouble, my Dear? For it will cause trouble. What's in a name?

THE QUEEN My love, Dearest; in that name, all my love for you.

(To this fond outburst the PRINCE *does not respond. He is looking at something.* THE QUEEN, *perceiving his attention riveted, asks)*

What are you looking at?

ALBERT A match! There is a burnt match lying on the floor. How did it come there?

(He looks round sharply and inquisitorially.)

And those curtains have been drawn open. Someone must have been in.

(He gets no further. From under the sofa comes a sound.)

THE QUEEN Hush! What is that? *(She points.)* Somebody is there!

ALBERT Stand away, Dearest!

(He goes to the sofa, and lifts the dust-sheet.)

Who is that under there? . . . Who are you? . . . Come out! . . .

(Compelled by the stronger will, the INTRUDER *emerges, and rises slowly to his feet.)*

THE QUEEN Oh, take care, Albert! Take care! He may be going to shoot you.

ALBERT How did you get in here?

(The INTRUDER *turns slowly, and points.)*

INTRUDER Through yon door.

ALBERT How did you get in at all?

INTRUDER I come through the stables.

ALBERT And then?

INTRUDER Through the kitchen.

ALBERT When?

INTRUDER After they'd done cooking the dinner . . . when they was all busy washing-up.

ALBERT What did you come for?

> (*There is a pause. The* INTRUDER *stares round, but does not answer.*)

I ask you—what did you come for?

INTRUDER Just to see.

ALBERT To see what?

INTRUDER To see if I could see where the Queen lived, and what it was all like.

ALBERT Yes?

INTRUDER So as I could tell people.

ALBERT Did no one see you come in?

INTRUDER They may ha' done. No one didn't stop me.

ALBERT And when you had come, and seen—what did you intend doing? . . . Now, I mean, when everything is locked up?

INTRUDER I was just going to open a winder, and get out.

ALBERT Did you mean to steal anything?

INTRUDER No, Sir. But I thought as how I'd set fire to it, perhaps.

ALBERT Set fire? . . . Why?

207

INTRUDER So as to see it in the papers, to-morrer.

THE QUEEN (*whispering*) He's mad, Albert! He's mad!

ALBERT (*quietly*) Very likely. Go and ring the bell; and then go yourself—at once.

THE QUEEN (*after looking round for it*) There is no bell, Albert.

ALBERT Then go, go quickly!

THE QUEEN No, Albert; I am not going to leave you.

> (*So, for the present, the position has to remain unaltered.*)

ALBERT Which door did you say you came in at?

INTRUDER (*pointing*) There. . . . That one.

ALBERT Then go through it again, at once.

> (*The* INTRUDER *obeys, meek as a lamb. The* PRINCE, *following him up, closes the door behind him.*)

ALBERT No bell; but there is a key. (*He turns it.*) Now, Weibchen, do you feel that I am safe enough for you to leave me?

THE QUEEN Oh, Albert! How brave, how brave you are!

ALBERT Only sensible, my Dear. Now go quickly, and send somebody at once.

> (*She goes. Left alone, the* PRINCE *pauses, then goes to the door, unlocks it, opens it, and calls*)

You . . . fellow! Are you there? What are you doing? (*He looks in.*) Ah! gone . . . gone. . . . Yes, of course.

> (*As he turns away the* SERGEANT STEWARD *enters, panting, by the main door.*)

SERGEANT STEWARD Oh, your Royal Highness! I pray pardon! What has happened? . . . Her Majesty has sent me.

ALBERT (*sharply*) Who are you, Sir? What do you call yourself?

SERGEANT STEWARD Your Royal Highness, I am the Sergeant Steward.

ALBERT That means, I suppose, that you have the safety of the Palace in your keeping?

SERGEANT STEWARD Yes, your Highness. Yes.

ALBERT Of the Royal Family, also?

SERGEANT STEWARD That is so, your Royal Highness . . . at least . . .

ALBERT Then it may interest you to know that there is, at present, somewhere in the Palace, a lunatic at large, who was able to walk in here without anyone preventing; and whom I myself, and Her Majesty, found hiding under that sofa—

SERGEANT STEWARD (*horrified*) Oh! your Highness!

ALBERT —intending, so he told me, to set fire to the Palace; so that he might 'see it to-morrow in the papers.'

SERGEANT STEWARD And, where, your Royal Highness . . . where has he gone now?

ALBERT Where he is now hiding himself I do not know. He went through that door. You had better go after him. . . . I say, you had better go after him.

SERGEANT STEWARD (*quailing*) But, your Royal Highness, he may be armed.

ALBERT He may be . . . quite likely. But he didn't shoot *me*; so perhaps he will not shoot *you*. But you must go and see.

> (*The* SERGFANT STEWARD *moves irresolutely toward the door.*)

Oh, before you go, draw those curtains again!

> (*The* SERGEANT STEWARD *does so.*)

And pick up that match!

> (*The match is picked up.*)

It ought not to have been there. Now go and see where that man is.

SERGEANT STEWARD (*in abject supplication*) Your Royal Highness! . . .

ALBERT I order you to go and see!

> (*As a lamb to the slaughter, the* SERGEANT STEWARD *goes.*)

And don't leave the door open!

> (*The door is shut.* THE QUEEN *enters, still anxious.*)

THE QUEEN Albert, why are you laughing?

ALBERT I have told that man to go and see if he will get shot; and he does not like it. . . . If he does get shot, his widow must have a pension. If he does not get shot, you will have to dismiss him for his incompetence.

> (*Suddenly, in the distance, an alarm bell rings, and through the main doors come running in single file six Royal Footmen armed with shovels and pokers. Without perceiving the Royal Couple, they dash through in pursuit of whatever danger is ahead of them.*)

ALBERT Really, my Dear, this place *has* become a lunatic asylum. No wonder *he* found his way into it! . . . Come, let me go back to bed.

QUEEN But I shan't *sleep*, Dearest! After all this!

ALBERT (*fondly*) Oh, yes . . . you *will*—you will. Come, Weibchen!

(*He kisses her; and they go out hand-in-hand.*)

The Rose and the Thorn

The Rose and the Thorn

1846

THE QUEEN *is holding her Court at Windsor. A Footman opens the folding-doors of a small ante-chamber; and from its softly illumined interior one sees across the broad corridor, through looped curtains, the large music-room (where presently performance is to take place) brilliantly lighted. Under its crystal chandeliers, the Ladies and Gentlemen of the Court are beginning to gather. The small room has in it little furniture: away from the wall, on one side of the door, stands a small settee; on the other, a grand-piano. On the same side, lower down, is a smaller door. Into the room come four musicians, carrying their instruments: their conductor, the future* SIR JOHN OAKLEY—*now only* 'MR.' —*leading them.*

OAKLEY We must come in here, for a moment. Her Majesty does not allow any tuning-up to be done in her presence.

> (*He opens the piano, and strikes notes and chords for the musicians to tune by.*)

So. . . . You are all ready? Come, then!

> (*They go out, leaving the folding-doors open, and cross the corridor to the music-room. A little*

later, .he doors of the music-room are closed, and one hears from within, very softly, the performance beginning.

And now two Ladies of the Court enter: the one a very beautiful DUCHESS *of middle age,* THE QUEEN'S *Mistress of the Robes; the other her cousin,* LADY JANE, *small, young, and pretty.* THE DUCHESS, *leading the way, lays down on the settee a richly embroidered shawl, and a feather fan. Meanwhile the younger lady is speaking.)*

LADY JANE But, your Grace, it's so difficult!

DUCHESS My dear, Court life *is* difficult. Its difficulties are the larger part of its duties.

LADY JANE But to be suspected—and for nothing—is so humiliating!

DUCHESS Yes, my dear; high positions, when they are not the highest, involve humiliation for all of us. Do you think *I* never feel humiliated?

LADY JANE You! Your Grace?

DUCHESS When I am sent out of the room, as if I were a servant, I feel it.

LADY JANE But you do it so grandly—with such an air!

DUCHESS Yes: that is how one covers the humiliation. After all, Court life is mainly made up of formalities; and being sent out of the room is one of them. Ministers are dismissed, and so are we. Even Lord Palmerston had a narrow escape the other day.

216

LADY JANE Lord Palmerston!

DUCHESS Yes; and quite right, too!

LADY JANE (*who has gone to the mirror, to re-arrange the flowers in her hair*) What for?

DUCHESS Well, it wasn't the Queen who told me, or I shouldn't repeat it. He told me himself—cross, but half-laughing. He wanted the Prince out of the room, while he discussed Foreign Affairs with her. And, to avoid it, he sent off some despatches without first submitting them. So there was trouble.

LADY JANE I should think so!

DUCHESS Yes, my dear; anyone who touches the Prince, touches a bomb, which goes off. She's the bomb: *He* isn't.

LADY JANE (*reverting to her grievance*) But I haven't touched him!

DUCHESS No; but you've looked at him. That's enough.

LADY JANE But, your Grace, he's there to be looked at! And how can one help admiring him, when he's so handsome?

DUCHESS You needn't help it; but you mustn't be admired in return.

LADY JANE Oh, why doesn't she only have *plain* women about her?

DUCHESS Even that wouldn't always meet the difficulty. Plain women have often a way with them. And it wants something more than mere looks to attract *him*.

LADY JANE (*with a touch of spite*) He isn't a bit in love with *her*!

DUCHESS No; but he's very fond of her. The Prince is —what is so rarely found amongst Royalty—the domestic man; and he's not only domestic, he's conjugal.

LADY JANE Then why is she so jealous of him?

DUCHESS My dear, she can't help it: she's possessive, and she's in love with him.

LADY JANE But *I'm* not!

DUCHESS Of course not, my dear. I know you wouldn't take such a liberty.

LADY JANE I wish she'd send me away! If this goes on, I shall ask to resign my appointment.

DUCHESS No, no, my dear! Don't do anything so out of character. 'Hold your ground!' is the motto of our family. Hold it! . . . What, exactly, happened to-day?

LADY JANE We were out riding in the Park; and the Prince came and rode beside me, just for a moment. My reins had got caught, and he was putting them straight for me. And the Queen pushed her horse right in between us; and she said, 'Lady Jane, if you don't know how to ride properly, you had better not come out with us!' And the Prince said, 'Lady Jane rides very nicely and well.' Oh, you should have seen the Queen's look then! And it's true; I *do* ride nicely—better than she does; and she knows it!

DUCHESS And was that all that happened?

LADY JANE All that happened to *me*. But the Prince left the Queen, and went straight off, and rode with one of his Gentlemen. And then the Queen suddenly turned round, and we all had to ride back to the Castle. And of course everybody knew that something was the matter, for we hadn't gone half our usual round. And now, I believe, she has put Lady Maud to spy on me.

DUCHESS Oh, I don't think that's likely, my dear. The Queen wouldn't say anything to anyone—she's too proud.

LADY JANE Well, she *is* spying anyway—hoping perhaps to tell tales presently. If I catch her, I'll slap her face!

DUCHESS My dear, I think I'd better arrange for you to take a little holiday—change of air. You shall see your doctor, and he will advise it. But don't give up your post. If the Queen proposes to dismiss you, I shall say something. She won't dismiss *me*.

LADY JANE No; but perhaps she will send you out of the room.

DUCHESS Perhaps she will, my dear. She has done it before; and I have continued the conversation the next day, with the Prince there to help me.

LADY JANE To help you?

DUCHESS Oh, yes; she's always much more easy to reason with when he's there.

LADY JANE He has such beautiful manners to everyone, hasn't he?

DUCHESS He is a very good corrective; and she knows it. I'm very fond of her; but she needs managing; and he is the only person who can do it.

LADY JANE He didn't manage her this morning!

DUCHESS He didn't try. . . . You wait!

LADY JANE Oh, dear! I don't know that I *can* wait. Everybody knows I'm in disgrace; so they won't speak to me.

DUCHESS Now be brave, my dear, be brave! The unfortunate thing has happened, and now it's over. You keep under my wing; and you shan't look as if you've been sent to Coventry by anyone. . . . There's the music coming to an end. We must go back, or she will be missing us.

> (*Forgetting her shawl and fan, she goes towards the door of the music-room, followed by* LADY JANE. *At that moment the doors open: from within comes a polite murmur of applause. The Musicians come out, carrying their instruments, and pass down the corridor. Behind them comes* MR. OAKLEY; *in the doorway he turns and bows. He, also, is retiring, when one of* THE QUEEN'S GENTLEMEN *comes after him.*)

GENTLEMAN Her Majesty wishes to speak to you, Mr. Oakley.

> (THE QUEEN *appears in the doorway. She is followed by* PRINCE ALBERT, *who, with stiff formality, crosses the corridor, and enters the ante-room, while* THE QUEEN *stays to speak to* MR. OAKLEY.)

THE QUEEN That was very beautiful, Mr. Oakley. Thank you. It was your own composition, I believe?

OAKLEY It was, your Majesty.

THE QUEEN We should very much like to hear another piece presently.

220

OAKLEY Most honoured, your Majesty.

(*Leaving* MR. OAKLEY *to receive the congratulations of other members of his audience,* THE QUEEN *follows* THE PRINCE *into the ante-room.*)

THE QUEEN Albert, why are you so cold to me?

ALBERT It is a cold day, my Dear. And this morning we did not take enough exercise.

THE QUEEN You did not come to me afterwards. I have hardly seen you since—except with others.

ALBERT (*stiffly*) No; that is so.

THE QUEEN Albert, have I offended you?

ALBERT My Dear, you must not try to give me riding lessons—before others.

(*He moves away.*)

THE QUEEN I want to speak to you, Albert.

(*Paying no attention, he returns to the corridor, and seeing* MR. OAKLEY, *pauses to speak to him. The other members of the Court draw back respectfully. Meanwhile* THE QUEEN, *after standing for a few moments, angry and undecided, turns and goes quickly past them. At the music-room door she stops to exchange words with some of her Ladies. Meanwhile* THE PRINCE *is speaking.*)

ALBERT Ah, Mr. Oakley, I have some news that I hope will please you. We are expecting to have the great Mendelssohn with us again soon. He is coming to England in the Spring.

221

OAKLEY That is great news indeed, Sir. Will he also be coming to Windsor?

ALBERT We hope so. We have invited him to come.

OAKLEY For all who love music, as does your Royal Highness, it will be a great occasion.

ALBERT It will, indeed.

> (*Dismissing* MR. OAKLEY *with a courteous gesture,* THE PRINCE *turns towards the music-room; but at sight of* THE QUEEN *standing in the doorway, he re-enters the ante-room, where* THE DUCHESS, *followed by* LADY JANE, *has returned to pick up her fan and shawl. Just as* LADY JANE *is entering, a rose falls from her hair.* THE PRINCE, *with courtly grace, stoops and picks it up for her.*)

ALBERT Lady Jane, here is something that you have dropped.

> (*He presents the flower.*)

LADY JANE (*nervously*) Oh, your Highness, I am sorry! —sorry to have given your Highness the trouble!

ALBERT (*gallantly*) No trouble . . . a pleasure. . . . It is a colour that suits you.

> (*Meanwhile* THE DUCHESS *has moved to the door, and is looking back with an amused smile, when* THE QUEEN, *pushing past her, comes swiftly into the room. Trembling with rage, she advances upon* LADY JANE, *and snatches the flower from her hand. With an instinct for the emergency,* THE DUCHESS *closes the folding-doors: such a scene must have no spectators.*)

222

LADY JANE (*with tremulous courage*) Your Majesty must pardon me: that flower is mine.

THE QUEEN How dare you speak to me! Go! Go, instantly!

> (LADY JANE, *her head very erect, makes a swift, deep curtsy, and goes out of the room. Meanwhile* THE DUCHESS *is speaking to* THE PRINCE.)

DUCHESS (*urgently*) I beg your Royal Highness to allow me to explain. I saw just what happened.

> (THE PRINCE *hesitates for a moment, then turns abruptly, and goes out of the room by the other door. There is a pause.* THE QUEEN *stands crushing the flower in her hands.*)

THE QUEEN Go and tell the Prince to come back! I wish to speak to him.

DUCHESS Will your Majesty—

THE QUEEN At once! Do as I tell you!

DUCHESS Yes, Ma'am, yes; in a moment. But first I beg your Majesty to allow me to speak—to explain.

THE QUEEN There is nothing to explain.

DUCHESS But there is! There is! I saw everything.

THE QUEEN So did I. I saw the Prince give her this flower—this rose. Do you mean to deny it?

DUCHESS No, your Majesty, no; he did not give it her. She had dropped it.

THE QUEEN (*suspiciously*) Dropped it? Ah, yes!

223

DUCHESS No, Ma'am; quite by accident. It fell out of her hair. The Prince only picked it up and returned it to her.

THE QUEEN You saw that, you say? You know that—for certain?

DUCHESS I assure your Majesty it was so.

THE QUEEN Do you know, also, what happened this morning?

DUCHESS I do, Ma'am. My Cousin has told me everything.

THE QUEEN Did she try to explain it?

DUCHESS There was hardly anything to explain, Ma'am. It might have happened to anyone.

THE QUEEN Then why did she tell you about it?

DUCHESS She was very much upset at the way your Majesty had taken what was a mere accident.

THE QUEEN It may have been an accident: I don't know. What has happened now is much more serious.

DUCHESS *Very* much more serious, your Majesty.

(THE QUEEN *looks at her in surprise:* THE DUCHESS *does not flinch. There is a pause.*)

THE QUEEN (*defensively*) It was all so sudden—so unexpected. One hadn't time to think.

DUCHESS That is so. Your Majesty gave yourself no time—to think.

THE QUEEN I was too hasty, you mean?

DUCHESS Does your Majesty wish me to say more than I have said?

THE QUEEN I only wish you to tell me the honest truth.

DUCHESS I will, Ma'am. . . . At least, I will try. But the truth is sometimes difficult.

THE QUEEN It should not be.

DUCHESS Not even when it is—to a Queen, Ma'am?

THE QUEEN A Queen may need it sometimes, far more than others.

DUCHESS If she knows that she needs it, Ma'am, she is already on the side of truth.

THE QUEEN I do know it—I do! . . . Tell me!—is it possible that I have been unjust?

DUCHESS It is possible, your Majesty.

THE QUEEN I did not intend to be.

DUCHESS No one, who knows your Majesty, would think that for a moment.

THE QUEEN Thank you, dear Duchess, for saying that! In my position, I would wish never to be unjust to any-one. . . . Will you—will you ask your Cousin—Lady Jane—to come and speak to me?

DUCHESS (*hesitating*) I am not sure, Ma'am, that she will come—now.

THE QUEEN Will you say 'please' for me?

DUCHESS If I can say it, Ma'am, as you have said it— (*Her voice breaks; she kisses* THE QUEEN'S *hand, and goes.*)

225

(THE QUEEN, *left to herself, sits rigid—facing an ordeal which, for her, is of an almost unbelievable character. Nevertheless, she faces it. Presently the door opens, and* LADY JANE *enters. She halts at the door, and curtsies: the word 'please,' which has brought her, has been left unexplained, and the expression of her face does not make things easier for* THE QUEEN.)

THE QUEEN Lady Jane . . . I have sent for you to say . . . I am sorry. . . . Forgive me. . . . I was quite wrong.

(LADY JANE *curtsies deeply, but does not speak. Slowly* THE QUEEN *reaches out her hand.* LADY JANE *goes quickly forward, kisses it, and bursts into tears.*)

THE QUEEN I am sorry, so sorry to have upset you. You had better go to bed now, and rest. . . . And, Lady Jane, if you would like—only if you would like—to go away for a little, for a change—pray do so. I'm not asking you to go; but should you at all wish to do so, you have my permission.

LADY JANE I thank your Majesty for so kindly suggesting it.

THE QUEEN Then that shall be arranged. . . . And now will you tell the Prince—I mean, will you ask someone to tell the Prince that I wish to see him?

(LADY JANE *makes her final curtsy, and goes.* THE QUEEN *sits with bowed head, motionless: time passes.* THE PRINCE *does not come. Her head sinks lower; she is shaken by sobs. Then, very quietly, the door opens, and* THE PRINCE *enters.*

He comes gently towards her, stands at her side, and reaching down his hand, begins softly to stroke her hair. Neither of them makes any attempt to speak, or any further move. Presently, leaving her, he goes to the piano, seats himself, and begins playing. It has to be something very simple and familiar—otherwise she might miss its meaning. He plays a few bars; then, in a low undertone, sings words which she already knows by heart.)

ALBERT   Drink to me only with thine eyes,
    And I will pledge with mine;
Or leave a kiss but in the cup,
    And I'll not ask for wine.
The thirst that from the soul doth rise,
    Doth ask a drink divine:
But might I of Jove's nectar sup,
    I would not change for thine.

(As the first verse draws to its close, THE QUEEN rises, crosses slowly, and stands behind him. As he begins the second verse, timidly she lays a hand upon his shoulder; and when the verse is half-way through, she lets her head fall upon his; and is so standing, with her cheek resting against the beautiful hair, which is already beginning to grow thin, when the verse ends.)

I sent thee late a rosy wreath,
    Not so much honouring thee,
As giving it a hope that there
    It could not withered be.

227

But thou thereon didst only breathe,
  And sent'st it back to me:
Since when it grows and smells, I swear,
  Not of itself, but thee.

*(The song ends. What happens then—who knows?
  As the last chords are played, the curtain falls
  slowly; but neither of them has moved.)*

Aims and Objects

Aims and Objects

1849

In his private apartment at Buckingham Palace, PRINCE
ALBERT *sits writing; his back is to the door.* THE
QUEEN *enters, and moving softly across the room,
stands behind him. Very fondly she feasts her eyes on
the top of his head, which is growing prematurely bald.
He continues to write, unconscious of her presence.*

THE QUEEN Albert, leave off writing! I want to talk to
you.

ALBERT (*laying down his pen*) Yes, Weibchen; what is it?

THE QUEEN Albert . . . You *do* love me, don't you?

ALBERT My Dear, have you any doubt?

THE QUEEN No; but say it!

ALBERT (*kindly, but without fervour*) I love you.

THE QUEEN Say it again, *and* again!

ALBERT Certainly, my Dear, if you wish . . . I love
you . . . I love you . . . I love you. . . . Isn't that enough?

THE QUEEN I was waiting to see how long you would be
able to go on.

ALBERT Saying what is so unnecessary?

THE QUEEN Not unnecessary to me, Albert. For I shall never be quite sure that it will always be so.

ALBERT Why not?

THE QUEEN Because you are so much above me—in everything but rank. And *that* I am not allowed to alter. Every time I speak about making you King Consort, my Ministers won't hear of it.

ALBERT Does it matter?

THE QUEEN You know it matters, Albert. It means that to them you are still only just a foreign Prince, who has come to marry me, and give me children.

ALBERT We must be patient, my Dear.

THE QUEEN Patient! Have we not been patient for ten years? I am sick of being patient! I would like to go and tell them that, if they do not make you Prince, or King Consort, I shall resign! . . . That would make them do it, Albert!

ALBERT Yes, Frauchen, perhaps. But you must not do it.

THE QUEEN Why not, when I love you so much; when you are everything to me, and so much wiser, that I know it is really you that ought to be King?

ALBERT Because, Dearest, when I came here—when I accepted what you offered me—you were not able to offer me *that*: and I knew it. What they do not want now, I knew that they would never want. I accepted—not only the greatness of the honour, but its limitations. Therefore, Dearest—that is why.

232

THE QUEEN But, Albert, so much has happened since then. My children are your children; some day Bertie will be King. How *can* they still go on thinking of you as a foreigner, after all that?

ALBERT But they will, Weibchen; and nothing that we can do will change them—nothing!

THE QUEEN And yet, Albert, now that you are always with me when I see my Ministers—advising, directing, deciding—they must know that it is your reign as much as mine. Yet still they will not let you even be Prince Consort[1]—only Prince Albert! And you—you seem not to mind!

ALBERT Now that surprises me. Have I acted my part so well? I suppose I ought to be glad.

THE QUEEN You *do* mind?

ALBERT. I mind very much. I have your love, your trust; but here I am still in exile: and shall be—to the day of my death.

THE QUEEN Oh, don't say it, Dearest: don't say it! You mustn't die—before I do.

ALBERT But I shall, Weibchen: only—not yet. And listen! Here is something that shall a little console you. When that happens, they will no longer have to be suspicious, or afraid of me. They will not trouble to think of me as a foreigner when I am dead. Only till then . . . But no, no, you must not look so sad! Here is something more practical and important, which concerns us now. I have some plans to show you. See!

[1] The title of Prince Consort was not granted him till 1857.

(He takes up, and spreads out for inspection some large sheets of paper.)

THE QUEEN What are these, Albert?

ALBERT The designs for the building of the Great Exhibition, which the Royal Commission has accepted—if you agree. Mr. Joseph Paxton, the architect, has had a wonderful idea for it—quite new. It is to be all of glass.

THE QUEEN Of glass, Albert? But won't it break?

ALBERT Not if it is put into a frame—a metal frame, like a window. But this will be *all* window: not a solid wall anywhere. Look well at it; for this, perhaps, is what modern architecture is going to be.

THE QUEEN Oh, how beautiful, and how wonderful! All glass! How it will light up when the sun shines on it.

ALBERT Yes. . . . If all goes well it may become the symbol of your reign, my Dear; and of England leading the World to peace.

THE QUEEN And when it does, then it will be your doing, Albert. *(Then, as she examines the design)* Oh, yes; I am beginning to see it now; it will be far more beautiful than St. Paul's Cathedral, I'm sure—glass being so much more beautiful than stone. And so original!

ALBERT Yes; and so suitable for the purpose. That is what makes it so beautiful. And it will not take so long to build, either.

THE QUEEN Where is it going to be?

ALBERT In Hyde Park, if you will agree. To be in a Royal Park, it must first have your permission. You approve?

234

THE QUEEN Of course! I think it is going to be the most wonderful building in the world: yes, and the most beautiful. And the Exhibition itself will be one of the most wonderful things in History; and the invention and planning of it all yours! I have always wanted this Country to be as great in the Arts as in Industry and Commerce; and now it is going to—thanks to you! Oh, if only my People could know what you are doing for them, how happy we should be!

ALBERT We will still be as happy as we can, Weibchen; and perhaps some day more shall come of it. And, talking about Art, my Dear, is it not time that you gave Mr. Edwin Landseer some kind of a title?

THE QUEEN (*doubtfully*) A title?

ALBERT Yes. He is a great painter—especially of dogs, which you are so fond of. And now that he has also done his great picture of the Duke's visit last year to the Field of Waterloo, would it not be well to make him a Baronet, or a Knight?

THE QUEEN Oh, not a Baronet, Albert! that would be too much. Mr. Landseer is not a man of any Family; he only comes from the people.

ALBERT Well, make him a Knight, then.

THE QUEEN I don't want to do anything unusual, Albert. Titles mustn't be made too cheap. Till now it is only Presidents of the Academy, or Painters by Royal Appointment, who have received titles; and I don't think Mr. Landseer will ever be President. Mr. Eastlake, I am told, is almost certain to be the next.

ALBERT But Mr. Landseer is quite as great an artist, my Dear, as any who have previously received titles. Sir Thomas Lawrence himself was the only son of a village innkeeper. So don't you think that you might?

THE QUEEN Why, yes; that does make a difference, of course; other artists of less merit having received the same honour.

ALBERT Then, do you not think, my Dear, that we might, at the same time, buy one of his pictures?

THE QUEEN Oh, yes; but not a large one; for I do not think we could find room for it.

ALBERT I think room could be found. And there was one at the Academy this year, which I remember you liked. May I buy it for you?

THE QUEEN Yes, Albert, if you liked it also. But remember, when we do a painter the great honour of buying one of his pictures, we only pay a certain price for it— thirty pounds, I think. But General Grey is sure to know; he will tell you. Yes, I am almost sure that it is thirty pounds.

ALBERT Ah! a very good arrangement. Had I known that before, I might by now have made quite a collection for you of other artists—of Academicians, I mean.

THE QUEEN No, Albert, Dear, we mustn't make ourselves cheap; that would never do! You see, it is such an advantage to an artist to have a commission from *Us*. When we sat to Winterhalter, it got him quite a lot of other commissions. He stayed in England more than a year.

236

ALBERT Ah, very satisfactory—very improving to the English taste!

THE QUEEN So I don't think we ought to buy from more than one artist at a time. One in four or five years is quite enough, I think; except, of course, when we have to sit for our portraits. But Mr. Landseer is certainly my favourite painter—his subjects so appeal to me.

ALBERT Yes; what a pity we cannot sit to him as a family group of his favourite species—'Queenie, Prince, and their six puppies.'

THE QUEEN (*rather shocked*) Oh, Albert, dear!

ALBERT I was only laughing, my Love. But, speaking of the family reminds me that I have something now much more serious to talk about. Our son, Bertie, is now eight years old.

THE QUEEN Oh, not yet, Darling!

ALBERT He will be in November; and it is quite time for his real education to begin. As some day he will have to be King, we must no longer think of him as a child.

THE QUEEN Isn't it too soon—too early?

ALBERT Had you not to be Queen rather sooner than you might have wished, my Dear? But for it you had been trained. We must not be afraid to face the fact that it might happen to him also. So for that we must be prepared.

THE QUEEN Oh, yes; of course you are right, Albert; for he has not yet learned nearly as much as I had done when I was his age.

ALBERT So have I found out. We must make a change; he must not have a Governess any more—he must have Tutors. He must learn history, and languages, and how to write and spell correctly in all of them; also about politics, and the making of the English Laws and Constitution.

THE QUEEN Yes, of course, that is most important.

ALBERT So I have, this week, been drawing up a scheme —a schedule—of the work he must do. To begin with— till he is ten—his lessons will be only six hours a day; when he is ten they must be eight.

THE QUEEN How many Tutors ought he to have, do you think, Albert?

ALBERT He must have an English Tutor, of course, so as not to have a foreign accent; also a French and a German master—three times a week each. He must learn also to dance well, and to draw just a little; and every day he must drill, and he must ride. Also he must be taught the art of conversation. His manners he will get, let us hope, from us. I do not think he need have a Chaplain yet —perhaps not till he is twelve; but he must have religious instruction every day. You see, my Dear, we have to make him a really good man, with a taste for serious things— what your English Kings have so seldom been. The only one in the last five reigns who was good at all, went mad. It was a pity. Your Uncle George was not at all what he ought to have been—not at all!

THE QUEEN Poor Uncle George! I can just remember him picking me up and kissing me; and I noticed how fat he was, and how he smelt of brandy. But he was quite nice and kind to me; so please don't say anything against him now he is dead.

ALBERT No; for it is not necessary. But I am glad, my Dear, that you did not wish to have any of your children named after *him*.

THE QUEEN But George is a very popular English name, Albert—St. George being our Patron Saint: you mustn't forget that.

ALBERT No; and some day perhaps—with our grand-children—it will be safe for the name to be used again. But not yet. It will not be the name of the next King, at any rate.

THE QUEEN No; that will be 'Albert Edward.'

ALBERT Why not Edward the Seventh?

THE QUEEN Because, Albert, I intend that my People shall some day recognise what they owe to *you*; and *that* will do it.

ALBERT Then why not Albert alone?

THE QUEEN Oh, no, Dearest; that I could never allow! If he could be called 'Albert the Second'—yes! But Albert alone—just as if no other Albert had come first— would be an act of disrespect to you, not to be thought of!

ALBERT Perhaps it is a matter we shall not be allowed to decide, Weibchen.

THE QUEEN But I mean to! Oh, Albert, I do wish Bertie had Vicky's brains! She is going to be so clever; and I'm afraid he is *not* going to be.

239

ALBERT We must make his brain to grow like his body. It can be done; it is only a matter of proper education. That is why I have already drawn up this scheme, so as to begin in good time.

THE QUEEN (*who is now standing by the window*) Look, Albert! There he is, in the garden, playing with Vicky. How prettily he moves; and how fond they are of each other! Look!

> (*She turns toward* THE PRINCE, *who now also looks out.*)

> (*Suddenly he taps angrily on the glass, then opens the window, and calls.*)

ALBERT Ah! Do not do that! Come in here, Bertie, at once!

THE QUEEN What did he do?

ALBERT What he must be taught not to do. You did not see?

THE QUEEN No.

ALBERT Ah, it is quite time that we began to give him a real education, and a real training in how to behave. He must learn discipline.

> (*The door opens. Very timidly, fearful of the scolding which awaits him, the little* PRINCE OF WALES *creeps into the room, and stands holding the door.*)

ALBERT Come in! Come in! What were you doing?

THE PRINCE Only playing, Papa.

ALBERT Playing! I saw you throw a handful of gravel at your Sister.

PRINCE Only for fun. She didn't mind.

ALBERT You are not to do it! If the gravel had gone into her eye, it would have blinded her.

PRINCE (*his voice breaking*) I didn't throw it at her face, Papa!

ALBERT It might have hit her face.

PRINCE (*weeping*) But it didn't!

ALBERT Don't answer! Go up to your room!

(*The culprit retires weeping.*)

ALBERT (*loudly*) And shut the door after you!

(*The door is shut.*)

THE QUEEN I'm afraid he's going to be difficult, Albert.

ALBERT Children always are difficult, till you make them understand what you mean them to be, and whom they have to obey. . . . Patience, my Dear, patience! It will take time; and it will not always be easy, or pleasant. But it has to be done.

> (*And on these excellent intentions the curtain falls, to rise again, some twelve years later—when the directing hand has been withdrawn—on a specimen of genial but faulty humanity, which— could he but have seen it—would have made* 'ALBERT THE GOOD' *turn in his grave.*)

The 'Go-Between'

The 'Go-Between'

December 1851

MR. MACAULAY, *the eminent Historian, has not yet received the Peerage which is soon to descend on him. But the honour of a command call from* HER MAJESTY *has brought him to Windsor; and in the temporary absence of* PRINCE ALBERT, THE QUEEN *is doing her best to carry on an intellectual conversation with one who finds it difficult to make his conversation small, or other than informative. Apparently* MR. MACAULAY *has been talking on his pet subject—Constitutional Liberty, as exemplified by English History.*

THE QUEEN But when it gets to breaking the *law*, Mr. Macaulay, then liberty becomes licence!

MACAULAY It may, Ma'am, or it may not. . . . You can't make an omelet without breaking eggs, Ma'am.

THE QUEEN Eggs?

MACAULAY Yes, Ma'am; and then, if you find they are bad, you throw them away, and make your omelet without them. Sometimes the Law turns out to be a very bad egg indeed; and you have to get rid of it as quickly as possible.

245

THE QUEEN But can it ever be right for the people to rebel against their own Sovereign, Mr. Macaulay?

MACAULAY To a descendant of the House of Hanover, Ma'am, I think I may say 'yes.'

THE QUEEN But I am a *Stuart*, Mr. Macaulay.

MACAULAY Your Majesty is many things by ancestry and inheritance—not only Scottish, but Welsh also; Norman, Saxon, French, Danish, *and* German. The value of mixed blood is pre-eminently exemplified in your Majesty's ancestry and person.

THE QUEEN I don't like mixed blood, Mr. Macaulay.

MACAULAY Your Majesty does not like the phrase. But in the *fact* lie the very foundations of our history and of our race.

THE QUEEN Oh, indeed? Well, Mr. Macaulay, if you say so, I am not prepared to deny it. I wish the Prince were here; he could argue with you so much better than I can. . . . But take India—surely India is a case where the trouble all comes from mixed blood?

MACAULAY Not so much mixed blood, Ma'am, as mixed religion. Were all Indians of the same religion, the mixed blood would not matter.

THE QUEEN Ah, yes; Religion is the most important thing in the world, is it not?

MACAULAY It is, Ma'am; even politically nothing matters more.

THE QUEEN So sad that they should be able to believe such things—the Indians, I mean. If they could only become Church of England, or Presbyterian—I suppose, then, as you say, government would be quite easy.

MACAULAY If that miracle were to happen, Ma'am, India, as we know it now, would vanish off the face of the earth. What would take its place, I cannot imagine.

THE QUEEN Still, it would be a great improvement; the people would understand so much better that we only rule them for their own good. What a pity it is that Eastern races cannot accept a reasonable form of Religion like ours!

MACAULAY The East, Ma'am, has its own mind on that subject, which the West finds some difficulty in understanding. Similarly, the East has some difficulty in understanding how anyone can believe the things that *we* do.

THE QUEEN Really! now that surprises me! How very extraordinary! To me it seems all so simple, so unanswerable.

MACAULAY Yes, Ma'am. But your Majesty must not expect the Eastern mind to grasp so easily great truths, which to your Majesty seem self-evident.

THE QUEEN Ah, no. I suppose not. . . . And how is your *History* getting on, Mr. Macaulay?

MACAULAY Since your Majesty so graciously released me from the cares of office, very well indeed, Ma'am.

THE QUEEN I shall read it with great interest. And now, Mr. Macaulay—

> (*She rises from her seat, and is about to give* MR. MACAULAY *his dismissal, when* PRINCE ALBERT *enters.*)

247

ALBERT Lord John Russell is waiting to see you, my Dear. . . . Ah, Mr. Macaulay, are you just going?

MACAULAY I am, Sir. I fear I have been here too long. One who no longer holds office has no right to keep Her Majesty's Prime Minister waiting.

THE QUEEN I have been very much interested, Mr. Macaulay, in all you have told me. I wish you could have been here, Albert. . . . Good-bye. And I shall greatly look forward to reading your *History*.

MACAULAY If my industry needed any further incentive, your Majesty has now provided it. (*Then, as he bows himself out*) Your Majesty's servant . . . Your Highness.

THE QUEEN Did Lord John Russell tell you what he has come about?

ALBERT He has come in reply to your letter about that man, Pilgerstein.

THE QUEEN But we must take care not to call him Pilgerstein to Lord John. I so nearly did, the other day. Did you say I would see him at once?

ALBERT I said he was to be shown in as soon as you were disengaged.

THE QUEEN You have ready all the notes you made, Albert?

ALBERT I have them with me.

THE QUEEN Well, Albert, if I forget anything, will you please remind me? We must get this settled now, once and for all.

248

(The door opens: a Gentleman of the Court announces,
'LORD JOHN RUSSELL, your Majesty.' And the
Prime Minister bows himself briskly into the
room.)

THE QUEEN Good morning, Lord John. I am glad that you have been able to come so soon.

RUSSELL Instantly upon receiving your Majesty's command.

THE QUEEN It is upon a very unpleasant subject that I have to speak to you this morning.

RUSSELL I rather feared so, your Majesty.

THE QUEEN Yes. After hearing from you yesterday that Lord Palmerston had told you almost nothing about the way in which he has been treating me, I felt that I must see you at once.

RUSSELL I am sorry, Ma'am, that there should have been any misunderstanding.

THE QUEEN It is hardly a misunderstanding, Lord John. It has happened too often. I am now obliged to regard it as wilful disobedience.

RUSSELL I am sure, Ma'am, that Lord Palmerston never so intended it.

THE QUEEN Then he has let his lack of intention become a habit, which I cannot allow!

RUSSELL Will your Majesty be good enough to give me the full particulars of what your Majesty has to complain of?

THE QUEEN I will ask the Prince to read you the Memorandum which he has made for me, dealing with

249

the whole matter. We have gone into it together very thoroughly.

RUSSELL I am your Majesty's most attentive servant.

ALBERT (*producing the Memorandum*) I will begin first, Lord John Russell, by reminding you of the previous occasions on which Her Majesty has had to complain of Lord Palmerston's actions and inattentions. They cover a very considerable period.

RUSSELL I was under the impression, Sir, that those previous occurrences had already been discussed, and settled—satisfactorily.

ALBERT Not satisfactorily, Lord John, if there is any recurrence of the misconduct complained of.

RUSSELL Misconduct is a hard word, Sir.

ALBERT It is an accurate one. . . . Three years ago, Her Majesty had to complain that Lord Palmerston had failed to keep her properly informed of the despatches sent from the Foreign Office on important matters of policy: that he had got into the habit of letting them go without first submitting them for Her Majesty's approval. Lord Palmerston explained that he did not always have time; but he was unable to give any instance when the lack of time was due, in any way, to Her Majesty being unwilling, or unable to receive him. . . . A few months later, Her Majesty spoke to you again, at some length, of her growing dissatisfaction with Lord Palmerston's very independent way of conducting Foreign Policy; also with the rather provocative tone in which so many of his despatches were written. With Her Majesty's criticisms, you expressed yourself as being generally in agreement, but you said that Lord Palmerston's Foreign Policy had the approval of the Cabinet, and also that he was a difficult and dangerous man for you to deal with, on account of his general popularity. So *that* matter was 'satisfactorily settled' by nothing being done.

RUSSELL I ask pardon, Sir. Is this Her Majesty's Memorandum: or are these your Highness's own comments made upon it?

ALBERT They are the comments, arising from the Memorandum, which Her Majesty has herself made to me. If I say anything of which Her Majesty does not approve, she will correct me. . . . On a later occasion, when it was found that Lord Palmerston had sent off to our Legation at St. Petersburg a very important despatch, without first submitting it, he endeavoured to escape criticism by describing it as a private letter, individually addressed to a Member of the Legation, though this 'private letter' had been placed in the records of the Foreign Office.

RUSSELL I understood that Her Majesty accepted that explanation.

ALBERT Her Majesty accepted that explanation in the sense that she could not tell Lord Palmerston that she did not believe him.

RUSSELL I am sorry that Her Majesty should have been left in any doubt.

ALBERT So am I. It placed Her Majesty in a very difficult position. That difficulty has come more often than once.

RUSSELL That Her Majesty finds herself unable to *believe—*?

ALBERT That Her Majesty has found herself forced—or at least pressed—by her Prime Minister, to accept explanations which she did not think satisfactory.

RUSSELL (*stiffly*) I am not aware, Sir, that I have ever brought 'pressure' to bear upon Her Majesty, in offering my humble advice.

ALBERT Advice without pressure, on a difficult problem, Lord John, is rather like an engine without steam. I think I am not wrong in saying that Her Majesty is now putting pressure upon you—legitimate pressure. It is only of illegitimate pressure that Her Majesty would complain.

RUSSELL (*stiffly*) If your Highness would kindly specify any undue pressure of which I have been guilty, I should know better where I am.

ALBERT Shall we put it like this?—Is it legitimate to let a 'difficult and dangerous person' go on being dangerous because of his general popularity?

RUSSELL I believe I warned Her Majesty—and I think rightly—that Lord Palmerston was quite capable of destroying the Government; and, under certain circumstances, might not be unwilling to do so.

ALBERT The Government of which he was a member? What a *safe* sort of colleague to have to do with!

RUSSELL Cabinet Government has its difficulties, your Highness.

ALBERT We, also, find that. But while it *is* Cabinet Government, under a Reigning Sovereign, it is not right for any member of it—however popular—to go his own way, without first consulting those who have the right to be consulted.

RUSSELL I humbly submit, Sir, that while the Government, as a whole, still enjoys Her Majesty's confidence, and while that Government is not in disagreement over the main lines of the policy pursued by its individual members—it is the bounden duty of the Prime Minister (even if he has to compromise somewhat more than he would wish), to do all he can to keep that Government in being.

ALBERT That word 'compromise' has two meanings, Lord John. I am afraid Her Majesty feels that the compromise you sometimes thought necessary, has compromised *her*.

RUSSELL If what I have done ever seems to take on so serious a complexion as *that*, my resignation is always at Her Majesty's disposal.

ALBERT It is not *your* resignation, Lord John, that Her Majesty thinks necessary. We all make mistakes. But a mistake wilfully made, and wilfully repeated,—*that* cannot be tolerated.

RUSSELL If your Highness—

ALBERT Just a moment, Lord John. I will put you in possession of all the points that Her Majesty wishes you to consider: that factor of wilfully repeated disobedience being the most important. . . . Last year, Lord Palmerston, without previous consultation, ordered the British Fleet to the Piræus, to make a hostile demonstration against the Greek Government: an action which might have led to War.

RUSSELL Over that matter, Sir, Lord Palmerston was given a strong vote of confidence by the House of Commons.

ALBERT 'Without consultation,' I said. In the House of Commons that point was carefully not raised—was not even mentioned. You, yourself, considered that three weeks' grace should have been allowed before what Lord Palmerston ordered to be done in twenty-four hours.

RUSSELL The result was successful, your Highness.

ALBERT The result would have been equally successful, and more conciliatory in its effect, had more time been granted. Lord Palmerston, when it suits him, can be as dilatory as he is sometimes hasty. . . . Last year, over the Spanish question when he had again sent off a despatch without submitting it to Her Majesty, he was three weeks in answering her letter of complaint. It is conduct like that, which makes Her Majesty sometimes doubt whether Lord Palmerston is even a Gentleman.

RUSSELL (*uncomfortably*) I have to admit, Sir, that this is the first I have heard of so grave an omission in duty and courtesy toward Her Majesty. I think it must have been forgetfulness.

ALBERT We think not. But, in any case, manners though important (and, to one's Sovereign, a matter of loyal duty), are not the most important things in politics: though, I fear, it is the tone of Lord Palmerston's notes to Foreign Chancellories, far more than his policy (which Her Majesty has often approved) that has drawn down upon this Country the hatred of all the Governments of Europe.

RUSSELL Over the Greek question, I must remind your Highness that the whole Government was prepared to take over the blame (if there was any), and offer resignation. And I communicated that fact to Her Majesty. As Her Majesty was not willing to accept our resignation, I could have hoped that the matter had been disposed of—finally.

ALBERT It would have been, Lord John—as would also those other matters—had there not been this persistent repetition of a course of action which you, yourself, have never attempted to defend—this sending off of despatches without consultation. . . . And now we come to the present—to the gravest matter of all. We have been faced in France by the violent accomplishment of a *coup d'état*, which has shocked the moral sense of the whole Country. Pending a further decision, Her Majesty's Ambassador in Paris was instructed to maintain an attitude of strict aloofness, and by no word to express either approval, or acceptance, of what has taken place. Behind his back, and without a word of advice to Her Majesty, Lord Palmerston has written a letter of encouragement to the new Government; and Lord Normanby, our Ambassador, only hears of it by accident. Her Majesty now says that this cannot go on. And she wishes to know what you are prepared to do in the matter?

RUSSELL I must admit to your Majesty that Lord Palmerston's precipitate action on this occasion is greatly regretted by the whole, or at least by a large majority of your Majesty's Government. I have myself told Lord Palmerston that, in this matter, I shall be unable to excuse or defend him if your Majesty is determined to press the case against him. And having now been informed so fully of your Majesty's mind, I will see Lord Palmerston again, and represent to him how very gravely, in your Majesty's view, the matter stands.

THE QUEEN What you propose to do has my full approval.

RUSSELL If it is your Majesty's pleasure, I will do that at once; and I will, as soon as possible, come back and report to your Majesty the result of our interview.

THE QUEEN Please do so. And please understand, Lord John Russell, that *this* time there must be a result, which will admit of no further *pretence* of misunderstanding.

RUSSELL I will bear very carefully in mind your Majesty's command.

(*And so saying,* LORD JOHN RUSSELL *bows himself out.*)

ALBERT You did very well, my Dear.

THE QUEEN I hardly said anything.

ALBERT That is what I mean. Considering how strongly you feel in this matter, you showed great self-restraint. . . . Exit Mr. Pilgerstein!—I *think*.

SCENE II

In a very comfortable arm-chair before the fire, in his room at the Foreign Office, LORD PALMERSTON *is taking his afternoon nap. His feet rest upon a cushioned stool; a silk handkerchief of bright pattern covers his face. A Foreign Office* ATTENDANT *enters, and with studied diffidence rouses him from sleep. With a jerk and a grunt, his Lordship sits up: the handkerchief falls from his face.*

256

ATTENDANT I beg pardon, my Lord, for disturbing your Lordship. Lord John Russell is here, and hopes that he may see your Lordship.

PALMERSTON Oh, yes; ask him to come up!

> (*The* ATTENDANT *goes, while* LORD PALMERSTON *slowly picks himself up, yawns, clears his throat, gives a rub to his hair, and (taking his stand on the hearth-rug with his coat-tails over his arms) prepares to receive his Visitor.* LORD JOHN *enters with pursed lips, and a self-conscious expression of importance mingled with severity.*)

PALMERSTON Well, John?

RUSSELL It isn't well at all, Palmerston. I'm afraid that, this time, you've done it.

PALMERSTON Oh, you've been giving me away, have you?

RUSSELL You've given yourself away. . . . I've warned you! . . . I've warned you!

PALMERSTON Yes; and I've warned *you*. You wouldn't take my warning; I wouldn't take yours. So far we are a match; but there it stops: same Government—opposite camps.

RUSSELL Opposite, eh?

PALMERSTON Yes; it's the battle of Constitutional Government I've been fighting: and not one of you had the guts to back me up!

RUSSELL I was under the impression that I had stood

257

by you through a good many battles, at great personal inconvenience to myself.

PALMERSTON Bah! What would have been the good of all Wellington's battles, if he'd run away at Waterloo?

RUSSELL He wouldn't have won Waterloo, if he hadn't *waited*. That's been your mistake, Palmerston; it's your hunting instinct, I suppose: no sooner do you see a gate then you want to go over it. Now you've come a cropper.

PALMERSTON Oh, have I? Have you come to ask for my resignation?

RUSSELL (*temporising*) I've come to talk about it. You'll have to make a big concession, this time, to avoid it; and you'll have to *stick* to it. You know, Pam, about this French business, you are all wrong.

PALMERSTON Am I? D'you suppose that *coup d'état* is not going to succeed?

RUSSELL I'm afraid it has succeeded.

PALMERSTON Quite so! Well, the only proper policy for this Country in Foreign Affairs is not to let anyone do a damned thing we don't want 'em to do, if we *can* help it: but to put a cheerful face on it, if we *can't*.

RUSSELL There's not much morality in that, Palmerston.

PALMERSTON It's damned Scriptural! Making friends of the Mammon of unrighteousness, and getting yourself into everlasting habitations as a reward. Isn't it better to be friendly with France, than be a skulking, sulking enemy? There's Russia looming ahead, my Boy; and we can't tackle her alone.

RUSSELL But why couldn't you have *waited*? Our

attitude was perfectly correct: we didn't express any disapproval—officially.

PALMERSTON Papers did: Normanby did—privately.

RUSSELL He denies that.

PALMERSTON He can't prevent fools blabbing, if he talks to 'em. He was making mischief for us. I wanted to send that letter; I *meant* to send it. She wouldn't have let me— or *He* wouldn't! And that's my point. He's her legal husband; but he's not the legal husband of the British Constitution. And, by God! if I chose to stand up and fight him, and give all the facts, I could get a vote of censure passed on him in the House of Commons any day.

RUSSELL You couldn't.

PALMERSTON I'd have a damned good try, if it came to it! Or anyway, I could carry a counter-vote of confidence in myself; which would come to much the same thing.

RUSSELL If you tried that on *this* time, you'd get none of the Cabinet voting for you.

PALMERSTON Oh! Shouldn't I? . . . John, you are not a very good judge of character: you don't even understand mine.

RUSSELL Don't I?

PALMERSTON No. You think I'm a regular fire-eater. I'm not. . . . I'm a peaceful, easy-going fellow: hate trouble—don't like giving trouble to others. I'm charitable in my judgments—fond of my fellow-men, so long as they aren't Germans. . . . By God! if Albert had been on the front Opposition bench, he'd have got us out before now—*me*, anyway! Lord! how he hates me! . . . Oh, but the fellow's got a brain: and works like four cart-horses.

259

He's made *me* work, you know! Again and again, I'd have to be out of my bed by ten o'clock in the morning, to write those damned despatches he thinks he's got to correct before the mail goes.

RUSSELL (*put wise*) So getting out of bed has sometimes been the trouble, has it?

PALMERSTON Well! can you wonder? One can't keep the hours of a Gentleman since he got the pull of things. . . . It's a pity, John! . . . It's a pity! She's not the same woman she was—now. She's a deteriorated character.

RUSSELL Indeed! I should have said rather the reverse.

PALMERSTON Ah, you didn't go to Court as early as I did. In old Mel's day, she used to listen to jokes and stories she won't listen to now. . . . Mel used to tell 'em; so did I. And, i' gad! how she'd laugh at 'em! But after she got *him*— Lord! if I'd tried to tell one of my old stories then, she'd have ordered me out of the room!

RUSSELL Yes, Palmerston, but that isn't what I've come to talk about. This is serious, you know.

PALMERSTON Oh, is it? What did you say to them— or what did they say to you?

RUSSELL A good deal was said, first and last, up and down—more than I can remember. But the main point was this: that you'd done the same thing too many times for her to put up with it any more. And he had got it all down for her in black and white—dates and everything. There was no disputing the facts. I had to admit that you hadn't behaved as you should have done. . . . Over one complaint she made, you left her three weeks without an answer.

PALMERSTON Good Lord! I wish she'd leave *me* three weeks without an answer! It's the three answers a day I get from her sometimes, that drive me almost crazy! . . . Look here, John! Do you, in your senses, think it possible for me to run the Foreign Office with him putting his nose into every despatch that goes out? . . . Last year I signed and sent off twenty-eight thousand of 'em. Do they imagine that they can take on a job of that size, or anything like it? Ask 'em that!

RUSSELL Well, that certainly *is* a point.

PALMERSTON Of course it is! Why, there are thousands and thousands they don't ever set eyes on—and don't want to. But if just one happens to go, and they miss it—then I'm made to hear of it. Damned humbug!

RUSSELL Well, well, but what am I to say, Palmerston?

PALMERSTON Say what you damned well like! What should you like to say? What d'you *want* to say?

RUSSELL I would like to say—if possible—that if owing to certain irregularities inadvertently committed—you have failed to give satisfaction in the discharge of your duties as Foreign Secretary, you once more express your sincere regret; and further, that if, upon my recommendation, it were Her Majesty's pleasure, you would be willing to accept a change of office.

PALMERSTON Oh, indeed! What office?

RUSSELL Lord Lieutenant of Ireland.

PALMERSTON I'll be damned if I do!

RUSSELL Then, my dear Palmerston, I have no alternative but to ask for your resignation.

261

PALMERSTON Oh? . . . What does the Cabinet say to that?

RUSSELL I have consulted seven members of the Cabinet. They all agree.

PALMERSTON (*calculating the situation as thus presented*) Seven—and yourself eight, eh? . . . So you've got a majority. . . . Very well. Shall I write it now?

RUSSELL Please.

(LORD PALMERSTON *sits down, and begins writing.*)

PALMERSTON How do you spell 'resignation,' John? It's a word I've never written before.

RUSSELL You spell it with an 'R.'

PALMERSTON H'm! Glad you've got some sense of humour left in you. . . . There you are, my Lord John! (*He hands him the document.*) And, mind you, by making it a resignation, I'm doing the generous by both of you. By the Lord! if I made her dismiss me—what a hullabaloo there'd be in all the papers!

RUSSELL (*ingratiatingly*) I'm sure, my dear Pam, you would always wish to do what is best—not for yourself, but for the Country.

PALMERSTON (*not so sure, but unable to say so*) Oh? well . . . I suppose so! Is that correct enough for 'em? If it isn't, I'll write a more formal one later.

RUSSELL Thank you. . . . I'm sorry, Palmerston.

PALMERSTON Not as sorry as you pretend to be. Are you going back to Windsor now?

RUSSELL I said I would return directly I'd seen you. I'm sorry I have not been more successful.

262

PALMERSTON I think you've been very successful. . . . You've got what you wanted.

RUSSELL No, Palmerston. What I wanted—and offered —you refused.

PALMERSTON Ireland? You thought you'd send me to Ireland, eh? . . . I don't put my head into a sack with my eyes open. I'm not that sort. Well, be off with you to Windsor! Carry the glad news! You've finished with me —for the present . . . who are you having instead?

RUSSELL A while back they suggested—Granville.

PALMERSTON Got it all arranged, had they? Oh, he'll do the pretty-pretty all right, if that's all you want! Well, God be with you! And my best respects to both of them.

RUSSELL Good-bye, Palmerston. I say again, I'm sorry.

PALMERSTON You aren't! But some day you will be.

> (LORD JOHN *has gone out, and is closing the door, when* PALMERSTON *calls after him.*)

Hi! John, John!

> (LORD JOHN *re-opens the door.*)

RUSSELL Well?

PALMERSTON If she accepts my resignation (which I suppose she will) who d'you reckon is going to be next Prime Minister, after you? . . . I mean, when the Liberals come in again.

RUSSELL Really, I haven't thought.

PALMERSTON Oh? . . . Well, I'll tell you, then. . . . It'll be *ME*.

RUSSELL You?

263

PALMERSTON Yes; *me*. And I shall make you my Foreign Secretary. With a bit of training, you'll make a very good one. You'll write the despatches; I'll come in and correct them. . . . Easy enough correcting despatches, once someone else has written them.

RUSSELL (*with a wry smile*) Well, if that ever *should* happen, I might find life easier, working *under* you, than working *over* you!

PALMERSTON Oh? Think so?

RUSSELL *That* hasn't been easy, I can assure you! All the same, I'm sorry.

> (*He nods good-bye; then goes quickly, closing the door.* PALMERSTON, *listening to his hurried departure, grunts an amused commentary.*)

PALMERSTON Trot away, little Man! You are an ass; but you are a clever one.

> (*Then, as he goes to sit down again, he rings the bell. And while he is settling into his chair, the* ATTENDANT *enters.*)

PALMERSTON Oh, Peters, see that I'm not disturbed for the next twenty minutes or so. I want to finish my nap.

> (*Pulling out the silk handkerchief, he lies back, and again covers his face.*)

SCENE III

We are again at Windsor. A Gentleman enters, and announces: 'LORD JOHN RUSSELL, *your Majesty.' And the Prime Minister, fresh from his not very comfortable interview with* LORD PALMERSTON, *re-enters.*

THE QUEEN You have been very expeditious, Lord John. We hardly expected you so soon.

RUSSELL I could wish, Ma'am, that my expedition had the accompaniment of more personal satisfaction over the result.

THE QUEEN (*anxiously*) Has Lord Palmerston not agreed, then, to what you told him he must do?

RUSSELL Not in the way, Ma'am, that would have given me most satisfaction. I had hoped (with your Majesty's gracious permission), to advise that his resignation should be effected by a change of office; and that your Majesty might be pleased to appoint him Lord Lieutenant of Ireland—that post being about to fall vacant. But Lord Palmerston would not hear of it.

THE QUEEN (*frigidly*) I think that, perhaps, Lord Palmerston was right. To be my representative in Ireland, is one of the highest honours in the gift of the Crown.

RUSSELL It is, Ma'am.

THE QUEEN (*rubbing it in*) What else would Lord Palmerston '*not hear of*'?

RUSSELL I ask pardon, your Majesty: the phrase was an unfortunate one. . . . Lord Palmerston requests me to convey to your Majesty his humble duty, and his very deep regret that he should have seemed in any way inattentive to your Majesty's wishes and claims upon his service. He admits certain omissions complained of by your Majesty, as regards despatches sent out without their having first received the Royal sanction. But he submits— I was to put this before your Majesty—that, in the course of the year he has had (in the performance of his duties as Foreign Secretary), to send out no fewer than twenty-eight thousand despatches; and he questions whether your Majesty could possibly be expected to consider all of them with the attention that some of them may require.

ALBERT If Lord Palmerston has been able to give due consideration to twenty-eight thousand despatches in a year, so also can Her Majesty.

RUSSELL I would not, Sir, for a moment, question Her Majesty's willingness to do so. Those numbers were merely given as an illustration of the large amount of routine-work, which has to be dealt with by others. Lord Palmerston submits, therefore, that, in his omission to present certain despatches for your Majesty's consideration, he has merely made a mistake—not so much in principle, as in selection.

ALBERT (*caustically*) His selection has been sometimes rather unfortunate.

RUSSELL It has, your Highness: that I most fully admit.

THE QUEEN Then what does he propose now to do?

RUSSELL I have received from him, Ma'am—I have it here—his resignation of office, as your Majesty's Secretary of State for Foreign Affairs.

THE QUEEN (*correctively*) You mean, Lord John, that he asks my permission to resign. He cannot do *that*, without first obtaining my consent.

RUSSELL That is so, Ma'am, of course. What I hold now, was only written hurriedly. Lord Palmerston requested me to say that his more formal offer of resignation would be submitted later.

THE QUEEN That will be quite satisfactory. Thank you, Lord John. I am very glad that, at last, you have made him see reason.

266

RUSSELL On this occasion, he did not make any difficulty, Ma'am. . . . And his last words to me—*almost* his last words—spoken very feelingly: were a request that I would convey to your Majesty (and also to your Royal Highness) the expression of his most deep and dutiful respects.

> (LORD JOHN *is distinctly pleased with himself over this manipulation of the farewell message: 'respects' is true—verbally; and 'feelingly' is also true—in a way.*)

THE QUEEN When you next see him, Lord John, will you please to thank him for that message. But do not let there be any delay in his sending of a properly-worded request for permission to resign.

RUSSELL I will not, Ma'am.

THE QUEEN There was one occasion, you know, when —having offered resignation—he withdrew it the next day.

RUSSELL He will not do so on this occasion, Ma'am, I am quite sure.

THE QUEEN Of course, Lord John, if you would like me to offer him a Peerage, so that he may go to the House of Lords, I am quite willing to do so.

RUSSELL I think, Ma'am, that he hopes to be able still to serve your Majesty, with more efficiency, in the House of Commons. . . . In the House of Lords, he might feel himself rather lost.

THE QUEEN Very well; that shall be as he wishes. (*She rises.*) I thank you very much, Lord John, for what you have done for me to-day. You have taken a great load off my mind. It was quite wearing me out.

267

RUSSELL Well, Ma'am, in that case—though my errand has been a sad one—I have some cause for satisfaction.

THE QUEEN You have, indeed. Good-bye!

RUSSELL (*as he bows himself out*) Your Majesty's most humble servant! . . . Your Highness!

ALBERT (*returning his bow with stiff formality*) Good-bye, Mr. Prime Minister.

> (*No sooner has the door closed, than* THE QUEEN, *almost clapping her hands, runs to* THE PRINCE.)

THE QUEEN Oh, Albert, Albert! I must write to Uncle Leopold at once! How delighted he will be to hear that Pilgerstein has resigned at last!

ALBERT (*with more reserve*) Oh, yes: he will be quite pleased, I am sure.

THE QUEEN And it was *your* doing! I couldn't have managed it without you.

ALBERT No?

THE QUEEN So, at last—*you have won!*

ALBERT Yes: I suppose so!

THE QUEEN Is anything the matter?

ALBERT I was only thinking of something the Duke of Wellington once said—that there was nothing so sad as a Victory, except a Defeat. Poor Pilgerstein! How he must be feeling it now!

> (*But, as a matter of fact,* PILGERSTEIN, *having finished his afternoon nap, is as happy as anybody concerned; for now he sees plainly the Premiership waiting for him.*)

268

Royal   Favour

Royal Favour

1859

Into one of the spacious apartments at Windsor Castle the morning sun streams through a high window. In the light of it, tempered by blinds, sits QUEEN VICTORIA. *One of her Ladies is now reading the regulation portion of the morning Scripture.*

LADY-IN-WAITING Proverbs, the twenty-sixth, Ma'am. . . . 'As snow in winter, and as rain in harvest, so honour is not seemly for fools. A whip for the horse, a bridle for the ass, and a rod for the fool's back. Answer not a fool according to his folly, lest thou also be like him. As the legs of the lame are unequal, so is a proverb in the mouth of fools. As he that bindeth a stone in a sling, so is he that giveth honour to a fool.'

> (*The door opens, and* DR. STANLEY *is ceremoniously announced. Still young and pleasant-looking, not yet a Dean, he steps easily into the Royal Presence, and the obeisance he makes, though correct in form, is a friendly one. As he advances to bow over the hand graciously extended, he manages to give a glance of happy recognition to the Queen's Lady, who, when* THE QUEEN *rises, rises also. For this is* LADY

271

AUGUSTA BRUCE, *destined presently to become his wife; and perhaps they already know it.*)

THE QUEEN Oh, good morning, Dr. Stanley. How very good of you to come, and so punctually! I wanted you to be here this morning.

STANLEY If in any way I can serve your Majesty, I shall be only too happy.

THE QUEEN You are always so kind. And here was Lady Augusta also looking forward to seeing you.

(*Thus graciously permitted,* DR. STANLEY *and* LADY AUGUSTA *press hands.*)

But to-day I did rather especially need you, for more reasons than one.

STANLEY Then I am specially fortunate, Ma'am. May I enquire? . . .

THE QUEEN Oh, yes. Do, please, sit down; both of you. You see, Dr. Stanley, I and the Prince have always felt that we ought—as far as we could—to encourage our distinguished men of literature. But there is always this difficulty. It is quite impossible to have at my Court, in the ordinary way, those with whom I cannot take the lead . . . intellectually, I mean, in conversation. I can, of course, make certain exceptions. Mr. Tennyson comes to see me sometimes; and though I have not read many of his poems myself, he reads them to me; so conversation becomes unnecessary.

STANLEY And does your Majesty enjoy the readings?

THE QUEEN Oh, yes; for even without understanding the poems, one can praise his reading of them. He has a beautiful voice; and he is so picturesque—so like a poet, is he not?

STANLEY He is indeed, Ma'am.

THE QUEEN Besides, he really is, I suppose, a great poet.

STANLEY A very great poet, Ma'am. I might even say that your Majesty is unusually fortunate in having such a poet for Laureate.

THE QUEEN I am so glad to hear you say so. There was just a question of offering the post to Lord Macaulay, whose *Lays of Ancient Rome* are certainly the finest poetry I know. But it was thought that would perhaps be too political an appointment. Mr. Tennyson, I understand, has no politics.

STANLEY None that I know of, Ma'am; or not so well as I know his poetry.

THE QUEEN No? Well that is why Lord Macaulay was not chosen as I expected.

STANLEY The reason against it was sufficiently good, Ma'am. The alternative it led to was even better.

THE QUEEN Yes? Well, that was really settled for us by the Prime Minister. But often since, in other cases, it has been a great regret that one could not pay all the attention one would like—by commanding their attendance at Court—to those who, outside politics, have become eminent in literature.

STANLEY But at your Majesty's call, one meets certain eminent writers . . . Churchmen amongst others.

THE QUEEN Of course some of the Bishops have written books, I know. But it is as Bishops, not authors that they

273

come here. And of course, being Head of the Church, I feel myself their equal, though we don't talk theology. . . . Nor have we any difficulty about artists. Their minds are not remarkable in thought or conversation; they are quite quiet and modest, I mean—waiting until they are spoken to. Sir Edwin Landseer, for instance, is a great artist, one of the greatest of all ages; but when he talks, he is just like anyone else—quite modest and pleasant. And he does not mind his work being criticised; though, I believe, he knows more about dogs than I do.

STANLEY In that case, Ma'am, he must be a very great authority. Yet you·don't feel any difficulty about him?

THE QUEEN Oh, no! About dogs I don't mind. Books are different. If I am to meet an author, I feel I must have read one of his books, at least, and been able to understand it. And as I really have not time for doing so, that is one of the reasons why I cannot—except on very special occasions—have authors coming to my Court.

STANLEY And yet, Ma'am, I myself am an author.

THE QUEEN Oh, yes, Dr. Stanley; but you are not the kind of author I mean. Besides, on so many things we have the same opinions. But I really am dreadfully nervous this morning; for a really great writer—and a very famous one—is coming to see us. The Prince thought that we really ought to ask him.

STANLEY And may I be informed, Ma'am, who·it is that your Majesty is about to honour in so very special a——

(*The interrogation is interrupted by the entry of the* PRINCE CONSORT. DR. STANLEY *rises, and bows low.*)

274

THE QUEEN Oh, here is the Prince. It must be nearly time, then.

ALBERT How do you do, Dr. Stanley. We are very pleased to see you. Has the Queen told you about the plans we are making, in which we shall need your assistance.

STANLEY Her Majesty did tell me that you were expecting somebody.

THE QUEEN (*interrupting*) Oh, no; I haven't told him anything yet, Albert, about *that*. I was leaving it till you came. Where is Bertie?

ALBERT He is here, waiting within call. I told him not to come in yet.

THE QUEEN It is about our son, the Prince of Wales, Dr. Stanley, that we wished to consult you.

ALBERT Yes, my Dear; but this will hardly interest Lady Augusta, if Lady Augusta does not mind.

THE QUEEN Oh, of course not. Lady Augusta, you may go; and take those letters with you.

> (LADY AUGUSTA, *who has stood since the* PRINCE'S *entry, curtsies; and retires.* DR. STANLEY *opens the door for her*.)

ALBERT Yes, Dr. Stanley, the Prince is now eighteen—a difficult age.

STANLEY Yes, Sir, as those who have lived through it know.

ALBERT I lived through it without any difficulty, Dr. Stanley.

STANLEY Then your Highness was a happy exception.

275

THE QUEEN Of course he was, Dr. Stanley. (*Aside*) Albert, may not Dr. Stanley sit down?

ALBERT (*coldly*) If you wish him to, my Dear.

THE QUEEN (*submissively*) Oh, no.

> (*The* PRINCE CONSORT *seats himself.* DR. STANLEY *remains standing.*)

Well, it is about that . . . about the Prince, that we wished to have your advice, Dr. Stanley.

ALBERT Your help, that is to say.

THE QUEEN We think that perhaps next year he ought to go abroad, and see things for himself a little more. But we have to be so very careful whom he goes with.

STANLEY Of course, Ma'am, naturally.

ALBERT We have decided, Dr. Stanley, that it must be with someone not too old to take a share in his interests and pursuits, but at the same time one whom we can trust to exercise a certain amount of discipline and control—and, when necessary, to insist on securing obedience.

STANLEY A difficult task, Sir, when two are travelling abroad together—the two alone.

ALBERT A difficult task, as you say. It is for that reason that we ask you to undertake it.

STANLEY But, indeed, Sir, I—

ALBERT There is no one else in whom we can place such complete trust and confidence as yourself. You have the qualifications, and the gifts. Though so much his senior, the Prince will come to look upon you as his friend.

STANLEY I am very reluctant, Sir.

ALBERT That is understandable. You are probably aware that the Prince has already become a difficulty. He has now been at the University for his first term. . . . It has been indicated to us that College life does not suit him, and that he had better leave as soon as other arrangements can be made. That is the position, Dr. Stanley, in which we come to you for help.

STANLEY Sir, I feel quite at a loss why I should have been chosen.

THE QUEEN Oh, surely, Dr. Stanley, you will not say no to *me*.

STANLEY If it is, indeed, your Majesty's fixed wish, then I can say no more.

ALBERT Ah, very good! That is settled, then.

(*The* PRINCE CONSORT *goes to the door, opens it, and calls through.*)

Bertie! Are you there? You may come in.

(THE PRINCE OF WALES *enters. He stands, shy and sullen, and does not advance.*)

Come on in . . . and shut the door!

(*The* PRINCE *shuts it.*)

Don't stand there! Here is Dr. Stanley waiting for you to speak to him.

THE PRINCE OF WALES (*perfunctorily*) How do you do?

STANLEY How do *you* do, Sir? How did your Royal Highness like Cambridge?

277

PRINCE Hated it.

ALBERT Then you won't have to hate it much longer, Sir. Next year we are sending you abroad; and Dr. Stanley goes with you.

PRINCE I don't want to go abroad—with anybody.

ALBERT That is not for you to decide. We have decided it for you; and Dr. Stanley has most kindly consented to take charge of you. Now, what do you say to that?

PRINCE As I'm not to say anything, there's nothing for me to say.

THE QUEEN Bertie! Speaking to your Father like that!

PRINCE Well, what *am* I to say?

ALBERT You might, at least, say 'Thank you' to Dr· Stanley.

PRINCE (*sullenly*) Thank you.

STANLEY Oh . . . pray, don't mention it!

(*There is a pause.*)

PRINCE Can I go now?

ALBERT No, Sir, you may *not* go. Wait here, and have your mind improved a little. We are expecting a visit from a very eminent man of letters; you will never have heard of him, of course. Well, stay and listen to him.

PRINCE I shan't understand a word he says.

ALBERT I dare say not. . . .

PRINCE (*sotto voce*) . . . And shan't want to!

ALBERT (*following on*) But you can, at least, try. And, while in the presence of others, you might also try to look a little less of an injured martyr.

278

PRINCE Well, I can't pretend to look pleased, when I'm not.

> (*A Gentleman of the Court enters, and, seeing* THE QUEEN *engaged in conversation with* DR. STANLEY, *goes and delivers his message to the* PRINCE CONSORT.)

THE QUEEN You must not mind, Dr. Stanley, if just at first there is this little unwillingness. Bertie so dislikes having to make up his mind about anything.

ALBERT Yes, Her Majesty is ready to receive him.

> (*The Gentleman bows and retires.*)

STANLEY I must confess, Ma'am, that the unwillingness was shared by your most humble servant. I might even say that, in each case, our minds have been made up for us. So, naturally, there is at first a little difficulty in getting used to the prospect.

ALBERT Our expected visitor is due, my Dear. I said that you would receive him as soon as he arrived.

THE QUEEN Yes, I hope he will be punctual.

> (*As she speaks, the clock on the mantelpiece strikes the hour.*)

STANLEY (*with a gesture towards the* PRINCE, *who stands moodily looking out of the window*) Would it not be well, Ma'am, to begin our better acquaintance now? May I go and speak to him?

THE QUEEN Oh, do, Dr. Stanley, do! It is very kind of you.

ALBERT I think I hear him coming

THE QUEEN Oh, Albert, this is going to be very difficult. You must do all the talking, please.

ALBERT We have Dr. Stanley to help us, my Dear. It will be all right.

> (*The door opens; an* USHER *enters followed by the much-expected Celebrity.*)

USHER If it please your Majesty, Mr. Martin Tupper.

> (MR. MARTIN TUPPER *bows himself in with more bows than the three which etiquette requires. He bows to everyone as long as time is left to him for bowing.*)

THE QUEEN (*rising*) How do you do, Mr. Tupper?

ALBERT How do you do?

> (MR. TUPPER *reverentially touches the Royal hands, and says in a voice sonorous with emotion*)

TUPPER So honoured, your Majesty! Your Royal Highness, so honoured!

THE QUEEN We are so pleased to meet you, Mr. Tupper.

ALBERT Having often heard of you . . . having also *read* you.

TUPPER Ah, Sir, that is, indeed, for a writer, the reward of rewards—to be read!

ALBERT Bertie, come and shake hands with Mr. Tupper. Mr. Tupper, this is my Son, the Prince of Wales.

PRINCE (*getting it over*) How do you do?

TUPPER How do *you* do, Sir. . . . Most honoured!

THE QUEEN Dr. Stanley, you and Mr. Tupper already know each other, I expect?

STANLEY (*bowing*) I have not had the honour.

TUPPER The honour is mine, Sir.

(*There is a slight pause.* THE PRINCE OF WALES *draws furtively away. Presently he stands by the window and takes up a book, turning its pages, merely to pass the time.*)

ALBERT Mr. Tupper, I was reading one of your books to Her Majesty, only last night.

THE QUEEN Yes, and I enjoyed it—very much.

TUPPER May I be allowed, Sir, to ask which?

ALBERT Your *Proverbial Philosophy*, Mr. Tupper.

TUPPER Ah! then your Majesty would, I am sure.

THE QUEEN Yes; there are so many things in it with which I so thoroughly agree.

TUPPER (*enthusiastically*) Thousands and thousands of your Majesty's loyal subjects have done the same, Ma'am. That book, I am proud to tell your Majesty, has already gone into fifteen editions—large ones.

ALBERT How many editions, Mr. Tupper?

TUPPER Fifteen, your Royal Highness.

ALBERT Oh, I thought you said fifty. . . . I could have wished it had been fifty.

TUPPER It will be fifty, some day, your Royal Highness, I don't doubt. The sales never diminish, Ma'am, never. That book, your Majesty, brings me in a steady income every year.

281

THE QUEEN How very gratifying for you; and how satisfactory for the publishers.

TUPPER Satisfactory for the publishers, you say, Ma'am? Alas, still more satisfactory for the pirates!

THE QUEEN The pirates?

TUPPER (*with emotion*) Millions of my books, your Majesty—complete editions—have been stolen from me by American pirates across the sea. And they call it the Land of Liberty.

THE QUEEN American pirates! I did not think such things still existed. Most extraordinary!

STANLEY Mr. Tupper is speaking of book-pirates, your Majesty—a product of the American copyright laws. It involves not loss of life; only loss of property.

THE QUEEN Still, that is very wrong.

TUPPER Most wrong, your Majesty. My book, *Proverbial Philosophy*, has been translated into sixteen languages throughout the world. And in every country it has been honestly paid for, except in America. And they call themselves a civilised nation! Your Majesty must pardon me if I let my indignation carry me away.

THE QUEEN But what you say is so interesting, Mr. Tupper. And I can share your indignation over a thing like that. I can quite understand it.

TUPPER Your Majesty is very good to say so. It consoles me, nay more, it makes up for the monetary loss it has been to me, that I have your Majesty's kind sympathy.

(*There is a pause.*)

ALBERT How do you write your books, Mr. Tupper?

TUPPER How do I write them, Sir?—In what way?

ALBERT Precisely, 'In what way?' Do you write them slowly, with difficulty; or do they arise naturally and spontaneously to your mind, without effort?

TUPPER Oh, they come very quickly, your Royal Highness, very quickly indeed! I would not say without any effort of a kind—without strain. Emotional strain on the nervous system there must be, of course. But no delay in the actual expression—or the choice of words. They come entirely as they like. Sometimes I see them there on the paper before me, almost without having become aware that I had written them.

PRINCE (*sotto voce*) Good Lord! What an ass!

THE QUEEN How very interesting. Most extraordinary!

TUPPER Yes, your Majesty, I have to admit that it is extraordinary. But that is what being a writer of free, spontaneous verse—the form in which it comes to me— must necessarily mean.

ALBERT Indeed? Most interesting. . . . Well, I am sure you have given us a great deal to think about, Mr. Tupper. And if we had time for a longer conversation, we should learn more. Perhaps, on some other occasion.

(*This is a covert indication to* THE QUEEN *that the time for terminating the interview has arrived. She rises.*)

THE QUEEN Mr. Tupper, before you go, will you sign your book for us?

283

TUPPER Oh, your Majesty! let me not only sign it, but let me inscribe in it a few lines of impromptu verse, inspired by the occasion!

THE QUEEN Do . . . please! We should value it greatly. Where is the book, Albert?

ALBERT Why, there is Bertie reading it!

> (*At that moment the* PRINCE *is cursorily reading it. As though detected in an act of guilt, he puts it down hurriedly.*)

ALBERT Bertie, let Mr. Tupper have his book for a moment. You will find pen and ink at that table, Mr. Tupper.

TUPPER I thank your Royal Highness. I shall not be a moment.

> (*He goes across to the table, takes up the book, and opens it at the fly-leaf.*)

THE QUEEN (*seating herself again*) Would you like us to be silent, Mr. Tupper, while you are composing the lines?

TUPPER No, no! Oh, no, your Majesty! Pray do not think of it. When the Muse inspires me, I am so carried away that I hear nothing, I assure you. Would your Majesty believe, now, that I wrote one of my best poems while a Punch-and-Judy show was performing under my very window?

PRINCE (*sotto voce*) *I* would!

THE QUEEN How extraordinary! And you were able to finish it, Mr. Tupper?

TUPPER I was, Ma'am.

284

PRINCE But you *did* hear it?

TUPPER Hear it? . . . Hear what, your Royal Highness?

PRINCE The Punch-and-Judy show.

TUPPER Oh, yes; I certainly heard it.

PRINCE Then, that time, you were not so inspired?

TUPPER Oh, I see what your Highness means. No, no. The Punch-and-Judy show took longer than the inspiration. I heard the beginning of it; and I heard the end of it: but not—not while I was composing. . . . May I sit down, your Majesty, while I am writing?

THE QUEEN Please do.

(*He sits down. . . . Inspiration descends on him.*)

ALBERT Bertie, you had better come away over here. You shouldn't talk so much.

(*The* PRINCE *moves away from the writing-table, but turns, and from a distance watches the process of composition which has now begun.*)

THE QUEEN (*speaking in a low voice*) Dr. Stanley, you will stay to lunch, will you not? Mr. Disraeli, the Minister-in-Attendance, will be here. You would like to meet him. He is so interesting, so amusing.

STANLEY Charmed, your Majesty, if I may, indeed, have the honour.

THE QUEEN Then do.

PRINCE (*imitating 'Punch'*) Judy! Judy!

THE QUEEN Bertie!

ALBERT If you can't behave yourself, you had better leave the room.

PRINCE Very well.

(*He moves to the door.*)

ALBERT Stay where you are! But you will take your lunch alone to-day, in your own room.

(MR. TUPPER *rises from his seat.*)

Ah, Mr. Tupper, have you done it all already?

(MR. TUPPER *bows, book in hand.*)

Then I am sure Her Majesty would like to hear it.

TUPPER If Her Majesty will understand that it is only a very slight effort.

THE QUEEN Please!

TUPPER   To England's Queen
    This book I give,
   That here kept green
    It still may live.
   From youth to age,
    Whene'er you need it,
   Oh, Madam, turn the page,
    And read it.

THE QUEEN Oh, thank you!

TUPPER (*with a gesture*) Pardon, Ma'am . . . just two more lines.

   And should you ever
    Deign to quote it,
   Happy will be
    The Heart that wrote it.

(*He lays the book down.*)

286

THE QUEEN Very pretty indeed! Thank you, Mr. Tupper. (*She rises.*) We looked forward very much to meeting you, and it has been a very, very great pleasure. . . . Good-bye.

ALBERT Good-bye, Mr. Tupper. We are glad to have had this opportunity of meeting you. Some day, I trust, we may meet again.

> (*Over this last adieu,* MR. TUPPER *has been unable to voice his emotion. But at the door he turns, and bows.*)

TUPPER Your Majesty's most humble, and grateful servant.

> (*The door, with liveried mechanism, opens to let him out, and closes again behind him.*)

THE QUEEN (*as she sits*) How very pleasant he was, to be sure. And so well-informed.

STANLEY (*dryly*) About his own writings? Yes, Ma'am.

THE QUEEN He *must* be well-informed to be able to write them.

STANLEY (*assenting, in a non-committal tone*) Oh, yes; I suppose so.

THE QUEEN You have read his book, Dr. Stanley?

STANLEY Ah, no. But I have been meaning to—now and then.

THE QUEEN Oh, but you must! You would find things in it so useful in your sermons. Indeed they remind me of sermons a good deal . . . only put in such beautiful language.

STANLEY Then I must, Ma'am—I must, indeed.

(*The door opens, and, with due announcement,* MR. DISRAELI *enters.*)

THE QUEEN (*rising to meet him*) Oh, Mr. Disraeli, I am sorry you did not come a little sooner.

DISRAELI I am always sorry, Ma'am, not to come sooner into so gracious a Presence. I am sorry when I have to leave it.

THE QUEEN Ah, but I meant for quite a different reason, Mr. Disraeli. Had you come sooner you would have met a distinguished man of letters, like yourself.

DISRAELI Like myself, Ma'am? To what other man of letters, in your Majesty's estimation, have I the honour of resemblance?

THE QUEEN Oh, I only meant both being famous writers. . . . Mr. Martin Tupper.

DISRAELI (*becoming inscrutable*) Ah? . . . Mr. Martin Tupper?

(*Meanwhile the* PRINCE CONSORT *has been at the writing-table, examining the newly autographed book with apparent interest. Thus, from a distance he has been able to acknowledge the entry of a Minister whom he dislikes, by a mere bow. Now he comes forward and joins in the conversation.*)

ALBERT We understand that he has a great reputation.

DISRAELI And a great circulation, Sir, to confirm it.

ALBERT You read his books, Mr. Disraeli?

288

DISRAELI I have not read them, Sir. It is an infirmity I have to confess, that, to read the works of men so greatly my superior in popular esteem, depresses me. I lose inspiration.

THE QUEEN That is a pity.

DISRAELI Yes, Ma'am, a great pity!

THE QUEEN But do you not read Shakespeare, Mr. Disraeli?

DISRAELI Oh, yes; I read Shakespeare, Ma'am. Shakespeare belongs to another age. He does not overshadow me, in popular esteem, in the same way as Mr. Martin Tupper. Of Shakespeare I have no jealousy . . . none.

THE QUEEN But you are jealous of Mr. Tupper?

DISRAELI Ah, Ma'am! do not probe, I beseech you, the dark and secret places of the human heart. What I feel about Mr. Tupper, with your Majesty's permission, I would rather not say.

THE QUEEN He has written some verses in his book for me; would you like to see them?

DISRAELI Any command of your Majesty's, I obey.

ALBERT Bertie, give Mr. Disraeli the book.

> (DISRAELI *takes the book, and reads.* THE QUEEN *is watching his face; but his expression, made suitable at the beginning of the reading, does not change. He lays the book down.*)

THE QUEEN Very beautiful, don't you think?

DISRAELI Ah, Ma'am, could I write poetry like that, not another of my own poor works would I be able to publish.

(LADY AUGUSTA *re-enters.*)

THE QUEEN Dear Lady Augusta, come and talk to Dr. Stanley. You will sit together at luncheon, please. Albert, I want to speak to you for a moment.

(*They go to the window together; and with their backs to the others they stand talking.*)

PRINCE Mr. Disraeli, you didn't miss anything. . . . I'm glad he's gone.

DISRAELI So am I, Sir.

PRINCE An awful ass!

DISRAELI I feel bound to respect your Highness's judgment.

(*And now the colloquy of* THE QUEEN *and the* PRINCE CONSORT *is over.*)

ALBERT Don't you think, Mr. Disraeli, that, for the next Honours List, we might suggest to the Prime Minister, that he should submit Mr. Martin Tupper's name for inclusion?

DISRAELI Your Highness means in the next *Birthday* Honours, I presume?

ALBERT Why the Birthday Honours, specially?

DISRAELI The New Year's Honours being, as a rule, more political in character.

ALBERT Ah, yes, yes. Well, Mr. Tupper is *not* political—is he?

DISRAELI He has political views, Sir. And for that reason, I must regretfully suggest, that the submission of his name should be left—to the *next* Government.

THE QUEEN Oh, Mr. Disraeli, I am so sorry!

DISRAELI So am I, Ma'am. But I have to repeat that the inclusion of Mr. Tupper's name in *any* Honours List would be regarded by your Majesty's present advisers—as, politically, inexpedient.

ALBERT Now there, Mr. Disraeli, you have an instance of the difficulty in which we are always finding ourselves! Her Majesty is anxious to do honour to literature. And you see, immediately, something that has nothing whatever to do with literature arises and prevents.

DISRAELI How true, Sir! How very true! Something that has nothing whatever to do with literature, arises and prevents.

(*The door opens. A* FOOTMAN *appears.*)

FOOTMAN Your Majesty is served.

(*In due order, they go in to luncheon.* THE PRINCE OF WALES, *who is not to be of the company, stands back, and waits for* MR. DISRAELI *to pass him.*)

PRINCE Well stopped, Sir!

(MR. DISRAELI *bows his acknowledgment; he smiles, but says nothing.*)

291

Intervention

Intervention

30th November 1861

On THE QUEEN's *writing-table a Government Despatch-box lies open.* GENERAL GREY, THE QUEEN's *Private Secretary, stands reading to Her Majesty the despatch which* LORD RUSSELL, *the Foreign Secretary, has addressed to Lord Lyons, the British Ambassador at Washington, on the seizure upon the High Seas, from the British ship* Trent, *of the two Confederate officers, Slidell and Mason.*

THE QUEEN Before you go on, General Grey, will you ring, please.

(THE GENERAL *rings, and continues reading. . . . One of* THE QUEEN's GENTLEMEN *enters.*)

Has His Royal Highness not returned from Sandhurst yet?

GENTLEMAN A few minutes ago, he had not, your Majesty.

THE QUEEN But it is so late! Was not the ceremony to have been over by midday?

GENTLEMAN I believe so, your Majesty. It is possible that His Royal Highness *may* have just returned.

295

THE QUEEN Please to go and see; and, if he has, bring back word at once. . . , General Grey, this looks very serious indeed! Is the Messenger who brought it still waiting?

GENERAL GREY I am not sure, Ma'am.

THE QUEEN Will you please to find out? And if he has not gone, say that he is to wait. . . . I do wish the Prince would come! It is so urgent; and with Lord Palmerston Prime Minister, one never knows what he may not do next, without waiting for *our* instructions.

GENERAL GREY Indeed no, Ma'am.

THE QUEEN At once, please!

(*As the* GENERAL *goes, the* GENTLEMAN *returns.*)

GENTLEMAN His Royal Highness has just returned, your Majesty. He has gone up to his room.

THE QUEEN Then go and ask His Royal Highness to come at once. Say that the matter is most urgent.

(*The* GENTLEMAN *goes.* THE QUEEN *takes up the despatch, and is re-reading it when* GENERAL GREY *returns.*)

GENERAL GREY The Messenger has gone, your Majesty.

THE QUEEN Without waiting!

GENERAL GREY He waited for an hour, Ma'am, I'm told.

THE QUEEN An hour! He should have waited all day, if necessary. Messengers from my other Ministers know that they have to wait. Why do not Foreign Office Messengers

296

wait too? This is what is always happening: and then they pretend that the delay it causes is our fault, not theirs.

GENERAL GREY Cannot one of your Majesty's Messengers go, Ma'am—the matter being so urgent?

THE QUEEN Yes, he must. Tell one of them to be ready to start instantly.

> (*As the* GENERAL *is going,* THE PRINCE CONSORT *enters. He looks haggard and tired.*)

THE QUEEN Oh, Albert, why did you wait to change? I have been so wanting you!

ALBERT My uniform was wet through, my Dear; and I was feeling very cold.

THE QUEEN (*taking his hand*) You are cold still, Dearest! your hand is like ice. Oh, why did you go in such weather, when I begged you not to?

ALBERT I had to, my Dear. . . . What is the matter?

THE QUEEN It's about that trouble with America, for having taken the Confederate Envoys off one of our ships. And most wrong of them it was! This is the despatch Lord Russell is sending to our Ambassador in Washington about it. He wants it to go to-night.

ALBERT (*taking it*) Is the Messenger waiting?

THE QUEEN No; he's gone.

ALBERT (*sharply*) Gone? Ah! That is what one has now to expect, I suppose!

THE QUEEN Yes; it's that Pilgerstein again. Troublesome man!

ALBERT Yes; though this time it is Lord Russell that does it; that Go-between, who was always so apologetic and nice to us. Hah! But it is Pilgerstein—as you say—still. Oh, yes!

THE QUEEN Read it quickly, Albert. I want to know what you think about it.

(GENERAL GREY *re-enters.*)

GENERAL GREY I have given your Majesty's order. A Messenger is ready and waiting.

THE QUEEN Very well. And now that the Prince is here, General Grey, I shall no longer need you.

(*The* GENERAL *goes.* THE QUEEN *sits watching the* PRINCE CONSORT *as he reads. Not till he has finished it does he speak.*)

ALBERT This means War.

THE QUEEN Yes; I was afraid so. How foolish of them not to give in! For they must know they are in the wrong. And everything that Lord Russell says is true, is it not?

ALBERT (*deep in thought*) Quite. . . . Quite. . . . But—it won't do.

THE QUEEN But, Albert, as we are in the right, what else can we do?

ALBERT Alter a few words. . . . Say it; but say it differently. Often it is just the way a thing is said that decides whether it shall be peace or war. It is the same when two people quarrel. You and I, Weibchen, might often have quarrelled, had we said the same thing that we did say—differently. . . . Russell? Oh, no: this is Pilgerstein, I think! He is the man that would *like* to have war
298

with America. He has worked for it; and this is his opportunity—that we are in the right! . . . He shall not have it! War? Oh, yes; and this time we should win. But another time would come, and we should *not* win.

THE QUEEN But we could always beat America now, Albert.

ALBERT Ah, so? What if we were fighting someone else, Vicky; and America chose her time then? No; that is what these 'patriots' never think about. . . . It is always —'*This* time, *this* time! We are *right*, and we shall do what we like!' What fools their patriotism makes clever men to be! And Pilgerstein the cleverest fool of them all, . . . And when he dies, they will say of this man—'Oh! yes; he had his faults; but he always upheld the Honour of his Country.' And when they say 'Honour,' they mean Pride. Again and again, he has been ready to sacrifice the Honour of his Country to its Pride. For Honour means that you are too proud to do wrong; but Pride means that you will not *own* that you have done wrong—at all. *That* is the difference.

THE QUEEN Then that applies to America, now.

ALBERT Yes. Here is America: she has done wrong, and she knows it. . . . Invite her to reconsider—a mistake: something done by her agents without her instructions. She will think, and will behave reasonably. . . . But say 'I order you!' and she will *not*.

THE QUEEN But, Albert, ought we to make it so easy for them as all that?

ALBERT Yes; because we should do just the same ourselves, if we were ordered. And we should call it

299

'Honour.' And for that Honour we should send thousands and thousands to die! What a wicked black thing Honour can become—when men make use of it—*so*!

THE QUEEN Then what are we going to do, Albert?

ALBERT We are going to alter this, *now*. . . . Sit down at once, and write! Say that this despatch is not to go, till he has heard from you. . . . And your Messenger must go now, at once, and must see Lord Russell himself. . . . This will take me more time; but you write your letter at once!

THE QUEEN Yes, Albert, yes!

> (THE QUEEN *seats herself at one writing-table. The* PRINCE CONSORT *goes to another.* THE QUEEN *begins to write, then rings, and continues writing. A* GENTLEMAN *enters, and stands waiting, while the letter is being finished.*)

THE QUEEN Tell the Messenger to take this to Lord Russell, at the Foreign Office. He is to see him, and is to bring an answer.

> (*The* GENTLEMAN *takes the letter, and goes.* THE QUEEN *goes across to the* PRINCE CONSORT. *She puts her hand on his shoulder, and leans over him.*)

ALBERT (*gently*) Will you leave me alone, my Dear, while I do this? I shall try not to be long.

*

> (*As the scene closes, the clock on the mantelpiece strikes four. When it opens again, some hours have passed. Candles are lighted.* THE

PRINCE *is still at his desk, writing. He sits up; the pen falls from his hand.*)

ALBERT That is done . . . *done!*

(*Slowly he reaches out, takes up a hand-bell, and rings. A* GENTLEMAN *enters.*)

Tell Her Majesty that I have finished. . . . Ask Her Majesty to come.

(*The* GENTLEMAN *bows, and goes out.* THE PRINCE *tries to rise, sinks back into his seat: resting his hands on the table, he bends slowly forward; his head drops to the table.*

(THE QUEEN *enters.*)

THE QUEEN Albert, what is the matter? Are you ill?

ALBERT (*raising himself with difficulty*) I have done. Read it! If you approve, send it!

(THE QUEEN *takes up the amended despatch and reads it. While she does so, the clock strikes seven.*)

THE QUEEN (*reading*) Yes. . . . Yes. . . . Yes. . . . I do —I do approve—every word.

ALBERT Then let it go—*now!*

(THE QUEEN *rings. She puts the paper into the Despatch-box, and locks it. A* GENTLEMAN *enters.*)

THE QUEEN See that this goes at once!

(*The* GENTLEMAN *goes.* THE PRINCE *has once more taken up his pen: he tries to write. The pen falls from his hand. He reaches out to* THE QUEEN, *with a gesture of helplessness.*)

301

ALBERT Take me to bed! . . . Take me to bed, Weibchen! . . . Ich bin so schwach. Ich habe kaum die Feder halten können!

> (*Again he tries to rise, fails, and falls back into his chair.* THE QUEEN *throws her arms round him.*)

THE QUEEN Albert!

Death and the Doctors

Death and the Doctors

14th December 1861

At Windsor: a large ante-room, plainly furnished, with side-entrances to right and left. In the centre are folding-doors. The subdued sound of a bell, ringing in the room to the left, is heard. Immediately the door opens; a Nurse enters, and advancing towards the folding-doors, taps softly, and waits. One half of the folding-door is opened: the HEAD NURSE *appears, and handing out certain sick-bed appliances, gives her orders in a quiet undertone.*

HEAD NURSE More hot water, Nurse; quick, please.

> (*As the Nurse goes on her errand, the* HEAD NURSE *is about to close the door again, when, from within, comes* THE QUEEN'S *Physician,* DR. JAMES CLARK. *She stands aside for him to pass. He comes out, and beckons her to follow him.*)

DR. CLARK The room wants airing; you must open a window. But you can't have it in there: open one of these, and then put open the doors.

> (*The* HEAD NURSE *goes to the window, hitches back the half-drawn curtains, raises the lowered blind, and opens the window. Meanwhile the Doctor is on the point of departure, by way of*

305

*the room used by the Nurses, when through the
curtained entrance on the right* PRINCESS ALICE
enters.)

PRINCESS ALICE Dr. Clark, don't go!

DR. CLARK (*excusingly*) Only for a moment, your
Highness; just to wash my hands.

PRINCESS ALICE (*urgently*) Yes; but wait! I must speak
to you before Mamma comes. . . . How is Papa?

DR. CLARK Very much the same; the change we are
hoping for hasn't come yet.

PRINCESS ALICE (*anxiously*) *Will* it?

DR. CLARK Oh, undoubtedly . . . undoubtedly. . . . At
least, we must hope so.

PRINCESS ALICE Dr. Clark, Mamma does not know—
does not in the least realise how ill Papa really is. She
won't listen to any of us. She *must* be told! And it's only
you who *can* tell her.

DR. CLARK I assure your Highness that I have given
Her Majesty my confidence as fully as she has given me
hers—which is saying a great deal. When she asks me, I
tell her everything—everything that I *know.* What I am
not certain about, I don't say—to anyone.

PRINCESS ALICE But have you told Mamma that he is
dangerously ill?

DR. CLARK 'Dangerously' is a frightening word: therefore, I don't use it. (*Then to the* HEAD NURSE, *who has
finished the opening of the window.*) Ah, yes, Nurse; that
will do nicely. In a quarter of an hour, shut it again;
but leave the door open.

306

(The HEAD NURSE *now goes and puts open the folding-doors; and through them we see the foot of the bed in which the Royal Patient is lying. She goes into the room, and passes out of sight. Meanwhile the* PRINCESS *and the* DOCTOR *are still talking.)*

PRINCESS ALICE But, Dr. Clark, Papa's illness is of a very serious kind, is it not?

DR. CLARK Very—very serious, your Highness: I would never suggest otherwise. But in this case, it is taking its normal course: normal—quite normal.

PRINCESS ALICE But even if it goes on being normal, don't people sometimes—die of it?

DR. CLARK That *has* happened, your Highness. But, in this case, we have no reason whatever for anticipating anything so unlikely—so disastrous. No, no! . . . And now, your Highness will excuse me, for I *must* go.

PRINCESS ALICE May I go in now?

DR. CLARK Oh, yes, yes, certainly! He will be waking presently. And when he does, Her Majesty wishes to be told, immediately.

PRINCESS ALICE *(meaningly)* If you are not here to tell her, Dr. Clark, may I do so?

DR. CLARK *(turning sharply)* Not that! Not that! I can't have my professional duties interfered with by anybody.

PRINCESS ALICE *(resignedly)* Very, well, Doctor.

(The DOCTOR *has made his escape. The* PRINCESS *goes in, pauses at the foot of the bed, then passes round it, and out of sight. The Nurse returns,*

307

carrying a hot-water bottle. She stops at the door; the HEAD NURSE *comes forward and takes it. Going to the foot of the bed, she effects the necessary exchange, and brings back the other to the waiting Nurse, who goes off with it. The* HEAD NURSE *is about to return to her Patient, when* THE QUEEN *enters.)*

THE QUEEN Who opened that window?

HEAD NURSE It was the Doctor's orders, your Majesty.

THE QUEEN What Doctor?

HEAD NURSE Dr. Clark, your Majesty.

THE QUEEN Oh! Then it may stay. . . . Is Her Royal Highness, the Princess Alice, in there?

HEAD NURSE Yes, your Majesty.

THE QUEEN Ask her to come, and speak to me.

(*The* HEAD NURSE *goes back into the room to give the message. The* PRINCESS *comes out.)*

THE QUEEN Is he awake yet?

PRINCESS ALICE Not yet, Mamma. But, just now, he seemed as if he were beginning to.

THE QUEEN Have those Doctors been?

PRINCESS ALICE No, Mamma dear, not yet.

THE QUEEN I do wish they would come, and get it over!

PRINCESS ALICE You will see them, Mamma, won't you?

THE QUEEN No; I don't wish to see either of them. Dr. Clark did not think it at all necessary for them to come; neither did I. But you all seemed so set on it!

308

PRINCESS ALICE Yes: we wished it very much. And I do wish you *would* see them, Mamma.

THE QUEEN I have said I will *not* see them. . . . You may, if you like—if Dr. Clark has no objection.

HEAD NURSE (*coming in from the sick-room*) His Royal Highness is awake, your Majesty.

> (*With a gesture indicating that* PRINCESS ALICE *must wait her turn,* THE QUEEN *goes into the room. She goes round to the further side of the bed. We see her reach out her hand, and a hand taking it.*)

THE QUEEN Albert.

ALBERT (*heard, but not seen*) Weibchen! . . . Frauchen! . . . Liebe Frauchen!

THE QUEEN How are you, my Dearest? Better?

ALBERT I don't . . . know. . . . Sometimes . . . when one is better . . . one feels worse.

THE QUEEN But you are not feeling worse, my Darling, are you?

ALBERT No? . . . I don't know . . . I don't know . . . Weibchen. . . . Kiss me! . . . Kiss me! . . . Again! . . . Once again! . . . That will do . . . Frauchen; Kleine Frauchen!

> (*And now, into the outer room, returns* DR. CLARK.)

PRINCESS ALICE Papa is awake now, Doctor; Mamma is with him.

DR. CLARK Ah! I'm glad! That will do him more good than anything. . . . Always does. . . . But I think Her Majesty wished to speak to me. . . . Would your Highness very kindly—?

309

PRINCESS ALICE (*speaking through the open door*) Mamma, Dr. Clark is here.

(THE QUEEN *comes out.*)

THE QUEEN You may go in now, my Dear. Shut the door.

(*The* PRINCESS *goes in, closing the door behind her.*)

Dr. Clark, how do you find him this morning?

DR. CLARK No change, Ma'am; no change. I'm disappointed not to find the improvement that I was looking for. But there has been no apparent loss of strength; and that's always to the good, when one is fighting against time.

THE QUEEN Just now he spoke to me—quite himself again. His mind wasn't wandering, as it has been doing so much lately. That is what I find so distressing—when he doesn't know me.

DR. CLARK Ah, yes, Ma'am; that one can understand, of course. To the feelings, very trying; but, medically speaking, it is quite a normal symptom—quite normal. It need not add to your Majesty's anxiety in any degree whatever. Nothing unexpected has occurred—nothing, nothing.

THE QUEEN He *is* going to get well, isn't he?

DR. CLARK I have not a doubt, Ma'am: not a doubt.

THE QUEEN Nor have I, Dr. Clark. If I had, I couldn't bear it. . . . But there are others here, who haven't my confidence and courage. I feel it: it's very trying! . . . Those Doctors! *I* didn't want them; but I had to give in —for the sake of others. I wish now that I had not. . . .

310

His knowing me, and speaking to me again, gives me such hope.

(*The clock of the Castle is heard striking three.*)

DR. CLARK Your Majesty is quite right to hope. There is no use in being anything *but* hopeful, and no reason not to be.

THE QUEEN That was three o'clock striking. Wasn't that the time the Doctors were to be here?

DR. CLARK It was, Ma'am.

THE QUEEN Then I think I'd better go! I don't wish to meet them. You quite understand, Dr. Clark, that it was no lack of confidence, on *my* part, which required these others to be called into consultation.

DR. CLARK I quite understand, Ma'am; and I appreciate greatly the confidence which your Majesty has placed in me.

THE QUEEN I hope they won't be here long.

DR. CLARK They will not be, Ma'am, I am sure. I shall not encourage it. The case, though serious, is quite a simple one.

THE QUEEN Very well; then now I will go.

(*As* THE QUEEN *goes out, the* HEAD NURSE *comes in to close the window. A* SERVANT *enters.*)

SERVANT Sir Henry Holland, and Dr. Watson, to see you, Sir.

DR. CLARK Oh, yes; let them come up: I'll see them here. . . . Nurse, just see that nobody comes in while we are having our consultation. Go in now, and have everything ready. And, when I bring them in to see His Royal Highness, you will go out.

HEAD NURSE Yes, Sir.

(*She goes in, as the two Doctors make their appearance.*)

DR. CLARK Oh, good afternoon, good afternoon, Gentlemen! I'm sorry you should have been troubled: I don't think it was necessary—not at all necessary. Nor can I say that Her Majesty actually wished it. But in view of all the circumstances—the exalted position of my Patient, the public anxiety, and—and—things in general —others *did*. And so, Her Majesty. . . . Well, you are here; and I shall be willing—willing, after you have examined His Royal Highness—to hear anything you may have to say on the case.

SIR HENRY You have no doubt, I suppose, Dr. Clark, as to what the disease actually is?

DR. CLARK Oh, none, none! Gastric fever, just gastric fever—that's all.

DR. WATSON Nothing else? No complications?

DR. CLARK No, no; quite normal. But these three weeks of it, and all the responsibility have been a great strain to me. And Her Majesty is quite aware of it. . . . Well, will you come in? . . . I've prepared His Royal Highness for your arrival; but he probably won't know you. It's only at intervals—just now and then—that his mind does not wander somewhat. I'll go in first, if you don't mind. A moment, just a moment.

(*So saying, he disappears into the room.*)

SIR HENRY Well? How does that little exhibition strike you?

DR. WATSON Oh, professional jealousy, I suppose. One must expect it.

SIR HENRY I don't mind his jealousy. It's his incompetence I'm afraid of. He's an old duffer, with a mind of yesterday.

DR. WATSON Court Physicians-in-Ordinary generally are, I'm afraid.

DR. CLARK (*returning*) Come in, Gentlemen.

> (*They go in. The* HEAD NURSE *comes out, carrying a tray of medicine bottles and glasses. She sets this down, in order to close the door. Then, taking it up again, goes to the door on the left, and calls, 'Nurse.' The second Nurse answers the call.*)

HEAD NURSE Take these.

> (*As the tray is being handed over,* PRINCESS ALICE *enters from the other side.*)

PRINCESS ALICE Have the Doctors come?

HEAD NURSE Yes, your Royal Highness; they've just gone in.

PRINCESS ALICE Will you, please, send word to Her Majesty, as soon as they have gone?

HEAD NURSE Yes, your Royal Highness; I will.

PRINCESS ALICE Nurse, how is he, do you think— really?

HEAD NURSE (*hesitating*) I don't know, your Royal Highness: I can't say. . . . I oughtn't to say anything.

PRINCESS ALICE You are quite right, Nurse; I ought

313

not to have asked you. Dr. Clark seems hopeful; but he does not tell one anything.

HEAD NURSE No, your Royal Highness.

PRINCESS ALICE Have you attended many cases like this?

HEAD NURSE Not quite like this, your Royal Highness. Patients are so different. Some take it one way, some another. I've never seen two cases quite alike.

PRINCESS ALICE But it is always a very—serious kind of illness, isn't it, Nurse?

HEAD NURSE Yes, your Royal Highness. But people do recover from it. There's always hope, if they can hold out long enough.

PRINCESS ALICE Is three weeks a long time?

HEAD NURSE Sometimes it's four, your Royal Highness: not often.

> (*At this moment another and a younger* PRINCESS *tip-toes into sight. She comes from the improper direction of the Nurses' waiting-room. She is about fifteen.*)

PRINCESS ALICE (*reprovingly*) Nellie!

PRINCESS HELENA I *had* to come! Don't tell Mamma: she said I wasn't to. . . . How is he?

PRINCESS ALICE The Doctors are in there now, having a consultation.

PRINCESS HELENA How many?

PRINCESS ALICE Three.

PRINCESS HELENA Who are they?

PRINCESS ALICE I don't know—except, of course, Dr. Clark.

PRINCESS HELENA Why had the others to come?

PRINCESS ALICE Because it was so much better to have other opinions.

PRINCESS HELENA Isn't Dr. Clark's good enough? . . . When are they going to let me see Papa?

PRINCESS ALICE I don't know, Dear.

PRINCESS HELENA I haven't seen him now—for ten days. I want to! . . . May I just look in?

PRINCESS ALICE You can't now, possibly—not while the Doctors are there.

PRINCESS HELENA I'll come again, then, when Mamma isn't here. . . . You'll let me, won't you, Ally?

PRINCESS ALICE (*tenderly*) Yes, my Dear, I'll let you.

PRINCESS HELENA Oh, Ally, there's Mamma coming! I must run!

> (*She bolts back by the way she came.* THE QUEEN *enters.*)

PRINCESS ALICE (*quietly*) You had better go, Nurse, and wait in the other room.

> (*The Nurse, with a curtsy to Her approaching Majesty, withdraws.*)

THE QUEEN Haven't they gone? Haven't they gone yet?

PRINCESS ALICE No, Mamma; they are still there.

THE QUEEN (*angrily*) Why did they come? I didn't want them to come! But you all so insisted.

PRINCESS ALICE Yes, Mamma: isn't it always right, in serious cases, to call other Doctors into consultation?

THE QUEEN I don't see why! I trust Dr. Clark more than any of them. Having attended us both for so long, of course he knows best what to do. If they differ from him, it only makes trouble; and if they agree, what more good does that do?

PRINCESS ALICE It should give Dr. Clark more confidence, Mamma dear.

THE QUEEN He has all *my* confidence; and that's all he needs.

PRINCESS ALICE (*hearing the bell ring in the Nurses' waiting-room*) I think they are coming, Mamma. Won't you wait and see them?

THE QUEEN No, I can't—I won't see them! I'll see Dr. Clark, after they've gone. . . . You are not to see them, either. Come!

> (THE QUEEN *goes out, followed by* PRINCESS ALICE, *just as the* HEAD NURSE, *in answer to the bell, returns to take up her duty again. As she approaches the door, the Doctors come out.*)

DR. CLARK Well, Gentlemen, now that you have examined my Patient, if you wish to make any recommendations as to different, or further treatment, I am quite ready to hear them.

SIR HENRY I fear, Dr. Clark, that His Royal Highness's condition is more serious than you led us to suppose.

DR. CLARK I have always regarded his condition as serious—very serious, Sir Henry.

SIR HENRY Yes. . . . A question of degree.

316

DR. CLARK What degree of seriousness do you suggest, Sir Henry?

SIR HENRY I don't want to say there is no hope. But I'm very much afraid of what may happen in the next few hours, if there is not a change. . . . What do you say, Watson?

DR. WATSON I agree.

SIR HENRY I think, then, that Her Majesty ought to be told.

DR. CLARK Told what, Sir?

SIR HENRY What we have just told *you*, Dr. Clark.

DR. CLARK I cannot take that responsibility. It is highly important that His Royal Highness should not be subjected to any undue disturbance, or shock. If Her Majesty were told anything so alarming as what you propose—then, Gentlemen, undoubtedly the shock of it would communicate itself to my Patient also. Up till now, I consider that his strength has been largely sustained by the extraordinary courage, and confidence in his recovery which Her Majesty has exhibited. From her it goes to him: deprive him of that sustaining force, and I cannot answer for the consequences.

SIR HENRY Well, Dr. Clark, we have told you what we think. The matter is in your hands. . . . Does Her Majesty wish to see us before we go?

DR. CLARK I think not, Sir.

SIR HENRY Perhaps that is as well—since we do not find ourselves in agreement.

DR. WATSON Very much better; for if Her Majesty were to ask for my opinion, I should be bound to give it.

317

SIR HENRY If you would like us to wait, Dr. Clark, within call—we will do so.

DR. CLARK I thank you, but I think not. I understood from Her Majesty that she would not require a second consultation. This was only done to satisfy others.

DR. WATSON If Her Majesty should ask you for a statement of our opinion of the case, Dr. Clark—what are you going to say?

DR. CLARK I believe that Her Majesty will be quite satisfied with my own statement of the case, without further inquiry. She has honoured me, so far, with her confidence; and I do not expect now to find that it has been withdrawn.

SIR HENRY Oh? . . . Then I think we had better say good afternoon, Dr. Clark. . . . I wish I had *your* confidence.

DR. WATSON Yes: sorry we could not be of more use. . . . Too late, too late!

> (*The Consultants part with frigid formality. As the two Doctors move towards the door by which they entered, gathering up each his hat and gloves as they go,* DR. CLARK *opens the inner door and beckons. The* HEAD NURSE *appears in time to see the intruders disappearing through the adjoining room.*)

DR. CLARK Nurse, just see there is somebody to show them out.

HEAD NURSE (*looking*) There is somebody, Sir.

DR. CLARK Oh, very well. Then, now send someone to tell Her Majesty that they have gone; but to say also,

318

that, for the present, I think His Royal Highness had better not see anybody. . . . I hope that, after this disturbance, he may sleep.

(*As the* HEAD NURSE *goes to perform her errand,* PRINCESS ALICE *is seen standing in the doorway.*)

PRINCESS ALICE I heard what you said, Dr. Clark. I will go and tell Mamma myself. And then—may I come back, and wait here?

DR. CLARK Oh, certainly, certainly. I am going myself now. I shall be back in about an hour.

PRINCESS ALICE (*anxiously*) You have no news for us? The Doctors said nothing that you can—?

DR. CLARK Nothing, your Highness: nothing, that I did not know already. . . . Nothing.

(*The Princess and the Doctor go out by opposite doors. The* HEAD NURSE *returns to the sickroom. Faintly, from a distance, come the sounds of the afternoon service in St. George's Chapel—the chanting of the Psalms. It is the 14th Evening of the month, and the 73rd Psalm is being sung. Presently the Princess returns; and, sitting down, she opens a Prayer Book and follows the words of the singing. Twilight begins to fall; time passes; it gets dark. Presently the Assistant Nurse, in answer to a bell from the sick-room, comes through, carrying a small shaded lamp. As she comes back, she sees* PRINCESS ALICE *seated at one of the windows.*)

NURSE Would not your Royal Highness like to have a reading-lamp?

PRINCESS ALICE No, Nurse: draw the curtains, and light the candles; that will do.

> (*The Nurse carries out the order, then goes. The Princess sits waiting. An hour passes. . . .*

*

> *In the adjoining room the bell rings sharply. As the Nurse enters in answer to the summons, the door of the sick-room opens, and the* HEAD NURSE *appears.*)

HEAD NURSE Call the Doctor! Quick!

> (*The Nurse runs out.*)

PRINCESS ALICE (*springing up*) Is he worse?

HEAD NURSE Oh, will your Royal Highness please tell Her Majesty to come!

> (*The Princess goes hastily out:* DR. CLARK *arrives, and entering the inner room, leaves the door half-open. A moment later* THE QUEEN *comes hurrying in, followed by the Princess. As they enter, the folding-doors are pushed back—the lower half of the bed can now be seen. A sound of heavy breathing is heard: it becomes more and more painful. The Nurse who has summoned the Doctor, now stands inside the outer door, waiting. The* HEAD NURSE *comes out; their eyes encounter; she shakes her head.*)

HEAD NURSE We are not to go in now: we are to wait here.

> (*They stand motionless, listening: only the heavy breathing is heard:* PRINCESS ALICE *comes hurriedly to the door.*)

PRINCESS ALICE Nurse, send word at once! Say that their Royal Highnesses are to come—immediately.

(*The Nurse goes out.*)

HEAD NURSE Oh, your Royal Highness, has the Doctor *said* anything?

PRINCESS ALICE Dr. Clark has just told us that there is no hope.

> (*She goes back into the room, where, in the subdued light,* DR. CLARK *is seen, passing across from the bed, and back again. The laboured breathing grows slower, and fainter.*
>
> *The Members of the Royal Family come in one by one. One sees them, as they enter, pause, stand for a moment, then pass round the bed, and kneel. . . . The heavy breathing dies down— ceases. There is a moment's silence, then from* THE QUEEN *comes a loud cry: and his name . . .* 'ALBERT!' *There follows a sound of weeping: and* DR. CLARK, *feeling that he is no longer needed, tiptoes softly out.*)

Bereavement

Bereavement

1861

In the deepest of widow's weeds, THE QUEEN *sits nursing a pet dog; and in the wistful gaze of the dumb beast she finds comfort, and a sympathy which she is less ready to accept when it is offered her by mere humans. She sits at her writing-table, having interrupted for a few moments the correspondence she is conducting on black-edged notepaper of the deepest dye.*

THE QUEEN Yes, you understand, don't you?—a little. No, you don't, you don't, Doggie! but you try to. That's the best you can do for me. It's all that anyone can do now. Nobody can really understand. . . . And now you must get down, dear; I must go on with my writing.

> (*She puts the dog gently down, and returns sadly to her correspondence. A* GENTLEMAN USHER *enters, and stands waiting for permission to speak.*)

THE QUEEN (*after a pause*) Yes?

USHER Mrs. Gladstone, your Majesty.

THE QUEEN Oh, yes. Let her come in. And while she *is* here, I do not wish to see anyone.

> (*The* USHER *bows, and goes.* THE QUEEN *takes up a portrait from the writing-table, and gazes at it fondly.*)

THE QUEEN Oh! Albert! Albert!

(*The door opens; the* USHER *enters, followed by* MRS. GLADSTONE.)

USHER Mrs. Gladstone, Your Majesty.

THE QUEEN Dear Mrs. Gladstone, how good of you to come, so soon!

MRS. GLADSTONE Directly—when I got your Majesty's command. I was so grateful that your Majesty wished it.

THE QUEEN There are very few I wish to see, now, Mrs. Gladstone; but you were one. You have always been so kind to me.

MRS. GLADSTONE The kindness has been your Majesty's.

THE QUEEN You have come to see an unhappy woman, the joy of whose life is over.

MRS. GLADSTONE Oh, I understand how your Majesty must feel! And I won't talk about time making any difference. But memories will. Your Majesty will find a great comfort in memories,—presently.

THE QUEEN They are a great pain to me. Almost more than I can bear.

MRS. GLADSTONE Yes, of course. But you would not be without them. They are already, Ma'am, are they not, the nearest to comfort—of anything?

THE QUEEN That is quite true, Mrs. Gladstone—quite true. Do, please, sit down! No; sit near me. . . . You also, at some time, must have known great sorrow.

MRS. GLADSTONE Yes, Ma'am; few of us can miss having it at some time in our lives.

326

THE QUEEN What has been your greatest sorrow, Mrs. Gladstone?

MRS. GLADSTONE My Sister, Ma'am, my only Sister. She was my closest and dearest friend.

THE QUEEN How long is it since you lost her?

MRS. GLADSTONE Four years, Ma'am.

THE QUEEN Does it seem long?

MRS. GLADSTONE No, Ma'am; she is still so much alive to me. At first she seemed dead—gone, utterly. She doesn't now. So much comes back; every day—new memories. Your Majesty will find that, too; I am sure.

THE QUEEN Thank you, Mrs. Gladstone; I hope so, too. But already I remember so much. I don't think there can be anything I have forgotten. As I read his diaries, and his dear letters, everything seems like yesterday.

MRS. GLADSTONE Yes: when we have loved much, time seems hardly to mean anything.

THE QUEEN You say the very thing I have been trying to say to myself, Mrs. Gladstone,—and to believe. It's a comfort to hear someone else saying it. . . . And, of course, now, *He* remembers everything too. So, in memory, we are together—still.

MRS. GLADSTONE Yes, Ma'am; and of one so really good as he was, what lovely and comforting memories you must have always with you.

THE QUEEN Yes, always; just as *he* was always with me. In all our married life, we were hardly ever apart; during twenty-two years only a few weeks. At first he was not with me so constantly—during the day, I mean. I had not found out then how much more he was fit to be King

327

than I was to be Queen. And people were jealous and afraid—even my own Ministers—lest he should have too much influence over me. And, just at first, sometimes we differed, he and I; but he was always right—always right! And before long, I found that I could do nothing safely without him. And there he was, always at my side—helping, advising, directing, guiding—often saving me from making mistakes; and my Ministers also. As time went on, they also learned to listen to him, and wished him to be present in all our consultations; all except just a few—Lord Palmerston sometimes. But even he has written and spoken to me, very kindly and feelingly, about what we owed to his great wisdom and foresight. The very last thing he did has, perhaps, saved us from war with America. Will people ever know what this Country owes to him? He ought to have been King: he was—almost; for I decided nothing till he had advised me about it. And now he is gone—I am alone; and though people don't know it, a new reign has begun—a Queen without her King! Oh, what shall I do? What shall I do without him?

MRS. GLADSTONE Is it not possible, Ma'am—your Son, the Prince, now being of age—that he may be of some help to your Majesty?

THE QUEEN (*with some asperity*) No! Indeed, no, Mrs. Gladstone! He has not either his Father's mind, nor his Father's character. I cannot allow him to take any part, at present, in my responsible work of Government.

MRS. GLADSTONE But he must do so some day, your Majesty; and it is a work for which he will need training.

THE QUEEN I have to hope, Mrs. Gladstone, that it will not have to be yet—not till he is a good deal older, and more—settled. At present, he is far too much the man of pleasure, and amusement. He is devoted to me, of course; as I am also to him. But he makes me very anxious.

MRS. GLADSTONE I think he has a very kind heart, your Majesty. Wherever he goes, he attracts and wins people.

THE QUEEN Yes; and not always of the best kind. Attracting people is sometimes his great temptation, and he does not feel—no, he does not *feel* his Father's death as he ought to do. . . . Just think! Only a fortnight after, I found him—*smoking*! It was a great shock to me; his Father having always forbidden it. *He* never smoked—never felt the need of it. So why should Bertie?

MRS. GLADSTONE But so many more do so now, Ma'am. It has become very much more common.

THE QUEEN Yes, 'common'! that is the word for it. How much the world is changing—from what *He* would have wished! But *I* shall never change—anything.

MRS. GLADSTONE To be faithful in all one's thoughts and wishes, is a great help, Ma'am, is it not? It makes one feel nearer.

THE QUEEN Dear Mrs. Gladstone, you do say such nice things! I wish we could have talked longer; it would have done me good, I'm sure. But even now the affairs of my Government have to go on; and I as the head of it. And I believe that already I have an appointment, and that one of my Ministers is waiting to see me. So now I must say good-bye to you. Thank you for coming. You must come again—soon.

> (*And as* MRS. GLADSTONE *curtsies over the hand offered her,* THE QUEEN *bends down and kisses her.*)

MRS. GLADSTONE Oh, yes, Ma'am, your Majesty has only to send for me. I wish—we all wish—that we could do anything that might be of use or comfort to your Majesty. But even love feels helpless sometimes.

THE QUEEN It is the only thing that can help now—that has helped me at all. . . . Good-bye!

(MRS. GLADSTONE *makes her last curtsy, and retires.* THE QUEEN *goes to the window, and stands looking out for a while; then, returning to the writing-table, she rings a bell. The* GENTLE-MAN *enters.*)

THE QUEEN If Lord Palmerston is here, I am now ready to see him.

USHER Lord Palmerston *is* here, your Majesty.

THE QUEEN Very well. Ask him to come in.

(*The* USHER *retires, and reappears, followed by* LORD PALMERSTON.)

USHER Lord Palmerston, your Majesty.

THE QUEEN Good morning, Lord Palmerston. You wrote that you wished to see me to-day, if possible.

LORD PALMERSTON I thank your Majesty for so graciously making the appointment. May I express the hope that your Majesty is now better?

THE QUEEN I am quite well, thank you, Lord Palmerston. You have come about something that requires my immediate attention, I believe?

LORD PALMERSTON I have, Ma'am, unfortunately. I would have been glad to have spared your Majesty, could it have allowed of postponement.

THE QUEEN Oh, no, please. I wish everything to go on as usual.

LORD PALMERSTON To-day, Ma'am, is the thirtieth of December; and the New Year's Honours still await your Majesty's approval and confirmation. To-morrow they must go to the Press, for next day's publication.

THE QUEEN Yes, of course. It would not do for there to be any delay in the usual announcements. . . . You have them with you?

LORD PALMERSTON I have, Ma'am. Lord Granville has communicated to me your Majesty's wish that Mr. Dilke should be made a Baronet, and that Mr. Bowring should be made a Companion of the Bath. Both those things will be done accordingly. But there are also three other persons, whose names I have for some time wished to submit to your Majesty for the dignity of Baronet; and, if your Majesty should be graciously pleased to approve of them, the list would stand as follows: Mr. Dilke (THE QUEEN *bows her assent*), Mr. William Browne, of Liverpool.

THE QUEEN Who is he?

LORD PALMERSTON A very wealthy and distinguished merchant, Ma'am, who has lately made a magnificent present of a Public Library to his fellow-citizens. . . . Mr. Thomas David Lloyd, a well-known and respectable gentleman of high standing, in the County of Carnarvon; and Mr. Matthew Rich, to whom the Government is under great obligation for political services—he having vacated his seat for Richmond, Yorkshire, to enable your Majesty's Solicitor-General to be elected in his place.

THE QUEEN Have they all sufficient means, Lord Palmerston, to support the dignity in a becoming manner?

LORD PALMERSTON Oh, yes, your Majesty; they are all men of wealth—great wealth, most of them.

THE QUEEN Then WE approve.

LORD PALMERSTON I thank your Majesty.

THE QUEEN Is there anything else?

LORD PALMERSTON Nothing, Ma'am, that cannot conveniently wait for a later occasion.

THE QUEEN (*rising*) Very well, Lord Palmerston. Then, for the present, that will do.

LORD PALMERSTON May I, with your Majesty's gracious permission, be allowed, before I withdraw, to express a fervent hope that the intensity of your Majesty's grief may not lead your Majesty to neglect the preservation of your health, which is so necessary for the care and welfare of your Majesty's Children, and hardly less for that of your Majesty's devotedly attached and affectionate subjects, of whom, Ma'am, I am ever one.

THE QUEEN Thank you, Lord Palmerston. I am keeping quite well. Good-bye.

> (THE QUEEN *inclines her head, but does not offer her hand.* LORD PALMERSTON *bows and retires.* THE QUEEN *sits down again, and with her eyes fixed upon the portrait, speaks.*)

Oh, Albert! Albert! Albert! Why did you leave me? How can I bear to go on living, and doing all this—*alone*!

The Queen: God Bless Her!

The Queen: God Bless Her!

1877

A Scene from Home-Life in the Highlands

The august Lady is sitting in a garden-tent on the lawn of Balmoral Castle. Her parasol leans beside her. Writing-materials are on the table before her, and a small fan, for it is hot weather; also a dish of peaches. Sunlight suffuses the tent interior, softening the round contours of the face, and caressing pleasantly the small plump hand busy at letter-writing. The even flow of her penmanship is suddenly disturbed; picking up her parasol, she indulgently beats some unseen object, lying concealed against her skirts.

QUEEN No: don't scratch! Naughty! Naughty!

> (*She then picks up a hand-bell, rings it, and continues her writing. Presently a fine figure of a man in Highland costume appears in the tent-door. He waits awhile, then speaks in the strong Doric of his native wilds.*)

MR. J. BROWN Was your Majesty wanting anything, or were you ringing only for the fun?

> (*To this brusque delivery Her Majesty responds with a cosy smile, for the special function of MR. JOHN BROWN is not to be a courtier; and, knowing what is expected of him, he lives up to it.*)

QUEEN Bring another chair, Brown. And take Mop with you: he wants his walk.

MR. J. B. What kind of a chair are you wanting, Ma'am? Is it to put your feet on?

QUEEN No, no. It is to put a visitor on. Choose a nice one with a lean-back.

MR. J. B. With a lean back? Ho! Ye mean one that you can lean back in. What talk folk will bring with them from up south, to be sure! Yes, I'll get it for ye, Ma'am. Come, Mop, be a braw little wee mon, and tak' your walk!

> (*And while his Royal Mistress resumes her writing, taking Mop by his 'lead,' he prepares for departure.*)

Have ye seen the paper this morning yet? Ma'am.

> (*The address of respect is thrown in by way of afterthought, or, as it were, reluctantly. Having to be in character, his way is to tread heavily on the border-line which divides familiarity from respect.*)

QUEEN Not yet.

MR. J. B. (*departing*) I'll bring it for ye, now.

QUEEN You had better send it.

J. B. (*turning about*) What did ye say? . . . Ma'am.

QUEEN 'Send it,' Brown, I said. Mop mustn't be hurried. Take him round by the stables.

> (*He goes: and* THE QUEEN, *with a soft, indulgent smile, that slowly flickers out as the labour of composition proceeds, resumes her writing.*)

336

(Presently enters a liveried FOOTMAN, *who stands at attention with the paper upon a salver. Touching the table at her side as an indication,* THE QUEEN *continues to write. With gingerly reverence the man lays down the paper and goes. Twice she looks at it before taking it up; then she unfolds it; then lays it down, and takes out her glasses; then begins reading. Evidently she comes on something she does not like; she pats the table impatiently, then exclaims:*

Most extraordinary!

(A wasp settles on the peaches.)

And I wish one could kill all wicked pests as easily as you.

(She makes a dab with the paper-knife, the wasp escapes.)

Most extraordinary!

(Relinquishing the pursuit of wasps, she resumes her reading.)

(In a little while MR. JOHN BROWN *returns, both hands occupied. The chair he deposits by the tent door, and hitches Mop's 'lead' to the back of that on which* THE QUEEN *is sitting. With the small beginnings of a smile she lowers the paper, and looks at him and his accompaniments.)*

QUEEN Well, Brown? Oh, yes; that's quite a nice one. . . . I'm sure there's a wasps' nest somewhere; there are so many of them about.

J. B. Eh, don't fash yourself! Wasps have a way of being aboot this time of year. It's the fruit they're after.

337

QUEEN Yes: like Adam and Eve.

J. B. That's just it, Ma'am.

QUEEN You'd better take it away, Brown, or cover it; it's too tempting.

J. B. (*removing the fruit*) Ah! Now if God had only done that, maybe we'd still all be running aboot naked.

QUEEN I'm glad He didn't, then.

J. B. Ye're right, Ma'am.

QUEEN The Fall made the human race decent, even if it did no good otherwise. Brown, I've dropped my glasses.

(*He picks them up and returns them.*)

QUEEN Thank you, Brown.

J. B. So you're expecting a visitor, ye say?

QUEEN Yes. You haven't seen Lord Beaconsfield yet, I suppose?

J. B. Since he was to arrive off the train, you mean, Ma'am? No: he came early. He's in his room.

QUEEN I hope they have given him a comfortable one.

J. B. It's the one I used to have. There's a good spring-bed in it, and a kettle-ring for the whisky.

QUEEN Oh, that's all right, then.

J. B. Will he be staying for long? Ma'am.

QUEEN Only for a week, I'm afraid. Why?

J. B. It's about the shooting I was thinking: whether it was the deer or the grouse he'd want to be after.

QUEEN I don't think Lord Beaconsfield is a sportsman.

338

J. B. I know that, Ma'am, well enough. But there's many who are not sportsmen that think they've got to do it —when they come north of the Tweed.

QUEEN Lord Beaconsfield will not shoot, I'm sure. You remember him, Brown, being here before?

J. B. Eh! Many years ago, that was; he was no but Mr. Disraeli then. But he was the real thing, Ma'am: oh, a nice gentleman.

QUEEN He is always very nice to me.

J. B. I remember now, when he first came, he put a tip into ma hand. And when I let him know the liberty he had taken, 'Well, Mr. Brown,' he said, 'I've made a mistake, but I don't take it back again!'

QUEEN Very nice and sensible.

J. B. And indeed it was, Ma'am. Many a man would never have had the wit to leave well alone by just apologising for it. But there was an understandingness about him, that often you don't find. After that he always talked to me like an equal—just like yourself might do. But Lord, Ma'am, his ignorance, it was surprising!

QUEEN Most extraordinary you should think that, Brown!

J. B. Ah! You haven't talked to him as I have, Ma'am: only about politics, and poetry, and things like that—where, maybe, he knows a bit more than I do (though he didn't know his Burns so well as a man ought that thinks to make laws for Scotland!). But to hear him talking about natural facts, you'd think he was just inventing for to amuse himself! Do you know, Ma'am, he thought stags had white tails like rabbits, and that 'twas only when they wagged them so as to show, that you could shoot them? And he thought that you pulled a salmon out o' the water as soon as you'd hooked him. And he thought that a haggis was made of a sheep's head boiled in whisky. Oh, he's very innocent, Ma'am, if you get him where he's not expecting you.

QUEEN Well, Brown, there are some things you can teach him, I don't doubt; and there are some things he can teach you. I'm sure he has taught me a great deal.

J. B. Ay? It's a credit to ye both, then.

QUEEN He lets me think for myself, Brown; and that's what so many of my Ministers would rather I didn't. They want me to be merely the receptacle of their own opinions. No, Brown, that's what we Stuarts are never going to do!

J. B. Nor would I, Ma'am, if I were in your shoes. But believe me, you can do more, being a mere woman, so to speak, than many a king can do.

QUEEN Yes; being a woman has its advantages, I know.

J. B. For you can get round 'em, Ma'am; and you can put 'em off; and you can make it very awkward for them— very awkward—to have a difference of opinion with you.

QUEEN (*good-humouredly*) You and I have had differences of opinion sometimes, Brown.

J. B. True, Ma'am; that *has* happened; I've known it happen. And I've never regretted it, never! But the difference there is, Ma'am, that I'm not your Prime Minister. Had I been—you'd 'a been more stiff about giving in— naturally! Now there's Mr. Gladstone, Ma'am; I'm not denying he's a great man; but he's got too many ideas for my liking, far too many! I'm not against temperance any more than he is—put in its right place. But he's got that crazy notion of 'local option' in his mind; he's coming to it, gradually. And he doesn't think how giving 'local option' to them that don't take the wide view of things, may do harm to a locality. You must be wide in your views, else you do somebody an injustice.

QUEEN Yes, Brown; and that is why I like being up in the hills, where the views *are* wide.

J. B. I put it this way, Ma'am. You come to a locality, and you find you can't get served as you are accustomed to be served. Well! you don't go there again, and you tell others not to go; and so the place gets a bad name. I've a brother who keeps an inn down at Aberlochy on the coach route, and he tells me that more than half his customers come from outside the locality.

QUEEN Of course; naturally!

J. B. Well now, Ma'am, it'll be bad for the locality to have half the custom that comes to it turned away, because of local option! And believe me, Ma'am, that's what it will come to. People living in it won't see till the shoe pinches them; and by that time my brother, and others like him, will have been ruined in their business.

QUEEN Local option is not going to come yet, Brown.

J. B. (*firmly*) No, Ma'am, not while I vote Conservative, it won't. But I was looking ahead; I was talking about Mr. Gladstone.

QUEEN Mr. Gladstone has retired from politics. At least, he is not going to take office again.

341

·J. B. Don't you believe him, Ma'am. Mr. Gladstone is not a retiring character. He's in to-day's paper again—columns of him; have ye seen?

QUEEN Yes; quite as much as I wish to see.

J. B. And there's something in what he says, I don't deny.

QUEEN There's a great deal in what he says, I don't understand, and that I don't wish to.

J. B. Now you never said a truer thing than that in your life, Ma'am! That's just how I find him. Oh, but he's a great man; and it's wonderful how he appreciates the Scot, and looks up to his opinion.

> (*But this is a line of conversation in which his Royal Mistress declines to be interested. And she is helped, at that moment, by something which really does interest her.*)

QUEEN Brown, how did you come to scratch your leg?

J. B. 'Twas not me, Ma'am; 'twas the stable-cat did that—just now while Mop was having his walk.

QUEEN Poor dear Brown! Did she fly at you?

J. B. Well, 'twas like this, Ma'am; first Mop went for her, then she went for him. And I tell ye she'd have scraped his eyes out if I'd left it to a finish.

QUEEN Ferocious creature! She must be mad.

J. B. Well, Ma'am, I don't know whether a cat-and-dog fight is a case of what God hath joined together;· but it's the hard thing for man to put asunder! And that's the scraping I got for it, when I tried.

342

QUEEN You must have it cauterised, Brown. I won't have you getting hydrophobia.

J. B. You generally get that from dogs.

QUEEN Oh, from cats too; any cat that a mad dog has bitten.

J. B. They do say, Ma'am, that if a mad dog bites you— you have to die barking. So if it's a cat-bite I'm going to die of, you'll hear me mewing the day, maybe.

QUEEN I don't like cats: I never did. Treacherous, deceitful creatures! Now a dog always looks up to you.

J. B. Yes, Ma'am; they are tasteful, attractive animals; and that, maybe, is the reason. They give you a good conceit of yourself, dogs do. You never have to apologise to a dog. Do him an injury—you've only to say you forgive him, and he's friends again.

(Accepting his views with a nodding smile, she resumes her pen, and spreads paper.)

QUEEN Now, Brown, I must get to work again. I have writing to do. See that I'm not disturbed.

J. B. Then when were you wanting to see your visitor, Ma'am? There's his chair waiting.

QUEEN Ah, yes, to be sure. But I didn't want to worry him too soon. What is the time?

J. B. Nearly twelve, Ma'am.

QUEEN Oh! then I think I may. Will you go and tell him: the Queen's compliments, and she would like to see him, now?

343

J. B. I will go and tell him, Ma'am.

QUEEN And then I shan't want you any more—till this afternoon.

J. B. Then I'll just go across and take lunch at home, Ma'am.

QUEEN Yes, do! That will be nice for you. And Brown, mind you have that leg seen to!

> (MR. JOHN BROWN *has started to go, when his step is arrested.*)

J. B. His Lordship is there in the garden, Ma'am, talking to the Princess.

QUEEN What, before he has seen *me*? Go, and take him away from the Princess, and tell him to come here!

J. B. I will, Ma'am.

QUEEN And you had better take Mop with you. Now, dear Brown, do have your poor leg seen to, at once!

J. B. Indeed, and I will, Ma'am. Come, Mop, man! Come and tell his Lordship he's wanted.

> (*Exit* MR. JOHN BROWN, *nicely accompanied by Mop.*)

> (*Left to herself* THE QUEEN *administers a feminine touch or two to dress and cap and hair; then with dignified composure she resumes her writing, and continues to write even when the shadow of her favourite Minister crosses the entrance, and he stands hat in hand before her, flawlessly arrayed in a gay frock suit suggestive of the period when male attire was still not only a fashion, but an art.*)

344

*Despite, however, the studied correctness of his
costume, face and deportment give signs of
haggard fatigue; and when he bows it is the
droop of a weary man, slow in the recovery.
Just at the fitting moment for full acceptance of
his silent salutation, the Royal Lady lays down
her pen.)*

QUEEN Oh, how do you do, my dear Lord Beaconsfield!
Good morning; and welcome to Balmoral.

LORD B. *(as he kisses the hand extended to him)* That
word from your Majesty brings all its charms to life!
What a prospect of beauty I see around me!

QUEEN You arrived early? I hope you are sufficiently
rested.

LORD B. Refreshed, Madam; rest will come later.

QUEEN You have had a long, tiring journey, I fear.

LORD B. It was long, Madam.

QUEEN I hope that you slept upon the train?

LORD B. I lay upon it, Ma'am. That is all I can say
truly.

QUEEN Oh, I'm sorry!

LORD B. There were compensations, Ma'am. In my
vigil I was able to look forward—to that which is now
before me. The morning is beautiful! May I be permitted to inquire if your Majesty's health has benefited?

QUEEN I'm feeling 'bonnie,' as we say in Scotland. Life
out of doors suits me.

345

LORD B. Ah! This tent light is charming! Then my eyes had not deceived me; your Majesty is already more than better. The tempered sunlight, so tender in its reflections, gives—an interior, one may say—of almost floral delicacy; making these canvas walls like the white petals of an enfolding flower.

QUEEN Are you writing another of your novels, Lord Beaconsfield? That sounds like composition.

LORD B. Believe me, Madam, only an impromptu.

QUEEN Now, my dear Lord, pray sit down! I had that chair specially brought for you. Generally I sit here quite alone.

LORD B. Such kind forethought, Madam, overwhelms me! Words are inadequate. I accept, gratefully, the repose you offer me.

> (*He sinks into the chair, and sits motionless and mute, in a weariness that is not the less genuine because it provides an effect. But from one seated in the Royal Presence much is expected; and so it is in a tone of sprightly expectancy that his Royal Mistress now prompts him to his task of entertaining her.*)

QUEEN Well? And how is everything?

LORD B. (*rousing himself with an effort*) Oh! Pardon! Your Majesty would have me speak on politics, and affairs of State? I was rapt away for the moment.

QUEEN Do not be in any hurry, dear Prime Minister.

LORD B. Ah! That word from an indulgent Mistress spurs me freshly to my task. But, Madam, there is almost

346

nothing to tell: politics, like the rest of us, have been taking holiday.

QUEEN I thought that Mr. Gladstone has been speaking.

LORD B. (*with an airy flourish of courtly disdain*) Oh, yes! He has been—speaking.

QUEEN In Edinburgh, quite lately.

LORD B. And in more other places than I can count. Speaking—speaking—speaking. But I have to confess, Madam, that I have not read his speeches. They are composed for brains which can find more leisure than yours, Madam—or mine.

QUEEN I have read some of them.

LORD B. Your Majesty does him great honour—and yourself some inconvenience, I fear. Those speeches, so great a strain to understand, or even to listen to—my hard duty for now some forty years—are a far greater strain to read.

QUEEN They annoy me intensely. I have no patience with him!

LORD B. Pardon me, Madam; if you have read *one* of his speeches, your patience has been extraordinary.

QUEEN Can't you stop it?

LORD B. Stop?—stop what, Madam? Niagara, the Flood? That which has no beginning, no limit, has also no end: till, by the operation of nature, it runs dry.

QUEEN But, surely, he should be stopped when he speaks on matters which may, any day, bring us into war!

347

LORD B. Then he would be stopped. When the British nation goes to war, Madam, it ceases to listen to reason. Then it is only the beating of its own great heart that it hears: to that goes the marching of its armies, with victory as the one goal. Then, Madam, above reason rises instinct. Against that he will be powerless.

QUEEN You think so?

LORD B. I am sure, Madam. If we are drawn into war, his opposition becomes futile. If we are not: well, if we are not, it will not be his doing that we escape that—dire necessity.

QUEEN But you *do* think it necessary, don't you?

> (*To the Sovereign's impetuous eagerness, so creditable to her heart, he replies with the oracular solemnity by which caution can be sublimated.*)

LORD B. I hope it may not be, Madam. We must all say that—up till the last moment. It is the only thing we *can* say, to testify the pacifity of our intention when challenged by other Powers.

QUEEN (*touching the newspaper*) This morning's news isn't good, I'm afraid. The Russians are getting nearer to Constantinople.

LORD B. They will never enter it, Madam.

QUEEN No, they mustn't! We will not allow it.

LORD B. That, precisely, is the policy of your Majesty's Government. Russia knows that we shall not allow it; she knows that it will never be. Nevertheless, we may have to make a demonstration.

348

QUEEN Do you propose to summon Parliament?

LORD B. Not Parliament; no, Madam. Your Majesty's Fleet will be sufficient.

> (*This lights a spark; and the royal mind darts into strategy.*)

QUEEN If I had my way, Lord Beaconsfield, my Fleet would be in the Baltic to-morrow; and before another week was over, Petersburg would be under bombardment.

LORD B. (*considerately providing this castle in the air with its necessary foundations*) And Cronstadt would have fallen.

QUEEN (*puzzled for a moment at this naming of a place which had not entered her calculations*) Cronstadt? Why Cronstadt?

LORD B. Merely preliminary, Madam. When that fortified suburb has crumbled—the rest will be easy.

QUEEN Yes! And what a good lesson it will teach them! The Crimea wasn't enough for them, I suppose.

LORD B. The Crimea! Ah, what memories—of heroism—that word evokes! 'Magnificent, but not war!'

QUEEN Oh! There is one thing, Lord Beaconsfield, on which I want your advice.

LORD B. Always at your Majesty's disposal.

QUEEN I wish to confer upon the Sultan of Turkey my Order of the Garter.

LORD B. Ah! how generous, how generous an instinct! How like you, Madam, to wish it!

349

QUEEN What I want to know is, whether, as Prime Minister, you have any objection?

LORD B. 'As Prime Minister.' How hard that makes it for me to answer! How willingly would I say 'None'! How reluctantly, on the contrary, I have to say, 'It had better wait.'

QUEEN Wait? Wait till when? I want to do it *now*.

LORD B. Yes, so do I. But can you risk, Madam, conferring that most illustrious symbol of honour, and chivalry, and power, on a defeated monarch? Your royal prestige, Ma'am, must be considered. Great and generous hearts need, more than most, to take prudence into their counsels.

QUEEN But do you think, Lord Beaconsfield, that the Turks are going to be beaten?

LORD B. The Turks *are* beaten, Madam. . . . But England will never be beaten. We shall dictate terms—moderating the demands of Russia; and under your Majesty's protection the throne of the Kaliphat will be safe—once more. That, Madam, is the key to our Eastern policy: a grateful Kaliphat, claiming allegiance from the whole Mohammedan world, bound to us by instincts of self-preservation—and we hold henceforth the gorgeous East in fee with redoubled security. His power may be a declining power; but ours remains. Some day, who knows? Egypt, possibly even Syria, Arabia, may be our destined reward.

> (*Like a cat over a bowl of cream, England's Majesty sits lapping all this up. But, when he has done, her commentary is shrewd and to the point.*)

350

QUEEN The French won't like that!

LORD B. They won't, Madam, they won't. But has it ever been England's policy, Madam, to mind what the French don't like?

QUEEN (*with relish*) No, it never has been, has it? Ah! you are the true statesman, Lord Beaconsfield. Mr. Gladstone never talked to me like that.

LORD B. (*courteously surprised at what does not at all surprise him*) No? . . . You must have had interesting conversations with him, Madam, in the past.

QUEEN (*very emphatically*) I have never once had a conversation with Mr. Gladstone, in all my life, Lord Beaconsfield. He used to talk to me as if I were a public meeting— and one that agreed with him, too!

LORD B. Was there, then, any applause, Madam?

QUEEN No, indeed! I was too shy to say what I thought. I used to cough sometimes.

LORD B. Rather like coughing at a balloon, I fear. I have always admired his flights—regarded as a mere *tour de force*—so buoyant, so sustained, so incalculable! But, as they never touch earth to any serviceable end, that I could discover—of what use are they? Yet if there is one man who has helped me in my career—to whom, therefore, I should owe gratitude—it is he.

QUEEN Indeed? Now that does surprise me! Tell me, Lord Beaconsfield, how has he ever helped you?

LORD B. In our party system, Madam, we live by the mistakes of our opponents. The balance of the popular

351

verdict swings ever this way and that, relegating us either to victory or defeat, to office or to opposition. Many times have I trodden the road to power, or passed from it again, over ruins the origin of which I could recognise either as my own work or that of another; and most of all has it been over the disappointments, the disaffections, the disgusts, the disillusionments—chiefly among his own party—which my great opponent has left me to profit by. I have gained experience from what he has been morally blind to; what he has lacked in understanding of human nature he has left for me to discover. Only to-day I learn that he has been in the habit of addressing—as you, Madam, so wittily phrased it—of addressing, 'as though she were a public meeting,' that Royal Mistress, whom it has ever been my most difficult task not to address sometimes as the most charming, the most accomplished, and the most fascinating woman of the epoch which bears her name. (*He pauses, then resumes.*) How strange a fatality directs the fate of each one of us! How fortunate is he who knows the limits that destiny assigns to him: limits beyond which no word must be uttered.

> (*His oratorical flight, so buoyant and sustained, having come to its calculated end, he drops deftly to earth, encountering directly for the first time the flattered smile with which the Queen has listened to him.*)

Madam, your kind silence reminds me, in the gentlest, the most considerate way possible, that I am not here to relieve the tedium of a life made lonely by a bereavement equal to your own, in conversation however beguiling, or in quest of a sympathy of which, I dare to say, I feel assured. For, in a sense, it is as to a public assembly, or

352

rather as to a great institution, immemorially venerable and august that I have to address myself when, obedient to your summons, I come to be consulted as your Majesty's First Minister of State. If, therefore, your royal mind have any inquiries, any further commands to lay upon me, I am here, Madam, to give effect to them in so far as I can.

> *(This time he has really finished, but with so artful an abbreviation at the point where her interest has been roused that the Queen would fain have him go on. And so the conversation continues to flow along intimate channels.)*

QUEEN No, dear Lord Beaconsfield, not to-day! Those official matters can wait. After you have said so much, and said it so beautifully, I would rather still talk with you as a friend. Of friends you and I have not many; those who make up our world, for the most part, we have to keep at a distance. But while I have many near relatives, children and descendants, I remember that you have none. So your case is the harder.

LORD B. Ah, no, Madam, indeed! I have my children— descendants who will live after me, I trust—in those policies which, for the welfare of my beloved country, I confide to the care of a Sovereign whom I revere and love. . . . I am not unhappy in my life, Madam; far less in my fortune; only, as age creeps on, I find myself so lonely, so solitary, that sometimes I have doubt whether I am really alive, or whether the voice, with which now and then I seek to reassure myself, be not the voice of a dead man.

QUEEN (*almost tearfully*) No, no, my dear Lord Beaconsfield, you mustn't say that!

353

LORD B. *(gallantly)* I won't say anything, Madam, that you forbid, or that you dislike. You invited me to speak to you as a friend; so I have done, so I do. I apologise that I have allowed sadness, even for a moment, to trouble the harmony—the sweetness—of our conversation.

QUEEN Pray, do not apologise! It has been a very great privilege; I beg that you will go on! Tell me—you spoke of bereavement—I wish you would tell me more—about your wife.

(*The sudden request touches some latent chord; and it is with genuine emotion that he answers.*)

LORD B. Ah! My wife! To her I owed everything.

QUEEN She was devoted to you, wasn't she?

LORD B. I never read the depth of her devotion—till after her death. Then, Madam—this I have told to nobody but yourself—then I found among her papers— addressed 'to my dear husband'—a message, written only a few days before her death, with a hand shaken by that nerve-racking and fatal malady which she endured so patiently—begging me to marry again.

(THE QUEEN *is now really crying, and finds speech difficult.*)

QUEEN And you, you—? Dear Lord Beaconsfield; did you mean—had you ever meant—?

LORD B. I did not then, Madam; nor have I ever done so since. It is enough if I allow myself—to love.

QUEEN Oh, yes, yes; I understand—better than others would. For that has always been my own feeling.

354

LORD B. In the history of my race, Madam, there has been a great tradition of faithfulness between husbands and wives. For the hardness of our hearts, we are told, Moses permitted us to give a writing of divorcement. But we have seldom acted on it. In my youth I became a Christian; I married a Christian. But that was no reason for me to desert the nobler traditions of my race—for they are in the blood and in the heart. When my wife died I had no thought to marry again; and when I came upon that tender wish, still I had no thought for it; my mind would not change. Circumstances that have happened since have sealed irrevocably my resolution—never to marry again.

QUEEN Oh, I think that is so wise, so right, so noble of you!

> (*The old Statesman rises, pauses, appears to hesitate, then in a voice charged with emotion says*)

LORD B. Madam, will you permit me to kiss your hand!

> (*The hand graciously given, and the kiss fervently implanted, he falls back once more to a respectful distance. But the emotional excitement of the interview has told upon him, and it is in a wavering voice of weariness that he now speaks.*)

LORD B. You have been very forbearing with me, Madam, not to indicate that I have outstayed either my welcome or your powers of endurance. Yet so much conversation must necessarily have tired you. May I then crave permission, Madam, to withdraw? For, to speak truly, I do need some rest.

QUEEN Yes, my dear friend, go and rest yourself! But before you go, will you not wait, and take a glass of wine with me?

355

(He bows, and she rings.)

And there is just one other thing I wish to say before we part.

LORD B. Speak, Madam, for thy servant heareth.

(The other SERVANT *is now also standing to attention, awaiting orders.)*

QUEEN Bring some wine.

(The ATTENDANT *goes.)*

That Order of the Garter which I had intended to confer upon the Sultan—have you, as Prime Minister, any objection if I bestow it nearer home, on one to whom personally—I cannot say more—on yourself, I mean.

(At that pronouncement of the royal favour the Minister stands, exhausted of energy, in an attitude of drooping humility. The eloquent silence is broken presently by THE QUEEN.*)*

QUEEN Dear Lord Beaconsfield, I want your answer.

LORD B. Oh, Madam! What adequate answer can these poor lips make to so magnificent an offer? Yet answer I must. We have spoken together briefly to-day of our policies in the Near East. Madam, let me come to you again when I have saved Constantinople, and secured once more upon a firm basis the peace of Europe. Then ask me again whether I have any objection, and I will own— 'I have none!'

(Re-enters ATTENDANT. *He deposits a tray with decanter and glasses, and retires again.)*

QUEEN Very well, Lord Beaconsfield. And if you do not remind me, I shall remind you. (*She points to the tray.*) Pray, help yourself!

(*He takes up the decanter.*)

LORD B. I serve you, Madam?

QUEEN Thank you.

(*He fills the two glasses; presents hers to* THE QUEEN, *and takes up his own.*)

LORD B. May I propose for myself—a toast, Madam?

(THE QUEEN *sees what is coming, and bows graciously.*)

LORD B. The Queen! God bless her!

(*He drains the glass, then breaks it against the pole of the tent, and throws away the stem.*)

An old custom, Madam, observed by loyal defenders of the House of Stuart, so that no lesser health might ever be drunk from the same glass. To my old hand came a sudden access of youthful enthusiasm—an ardour which I could not restrain. Your pardon, Madam!

QUEEN (*very gently*) Go and lie down, Lord Beaconsfield; you need rest.

LORD B. Adieu, Madam.

QUEEN Draw your curtains, and sleep well!

(*For a moment he stands gazing at her with a look of deep emotion; he tries to speak. Ordinary words seem to fail; he falters into poetry.*)

357

'When pain and anguish wring the brow,
A ministering Angel, thou!'

(*It has been beautifully said, they both feel. Silent
and slow, with head reverentially bowed, he
backs from the Presence.*)

(THE QUEEN *sits and looks after the retreating
figure, then at the broken fragments of glass.
She takes up the hand-bell and rings. The*
ATTENDANT *enters.*)

QUEEN Pick up that broken glass.

(*The* ATTENDANT *collects it on the hand-tray which
he carries.*)

Bring it to me! . . . Leave it!

(*The* ATTENDANT *deposits the tray before her, and
goes. Gently* THE QUEEN *handles the broken
pieces. Then in a voice of tearful emotion she
speaks.*)

Such devotion! Most extraordinary! Oh! Albert!
Albert!

(*And in the sixteenth year of her widowhood and the
fortieth of her reign, the Royal Lady bends her
head over the fragments of broken glass, and
weeps happy tears.*)

CURTAIN

His Favourite Flower

His Favourite Flower

1881

A Political Myth Explained

LORD BEACONSFIELD *has not been at all well. He is sitting up in his room, and his doctor has come to see him for the third time in three days. This means that the malady is not yet seriously regarded: once a day is still sufficient. Nevertheless, he is a woeful wreck to look at; and the doctor looks at him with the greatest respect, and listens to his querulous plaint patiently. For that great dome of silence, his brain, repository of so many State-secrets, is still a redoubtable instrument: its wit and its magician's cunning have not yet lapsed into the dull inane of senile decay. Though fallen from power, after a bad beating at the polls, there is no knowing but that he may rise again, and hold once more in those tired old hands, shiney with rheumatic gout, and now twitching feebly under the discomfort of a super-imposed malady, the reins of democratic and imperial power. The dark, cavernous eyes still wear their look of accumulated wisdom, a touch also of visionary fire. The sparse locks, dyed to a raven black, set off with their uncanny sheen the clay-like pallor of the face. He sits in a high-backed chair, wrapped in an oriental dressing-gown, his muffled feet resting on a large hot-water bottle; and the eminent physician, preparatory to taking a seat at his side, bends solicitously over him.*

361

DOCTOR Well, my dear Lord, how are you to-day? Better? You look better.

BEACONSFIELD Yes, I suppose I am better. But my sleep isn't what it ought to be. I have had a dream, Doctor; and it has upset me.

DOCTOR A dream?

BEACONSFIELD You wonder that I should mention it? Of course, I—I don't believe in dreams. Yet they indicate, sometimes—do they not—? certain disorders of the mind.

DOCTOR Generally of the stomach.

BEACONSFIELD Ah! The same thing, Doctor. There's no getting away from that in one's old age; when one has lived as well as I have.

DOCTOR That is why I dieted you.

BEACONSFIELD Oh, I have nothing on my conscience as to that. My housekeeper is a dragon. Her fidelity is of the kind that will even risk dismissal.

DOCTOR An invaluable person, under the circumstances.

BEACONSFIELD Yes; a nuisance, but indispensable. No, Doctor. This dream didn't come from the stomach. It seemed rather to emanate from that outer darkness which surrounds man's destiny. So real, so horribly real!

DOCTOR. Better, then, not to brood on it.

BEACONSFIELD Ah! Could I explain it, then I might get rid of it. In the ancient religion of my race dreams found their interpretation. But have they any?

DOCTOR Medical science is beginning to say 'Yes'; that in sleep the subconscious mind has its reactions.

362

BEACONSFIELD Well, I wonder how my 'subconscious mind' got hold of primroses.

DOCTOR. Primroses? Did they form a feature in your dream?

BEACONSFIELD A feature? No. The whole place was alive with them! As the victim of inebriety sees snakes, I saw primroses. They were everywhere: they fawned on me in wreaths and festoons; swarmed over me like parasites; flew at me like flies; till it seemed that the whole world had conspired to suffocate me under a sulphurous canopy of those detestable little atoms. Can you imagine the horror of it, Doctor, to a sane—a hitherto sane mind like mine?

DOCTOR Oh! In a dream any figment may excite aversion.

BEACONSFIELD This wasn't like a dream. It was rather the threat of some new disease, some brain malady about to descend on me: possibly delirium tremens. I have not been of abstemious habits, Doctor. Suppose—?

DOCTOR Impossible! Dismiss altogether that supposition from your mind!

BEACONSFIELD Well, Doctor, I hope—I hope you may be right. For I assure you that the horror I then conceived for those pale botanical specimens in their pestiferous and increscent abundance, exceeded what words can describe. I have felt spiritually devastated ever since, as though some vast calamity were about to fall not only on my own intellect, but on that of my country. Well, you shall hear.

363

(He draws his trembling hands wearily over his face, and sits thinking a while.)

With all the harsh abruptness of a soul launched into eternity by the jerk of the hangman's rope, so I found myself precipitated into the midst of this dream. I was standing on a pillory, set up in Parliament Square, facing the Abbey. I could see the hands of St. Margaret's clock pointing to half-past eleven; and away to the left the roof of Westminster Hall undergoing restoration. Details, Doctor, which gave a curious reality to a scene otherwise fantastic, unbelievable. There I stood in a pillory, raised up from earth; and a great crowd had gathered to look at me. I can only describe it as a primrose-crowd. The disease infected all, but not so badly as it did me. The yellow contagion spread everywhere; from all the streets around, the botanical deluge continued to flow in upon me. I felt a pressure at my back; a man had placed a ladder against it; he mounted and hung a large wreath of primroses about my neck. The sniggering crowd applauded the indignity. Having placed a smaller wreath upon my head, he descended. . . . A mockery of a May Queen, there I stood!

DOCTOR *(laying a soothing hand on him)* A dream, my dear Lord, only a dream.

BEACONSFIELD Doctor, imagine my feelings! My sense of ridicule was keen; but keener my sense of the injustice— not to be allowed to know *why* the whole world was thus making mock of me. For this was in the nature of a public celebration, its malignity was organised and national; a new fifth of November had been sprung upon the calendar. Around me I saw the emblematic watchword of the great

364

party I had once led to triumph: 'Imperium et Libertas,' 'Peace with Honour,' 'England shall reign where'er the sun,' and other mottoes of a like kind; and on them also the floral disease had spread itself. The air grew thick and heavy with its sick-room odour. Doctor, I could have vomited.

DOCTOR Yes, yes; a touch of biliousness, I don't doubt.

BEACONSFIELD With a sudden flash of insight—'This,' I said to myself, ' is my Day of Judgment. Here I stand, judged by my fellow-countrymen, for the failures and shortcomings of my political career. The good intentions with which my path was strewn are now turned to my reproach. But why do they take this particular form? Why—why primroses?'

DOCTOR 'The primrose way' possibly?

BEACONSFIELD Ah! That occurred to me. But has it, indeed, been a primrose way that I have trodden so long and so painfully? I think not. I cannot so accuse myself. But suppose the Day of Judgment which Fate reserves for us were fundamentally this: the appraisement of one's life and character—not by the all-seeing Eye of Heaven (before which I would bow) but by the vindictively unjust verdict of the people one has tried to serve—the judgment not of God, but of public opinion. That is a judgment of which all who strive for power must admit the relevancy!

DOCTOR You distress yourself unnecessarily, dear Lord. Your reputation is safe from detraction now.

BEACONSFIELD With urgency I set my mind to meet the charge. If I could understand the meaning of that yellow visitation, then I should no longer have to fear that I was going mad!

(*At this point the door is discreetly opened, and the* HOUSEKEEPER, *mild, benign, but inflexible, enters, carrying a cup and toast-rack upon a tray.*)

HOUSEKEEPER I beg pardon, my Lord; but I think your Lordship ought to have your beef-tea now.

BEACONSFIELD Yes, yes, Mrs. Manson; come in.

DOCTOR You are right, Mrs. Manson; he ought.

HOUSEKEEPER (*placing the tray on a small stand*) Where will you have it, my Lord?

BEACONSFIELD In my inside, Mrs. Manson—presently —he, he!

DOCTOR Now, let me take your pulse. . . . Yes, yes. Pretty good, you know.

(MRS. MANSON *stands respectfully at attention with interrogation in her eye.*)

BEACONSFIELD. Yes, you may bring me my cap now. (*Then to the* DOCTOR.) I generally sleep after this.

(MRS. MANSON *brings a large tasselled fez of brilliant colour, and adjusts it to his head while he drinks. She then goes to the door, takes a hot-water bottle from the hands of an unseen servant and effects the necessary changes. All this is done so unobstrusively that* BEACONSFIELD *resumes his theme without regarding her. When she has done she goes.*)

Ah! Where was I?

DOCTOR If you 'could understand,' you said.

366

BEACONSFIELD Ah, yes; understand. Again a strange faculty of divination came upon me. I stood upon the international plane, amid a congress of Powers, and let my eye travel once more over the Alliances of Europe. I looked, Doctor, and truly I saw, then, surprising shifts and changes in the political and diplomatic fabric which I had helped to frame. Time, and kingdoms had passed. I saw, at home and abroad, the rise of new parties into power, strange coalitions, defections, alliances; old balances destroyed, new balances set up in their place. I saw frontiers annulled, treaties violated, world-problems tumbling like clowns, standing on their heads and crying, 'Here we are again!' Power—after all, had solved nothing!

My eye travelled over that problem of the Near East, which, for some generations at least, we thought to have settled, to Vienna, Petersburg, Constantinople—and away farther East to Teheran and—that other place whose name I have forgotten. And, as I looked, a Recording Angel came, and cried to me in a voice strangely familiar, the voice of one of my most detested colleagues—trusted, I mean—'You have put your money on the wrong horse!'

And I had, Doctor; if what I saw then was true—I had! Yes, if ever man blundered and fooled his countrymen into a false and fatal position—I was that man! It wasn't a question of right or wrong. In politics that doesn't really matter; you decide on a course, and you invent moral reasons for it afterwards. No, what I had done was much worse than any mere wrongdoing. All my political foresight and achievements were a gamble that had gone wrong; and for that my Day of Judgment had come, and I stood in the pillory, a peepshow for mockery. But why for their instrument of torture did they choose primroses? Oh,

I can invent a reason! It was Moses Primrose, cheated of his horse with a gross of green spectacles cased in shagreen. But that was not the reason. For then came new insight, and a fresh humiliation. As I looked more intently I saw that I was *not* being mocked; I was being worshipped, adulated, flattered; I had become a god—for party purposes perhaps—and this was my day, given in my honour for national celebration. And I saw, by the insight given me, that they were praising me *for having put their money on the wrong horse!* Year by year the celebration had gone on, until they had so got into the habit that they could not leave off! All my achievements, all my policies, all my statecraft were in the dust; but the worship of me had become a national habit—so foolish and meaningless, that nothing, nothing but some vast calamity—some great social upheaval, was ever going to stop it.

DOCTOR My dear Lord, it is I who must stop it now. You mustn't go on.

BEACONSFIELD I have done, Doctor. There I have given you the essentials of my dream; material depressing enough for the mind of an old man, enfeebled by indisposition, at the end of a long day's work. But I tell you, Doctor, that nothing therein which stands explainable fills me with such repulsion and aversion as that one thing which I cannot explain—why, why primroses?

DOCTOR A remarkable dream, my Lord; rendered more vivid—or, as you say, 'real'—by your present disturbed state of health. As to that part of it which you find so inexplicable, I can at least point toward where the explanation lies. It reduces itself to this: primroses had become associated for you—in a way which you have forgotten—with something

368

you wished to avoid. And so they became the image or symbol of your aversion; and as such found a place in your dream.

> (*So saying the* DOCTOR *rises and moves toward the window, where his attention suddenly becomes riveted.*)

BEACONSFIELD Perhaps, Doctor, perhaps, as you say, there is some such explanation. But I don't feel like that.

DOCTOR Why, here are primroses! This may be the clue? Where do they come from?

BEACONSFIELD Ah, those! Indeed, I had forgotten them. At least; no, I could not have done that.

DOCTOR There is a written card with them, I see.

BEACONSFIELD Her Gracious Majesty did me the great honour, hearing that I was ill, to send and inquire. Of course, since my removal from office, the opportunity of presenting my personal homage has not been what it used to be. That, I suppose, is as well.

DOCTOR And these are from Her Majesty?

BEACONSFIELD They came yesterday, brought by a special messenger, with a note written by her own hand, saying that she had picked them herself. To so great a condescension I made with all endeavour what return I could. I wrote—a difficult thing for me to do, Doctor, just now—presented my humble duty, my thanks; and said they were my favourite flower.

DOCTOR And were they?

BEACONSFIELD Of course, Doctor, under those circumstances any flower would have been. It just happened to be that.

DOCTOR Well, my lord, there, then, the matter is explained. You *had* primroses upon your mind. The difficulty, the pain even, of writing with your crippled hand, became associated with them. You would have much rather not had to write; and the disinclination, in an exaggerated form, got into your dream. Now that, I hope, mitigates for you the annoyance—the distress of mind.

BEACONSFIELD Yes, yes. It does, as you say, make it more understandable. Bring them to me, Doctor; let me look my enemy in the face.

> (*The* DOCTOR *carries the bowl across, and sets it beside him. Very feebly he reaches out a hand and takes some.*)

My favourite flower. He—he! My favourite flower.

> (*Lassitude overtakes him—his head nods and droops as he speaks.*)

> A primrose by the river's brim
> A yellow primrose was to him,
>   And it was nothing more.

Who was it wrote that?—Byron or Dr. Watts? My memory isn't what it used to be. No matter. It all goes into the account.

My favourite flower!
'For I'm to be Queen of the May, mother, I'm to be Queen of the May!'

> (*The* DOCTOR *takes up his hat, and tiptoes to the door.*)

> Tell me, where is fancy bred,
> Or in the heart or in the head?
> How begot, how nourished?

370

(He breaks, and lets the petals fall one by one.)

(The DOCTOR *goes out.)*

> Let us all ring fancy's knell;
> I'll begin it—Ding-dong bell,
>   Ding-dong, bell.

(He goes to sleep.)

CURTAIN

Religious Difficulties

Religious Difficulties

THE DEAN'S *Study at Windsor is a comfortable room, lined with books. On the writing-table there is no parade of industry; and the chairs are beautifully easy for meditative minds to repose in. It is summer; the French windows are open, and one gets a glimpse of sunlit lawn, garden-path, and flower-border. From the garden comes the sound of tennis-players:* 'Play!' *is cried;* 'Fault!' . . . 'Another fault!' . . . *In through the open window steps a fair maiden, carrying a tennis-racquet of prehistoric design—a survival from the late* "Seventies,' *when lawn-tennis had barely begun, and the racquets were like egg-spoons. She is followed by a youth, not in flannels—for that is not yet the correct thing—he also carries a racquet.*

SHE This isn't the room! There are no strawberry-ices here.

HE Does it matter? Who wants a strawberry-ice? I want *you*! Come and sit down; and let's just talk!

SHE Nonsense! Don't be silly! This isn't the place, or the time for it. Come back at once! There's the Dean playing: and it's such fun watching him. We always try to make him win; but it's so difficult.

HE I don't care whether the Dean wins, or loses!

SHE (*slipping out again*) No; but *I* do.

> (*She has gone; and he goes after her.*

> *Along the path outside stroll two Ladies with raised parasols, in quiet conversation. An inner door opens, and with elaborate respect an elderly* MAN-SERVANT *bows into the room a Lady whose face everybody knows. But here, in such private surroundings, coming so unexpectedly, it takes a little time to recognise her. Only the wonderful way in which that figure of ample breadth, but diminutive stature, moves across the room assures us that it is* THE QUEEN *herself.*)

THE QUEEN What is going on here to-day?

MAN-SERVANT A garden-party, your Majesty.

THE QUEEN Then you must see the Dean alone, and tell him *privately* that I am here.

MAN-SERVANT Yes, your Majesty.

> (*And bowing to her back, he goes.*)

THE QUEEN And before you go, you had better close that window.

> (*But the order has come too late to be attended to; and* THE QUEEN, *finding herself alone, does not close it herself, but takes a seat a little away from it, with her face turned from the light. Thus, in her widow's weeds, she gives a sad finish to the quiet interior; and one of the guests, an* ELDERLY GENTLEMAN *in a white*

376

*waistcoat, strolling past the window with his
Wife, looks in, and sees her.)*

ELDERLY GENTLEMAN There's someone there, my
dear:—looking rather lonely, and out of it. Poor thing!
I think I'll just go in, and speak to her.

> *(And in he goes, while his Wife strolls on. Very
> affable, and pleased with himself, he advances,
> rubbing his hands; and in a kind, ingratiating
> tone he opens conversation.)*

I *think* I know the face?

> *(Does he? It gives him a haughty stare, then turns
> away, while his milk of human kindness con-
> tinues its inappropriate flow.)*

Such nice weather! So fortunate! All the young people
enjoying themselves.

> *(And then the door opens, and* THE DEAN *enters
> hurriedly.)*

THE DEAN Oh, your Majesty! I am so sorry to have
kept your Majesty waiting!

THE QUEEN Mr. Dean, send that man away!

> *(But there is no need. Like a worm with a broken
> spine, the Intruder collapses out of the room, to
> spend the rest of that nice day in abject explana-
> tion of the appalling mistake he has made. And
> though he himself will take many days to
> recover from it, it gives the garden-party an
> added success; the Guests are enormously
> pleased to know that* THE QUEEN *is there.
> Meanwhile* THE DEAN *is bestowing his
> sympathy where it is less needed.)*

377

THE DEAN Really, your Majesty, I am most sorry!—*most* sorry! Very unfortunate!

THE QUEEN Please do not apologise. It was my fault—not sending you word beforehand. I seem to have come on a wrong day.

THE DEAN Oh, no, your Majesty, not at all! Quite the reverse. Your Majesty's arrival gave me a respite for which I am truly grateful. I had foolishly let myself be persuaded to a game of tennis: which—at my age—

THE QUEEN Yes, indeed; very rash! *I* don't play tennis; I never did. Even croquet is now rather beyond me. You see, it doesn't do for the Queen always to be beaten; and when that happened, I left off.

THE DEAN I am sure your Majesty's decision was a wise one.

THE QUEEN Yes; but I can't always decide things as easily as that for myself. There are some things which I have to admit are quite beyond me.

THE DEAN Indeed, Ma'am, I should hardly have thought so.

THE QUEEN Oh, yes. And it is about something of that kind that I have come now. I want to consult you on a matter over which I am in real difficulty—

THE DEAN I feel truly honoured, Ma'am.

THE QUEEN It is on a matter of *faith*.

> (*At once* THE DEAN'S *manner undergoes a spiritual change: the correct sort of change, which (as one having authority) he feels to be expected of him.*)

378

THE DEAN Over any such matter as *that*, your Majesty has my deepest, my most earnest attention—and sympathy.

THE QUEEN I think, then, you had better close the window—

THE DEAN Ah, yes; I will, I will.

(*He does so.*)

THE QUEEN (*continuing*)—so that we can feel quite safe.

> (*As a further proof of sympathetic feeling, he lets down the blind.*)

Thank you. That will do nicely.

> (THE DEAN *is now all attention, in an atmosphere better suited to a consideration of religious difficulties than that afforded by an outlook on garden-party gaiety; and* THE QUEEN *begins.*)

THE QUEEN When I was in Scotland recently, I listened to a sermon from Dr. Donald Macleod, one of my Presbyterian Chaplains—with most of which I entirely agreed. But there was one part about which I felt a certain difficulty. He said that, as faithful Christians, we were bound to accept, without question, the story of Jonah and the Whale. Mr. Dean, is it really necessary that I should believe that Jonah *was* swallowed by a Whale?

THE DEAN (*ponderingly*) The question is a difficult one, Ma'am.

THE QUEEN Yes; that is why I ask it.

THE DEAN Difficult, I mean, to answer in a few words. There are, in fact—and that is what makes it difficult—*two* answers to the question.

379

THE QUEEN *Two* answers? It must be yes, *or* no.

THE DEAN It is yes, *and* no, Ma'am.

THE QUEEN That seems to me very puzzling, Mr. Dean.

THE DEAN I will endeavour to explain, Ma'am.

THE QUEEN Then do, please, sit down: for this may take a long time.

(THE DEAN *bows himself to a chair.*)

THE DEAN I was about to say, Ma'am, that we can have no doubt, since the story is given a very significant application in the New Testament—

THE QUEEN Yes; *that* was my trouble.

THE DEAN —that it was actually written under Divine inspiration, for our guidance and instruction. As an illustrative symbol of the great central Truth of our Christian Faith, it has a sanctity and a significance which cannot be denied. Nor, I think, ought we to say it could not *possibly* be also true literally, since with God all things *are* possible. And though, ordinarily speaking, there are biological difficulties, about which the scientists inform us—still, we must guard ourselves from saying that it was *impossible* for the Creator to 'provide'—for that is the word used—to provide a great fish fully capable of swallowing Jonah—had it been necessary.

THE QUEEN (*insistently*) But do you think that He *did*?

THE DEAN (*guardedly*) No, Ma'am, upon the whole, I do not think so.

THE QUEEN Neither do I!

THE DEAN But I also think He *could* have done so: which being granted—and we must faithfully grant it—
380

then, I think, we are quite free to believe that the story was used by our Lord merely for its illustrative value:—Here was something which all His hearers knew and believed, on high Scriptural authority; and He used it to tell them of a greater wonder yet to come, about which we ourselves can have no doubt whatever. Theologically speaking, therefore, we must accept the story as both possible, and—in its doctrinal significance—*true*; though, biologically, we are free to think that God did *not* find it actually necessary for Jonah to be swallowed by a whale, or by any other form of fish.

THE QUEEN Then, to my mind, that settles it.

THE DEAN We have also to remember, Ma'am, that metaphor and other figures of speech, are frequently used in Holy Scripture—in the Old and the New Testament alike. So I do not think that your Majesty's mind need be troubled over what may, after all, have only been a very striking example of poetical imagery, divinely chosen to enforce the great truth that with God all things are possible. Does that, Ma'am, meet your Majesty's difficulty; or does any other point still—?

THE QUEEN No, Mr. Dean, you have now quite satisfied me; and I am so much obliged to you. It was, as you say, a very difficult question; and you have lifted a great weight off my mind. . . . I do not usually discuss matters of this kind with *anybody*. Even to my dear Husband, the Prince, I seldom mentioned them; for I was aware that in his great mind—too deep for my understanding—he held theological views with which he did not wish to trouble me—for fear we might not agree. He was so considerate always!

THE DEAN He was, indeed, Ma'am.

THE QUEEN Had he been here still, I should have asked *him*. As it was, I first wrote to Sir Henry Ponsonby, who was away at the time, and whom, in smaller matters, I always find so helpful. It was he who advised me to come to you, as I have now done.

THE DEAN I am very glad, and most honoured that your Majesty did so.

THE QUEEN Yes; religion is sometimes very puzzling, is it not?

THE DEAN It has that quality, Ma'am; but the difficulties have their value. We should not wish them altogether away.

THE QUEEN Yet I always want to know more—about the next world, I mean.

THE DEAN That, Ma'am, is understandable—especially under the shadow of such a bereavement as your own. Life is a great mystery.

THE QUEEN But not so great a mystery as death.

THE DEAN No, no. Of course to us, here and now, death necessarily seems a terrible and overwhelming event —because life seems to end *with* it. But when we have got beyond it, will it not surely look very different?

THE QUEEN Yes, very different, no doubt: as one looks *down* a hill, after having come up it.

THE DEAN Quite so; and therefore, as one looks back, smaller and less important. If one may compare small things to great—a visit to the dentist provides us with a similar comparison. When one goes to have a tooth out, the ordeal beforehand seems great; but when it *is* out, the ordeal is over.

THE QUEEN Ah, yes! I have only had two teeth out in my life; and that was under gas; so I knew nothing about it.

THE DEAN Your Majesty has, indeed, been fortunate.

THE QUEEN And people, when they are dying, *are* generally unconscious, I believe?

THE DEAN Yes; I suppose that is so. A merciful provision.

THE QUEEN The Prince was so, during his last hours.

THE DEAN Ah, indeed? Yes.

THE QUEEN And that, of course—the added sense of separation while still alive—was a great grief to me.

THE DEAN But to him a blessing.

THE QUEEN I wonder how long the unconsciousness lasts?

THE DEAN After death, Ma'am?

THE QUEEN Yes. Do we wake up suddenly; or do we sleep for a time?

THE DEAN That, Ma'am, is one of the mysteries which it is not given us to know.

THE QUEEN Still, I would *like* to know. The Roman Catholics don't seem to have any doubt about it. Why should *we*?

THE DEAN The Roman Church, Ma'am, has always pretended to know more than we have any warrant for in Holy Scripture.

THE QUEEN Oh, yes; of course, I know they are often in many ways superstitious. Still, one would like, about a thing of that sort, to have some assurance. And why shouldn't one? When one goes into the next world—not to meet those who are *waiting* for us, without waste of time, seems such a pity!

THE DEAN It does, Ma'am, it does! To mere human understanding it must, indeed, seem so. Still, we are bound to believe that, in the other world, everything has been arranged for the best. Indeed, we *must* believe it.

THE QUEEN (*reluctantly*) Yes; I suppose so. . . . Life in the next world, when we really get to it, will be very interesting.

THE DEAN Very; very.

THE QUEEN So much to see—and hear—and learn.

THE DEAN Yes, indeed, Ma'am. Your Majesty has evidently thought deeply on these subjects.

THE QUEEN I have. Since my beloved Husband was taken from me, naturally my thoughts have followed him a good deal.

THE DEAN Ah, yes. Has your Majesty a great sense of —nearness, shall I say? As if death were something very slight and unreal?

THE QUEEN No. It's the separation I feel. I always think of him as he *was*, here with me on earth: so handsome, so thoughtful, so affectionate, so attentive to all my wishes. And taken from me so soon! No one ever knew his true value, his greatness, his goodness, as I did.

THE DEAN That, Ma'am, is understandable. Who could? It was a terrible bereavement.

THE QUEEN It would be very disappointing to me to think that death was not going to end it.

THE DEAN Oh, but it will, Ma'am, of course!

THE QUEEN *At once,* I mean.

THE DEAN But however long the unconsciousness may last, it will *seem* at once. When we wake we shall surely be in the presence of those we love.

THE QUEEN But there will be others, too.

THE DEAN Undoubtedly.

THE QUEEN *Many* others—of all ages.

THE DEAN Yes: parents and children—the old and the young together.

THE QUEEN I meant—of other ages, in history.

THE DEAN Ah, yes; and how interesting! To meet all the great characters of history.

THE QUEEN Yes; the English Kings. I wonder how many of them will be there. Not all, I'm afraid.

THE DEAN It will be a very interesting encounter for your Majesty: quite an historic event.

THE QUEEN Yes. I wonder what I shall think of them. Some of them were not what they should have been. Still, they were all my ancestors, or my relatives—quite near relations, some of them.

THE DEAN But most of them rather distant.

THE QUEEN Yes; and sometimes distance has its advantages.

THE DEAN And its interest also. So the further back you go in history, the more interesting it will be:—Julius Cæsar.

THE QUEEN One hardly thinks of Julius Cæsar as being in Heaven, does one?

THE DEAN I suppose not, Ma'am. Still, let us hope!

THE QUEEN Yes; hope is a Christian duty. But I haven't much of it in some directions.

THE DEAN Still, Ma'am, however far back in history we go, there will always be the great characters of Holy Scripture. Of them, at least, one may be certain: *They* will be there.

THE QUEEN Yes; that will be very interesting. Moses, and the Prophets; and Elijah—a most interesting character, especially in the way his life on earth ended. And Isaiah, who wrote so beautifully.

THE DEAN Ah, yes; and the great Psalmist, David. To meet him will indeed be—

THE QUEEN David? I hope not!

THE DEAN (*astonished*) I beg pardon, your Majesty?

THE QUEEN I said—'I hope *not*.' I do not wish to meet King David anywhere.

THE DEAN I really fail to know why your Majesty should—

THE QUEEN He was not the sort of person I could ever wish to know. His conduct about Bathsheba. . . .

THE DEAN One has to make allowance, Ma'am, for the age in which people lived. Moral standards have changed.

THE QUEEN He knew he was doing wrong, as well as I do.

386

THE DEAN He also repented.

THE QUEEN I'm not so sure about *that*!

THE DEAN Oh, but surely!

THE QUEEN There was Abishag, who came later. He wasn't married to Abishag.

THE DEAN Well, Ma'am, then what about Solomon?

THE QUEEN Solomon was a wise King, but he was foolish about women.

THE DEAN Your Majesty is a shrewd judge of character.

THE QUEEN I've had a good deal of experience, Mr. Dean: my Uncles—I don't mind telling you.

THE DEAN Ah, yes, yes. But at your Majesty's Court things have become so different—thanks to your Majesty.

THE QUEEN The Prince, my dear Husband, set such an example to everybody.

THE DEAN Ah, yes. Indeed, indeed!

THE QUEEN (*rising*) Well, Mr. Dean, I have taken up quite enough of your valuable time; and now—I must go. But don't play any more tennis. At your age it is too risky.

THE DEAN I will pay all attention to your Majesty's advice, for which I am duly grateful.

THE QUEEN Yes; for that *is* a matter on which I can advise, as you on this matter have advised *me*—and have made it all so clear. But I shall go on hoping that it wasn't really a Whale.

THE DEAN So, Ma'am, with due reservation, shall I.

387

THE QUEEN For I do think Religion ought to be sensible, and not too hard to understand.

THE DEAN I quite agree, Ma'am.

THE QUEEN And in these days—what with Darwin, and Huxley, and people of that sort—it has become so difficult.

THE DEAN It has indeed, Ma'am.

THE QUEEN Well, good-bye, Mr. Dean. I hope nobody is about. I don't want to meet anyone.

THE DEAN I think we shall find the way quite clear, Ma'am. Directly I heard your Majesty was here, I gave definite instructions. . . . This way, Ma'am: this way!

(And bowing her forward with courtly grace, he leads THE QUEEN *out.)*

'We Are Not Amused'

'We Are Not Amused'

1885

In one of the apartments at Buckingham Palace, four LADIES *sit in attendance, waiting to be called. It is morning. Their Royal Mistress has not yet sent for them: it is before her accustomed hour; so, though they are all supposed to be doing something, they are not working very hard. Two of them, at a table by the window, are opening and sorting letters. The two others are at needle-work of an ornamental kind, which implies taste rather than usefulness. With fingers gracefully employed, they have minds free for conversation; and the two who are sorting the letters stop occasionally to listen.*

FIRST LADY But I really *couldn't* afford a new dress just then; so I had my pink satin altered, and re-trimmed with black lace.

SECOND LADY Very becoming, my dear!

FIRST LADY Yes. But, of course, *She* found out; so I was never able to wear it again. The first time I appeared in it, she looked me up and down, very disapprovingly. 'You seem very fond of that dress, Miss Somers,' she said. 'since you wear it so often.' 'I have worn it four times, your Majesty,' I replied. 'I have seen it *seven* times,' she said.

SECOND LADY Had she?

FIRST LADY Yes: seven was the exact number. Isn't she awful?

THIRD LADY Well, but really! How can she expect us always to have new dresses, on three hundred a year? I spend four hundred, at least.

FOURTH LADY I don't spend it, but I owe it.

SECOND LADY Still, as we do like being at Court, we must expect to pay for it.

FIRST LADY We should be more encouraged to pay for it, if she spent a little more on dress herself. This Widow-business is one of her saving ways.

SECOND LADY Oh, my dear, I don't think you ought to say that!

FIRST LADY But I do! And with all that old lace of hers, she can cover up any old rag; and you can't see whether it's old or new. Two of us once tried exchanging dresses—with alterations, of course. I took one of Lady Charlotte's; she took one of mine. . . . The first time I ever wore it, the Queen said to me, 'Miss Somers, that dress doesn't suit you! You must get another.' And she said exactly the same to Lady Charlotte, when she saw her in mine. . . . She *knew* what we'd done!

THIRD LADY There's nothing she doesn't know, that she makes up her mind to know. She's got an eye like a gimlet.

FIRST LADY And a memory like a pin-cushion! Every-thing that goes into it—sticks.

(*A* FIFTH LADY *enters in agitated excitement.*)

FIFTH LADY Oh, my dears! I've just had such an escape!

SECOND LADY What from?

FIFTH LADY I almost met the Queen, coming out of her room—face to face!

SECOND LADY But why shouldn't you meet her?

FIFTH LADY Dear Innocence, when you've been here long enough to learn the ABC of Court Etiquette, and Queen's Whims, you'll know that to meet Her Gracious Majesty where you are not supposed to meet her—out of your proper place—is one of the unforgivable sins. . . . I was carrying a vase of flowers—down the Queen's private corridor, of all places! It was rather full, so I had my eye on it.

THIRD LADY The corridor?

FIFTH LADY No; the vase. . . . And all at once, I saw the Queen coming out of her room—with 'Mop.' I couldn't run; so I just dodged behind a window-curtain. . . . Mop came trotting down the passage, and stopped to smell at me. Had he started barking, I should have been done for. Luckily I'd spilt some of the water; that distracted his attention. Then up comes the Queen. And there was Mop; and there was the water. So, of course, Mop was suspected of a small misbehaviour.

FIRST LADY Oh, my dear! How thrilling!

FIFTH LADY She was so near me, I could have touched her. Mop had run on: she called him back, in a tone that at once made him look guilty, poor lamb! (*And now, carried away by the interest of her story, she starts, in tone and gesture, to mimic Her Royal Mistress.*) 'Mop! Mop! Come here at once! What's this? . . . Who did that? . . . Now don't pretend, and look as if you didn't know! You

393

are a very naughty, naughty, naughty, little dog. And you must be whipped for it.'

> (*The* LADIES, *who get so little in Court life to amuse them, go into squeals of laughter; and, in their paroxysms of mirth, do not perceive that the door is slowly opening.*)

LADIES Oh! how perfectly lovely. How exactly like her!

> (THE QUEEN *enters; they all rise precipitately, and curtsy.* THE QUEEN *advances in measured silence; then speaks.*)

THE QUEEN Like whom?

> (*There is an awful pause: nobody answers. With quiet precision,* THE QUEEN *repeats her question.*)

Like whom?

FIFTH LADY I was only trying to give an imitation, your Majesty.

THE QUEEN Yes. Of whom?

FIFTH LADY I really couldn't say, Ma'am. Of no one in particular.

THE QUEEN Oh? How do you give an imitation of 'no one in particular'?

FIFTH LADY I mean, Ma'am, it was such a bad imitation.

THE QUEEN I daresay. But—of whom? . . . I ask you —of *whom*?

FIFTH LADY (*wishing herself dead*) Of your Majesty.

THE QUEEN So I supposed. You will please to do it again.

FIFTH LADY Oh, I *couldn't*, your Majesty!

THE QUEEN And pray, why not?

FIFTH LADY I did it so badly. It was silly of me. It wasn't really like, at all. It was only— Oh, I'm sure your Majesty will excuse me!

THE QUEEN As I trust that you would do nothing behind my back, Lady Jane, that you would be ashamed of doing to my face, I tell you to do it again.

FIFTH LADY I don't think I can, your Majesty!

THE QUEEN I daresay you don't; but *I* do.

FIFTH LADY (*bracing herself for the ordeal*) I do beg your Majesty to pardon me!

THE QUEEN When you have done it again: not before.

FIFTH LADY If your Majesty would only allow me to explain.

THE QUEEN I have no doubt, Lady Jane, that it will explain itself. . . . Now . . . begin!

> (*In a very lack-lustre way, the imitation is repeated —with modifications.* THE QUEEN *has seated herself. Mop, who has joined the company, stands looking on. He hears himself named, but cannot understand why: for here nothing has happened.*)

FIFTH LADY 'Mop! . . . Mop! . . . Where are you? You naughty, naughty, little dog! Who did that? . . .'

THE QUEEN What does '*that*' mean?

FIFTH LADY (*with feeble invention*) A torn curtain, your Majesty.

THE QUEEN Oh? Indeed? Mop is not in the habit of tearing curtains, Lady Jane, any more than I am.

FIFTH LADY No, your Majesty.

THE QUEEN *No.* . . . It was *not* a torn curtain—nothing of the kind. . . . *We are* NOT *amused.*

(*She rises, and goes out.*)

FIRST LADY How awful! How very awful! She *knew!*

THIRD LADY Knew? Of course she knew! Why, it's only just happened.

FIFTH LADY Well, that settles it! After tea, I shall go and drown myself! *Then* she'll be sorry!

(*The door re-opens;* THE QUEEN *again enters.*)

THE QUEEN Lady Jane, as you seem to have been a witness of the incident, will you, please, take Mop, and whip him at once—before he forgets? And then—*send* somebody!

FIFTH LADY (*tremulously*) But. it *wasn't* Mop, your Majesty!

(*But she is too late. Believing in Mop's guilt,* THE QUEEN *has already gone.*)

FIRST LADY Hadn't it better be?

FIFTH LADY (*miserably*) Yes, I suppose so! For if I don't do it, she'll find out. . . . Poor Mop! Come and be whipped!

(*She takes up the vicarious sacrifice in her arms, and goes out, leaving the door open. And presently, from far down the passage, we hear the mild yelpings of a small dog, who is being whipped—not, perhaps, very severely. But the accompanying words—'Naughty! Naughty!' are loudly given, so that—reaching* THE QUEEN'S *ear—Her Majesty may be satisfied that her order has been obeyed.*)

396

The Blue Ribbon

The Blue Ribbon

1887

Monsieur Benjamin Constant's portrait of the Queen, sitting crowned and enthroned in a soft cascade of sunlight, is so well known that the fact of its back being now to the spectator hardly matters. MONSIEUR CONSTANT *has himself arranged it in the best light available; but the windows of Windsor Castle do not give quite the light that he would wish. Still, though the opportunity for favourable display is not all that the Artist could desire, the honour conferred by the Royal command more than compensates.* MONSIEUR CONSTANT, *ceremonially arrayed, flutters in front of his masterpiece; and the* COURT OFFICIAL *who has charge of him, stands quietly looking on, admiring the gestures with which, almost as much as with words, the distinguished visitor conducts his conversation.*

COURT OFFICIAL I hope the light is as you wish, Monsieur?

CONSTANT The light? Oh, yes, as you cannot change the windows—it must do!

COURT OFFICIAL We can, if you like, Monsieur, have the windows closed, and the chandeliers lighted.

CONSTANT Ah, no, no, no, no, no! That might make my collars to look untrue. And my collars are very actually chosen.

> (*The* COURT OFFICIAL *realises, after a moment, that it is his picture, not his clothes, that* MONSIEUR CONSTANT *is referring to. He turns to study it with the respect due to its vast size.*)

COURT OFFICIAL It is a remarkable picture, Monsieur Constant.

CONSTANT (*with proud humility*) Of so remarkable a Personage, it would be difficult *not*.

COURT OFFICIAL In Paris—it has been popular?

CONSTANT Popular? Ma foi! mais oui! It has struck the conscience of the whole Nation. They look: 'Ah! a Queen!' they say. 'Why have we not still Kings and Queens?' Our Government was quite glad that I brought it away to Bond Street—to relieve the political situation.

COURT OFFICIAL Dear me! And in Bond Street, also, it has been a great success?

CONSTANT Ah! If your Queen Victoria had not been popular before, this would have made her to be so!

COURT OFFICIAL You had no sittings from Her Majesty, Monsieur? But you must surely have come over to England to paint the Throne, and that background. The House of Lords, is it not?

CONSTANT Ah, yes; no! For that, photographs were sufficient. The rest—myself!

COURT OFFICIAL Indeed? And the light—the effect of light coming down from above—that is wonderful!

CONSTANT The light? Ah! yes, the light! Ah! that is my forte. That is where I excel in my imagination.

COURT OFFICIAL Remarkable!

(And then the COURT OFFICIAL *has a duty to perform, which must be done delicately.)*

Monsieur Constant, you have met Royalty before?

CONSTANT Ah, no! In Republican France, hélas! we do not have much opportunity for to meet Royalty.

COURT OFFICIAL I only asked because we have a certain etiquette—as to which I am sure you will find no difficulty. Our manners at Court are more like the French manners than the English.

CONSTANT More civilised, you would say?

COURT OFFICIAL Well, in your country you have more ceremony—more grace: so you will understand. . . . When Her Majesty enters, she will only bow to you. When she leaves she may give you her hand. If, then, she raises it slightly, you will kiss it—not otherwise. In conversing with Her Majesty, you will always say 'Your Majesty' or 'Ma'am'—pronounced so.

CONSTANT Ah! Parfaitement! 'Même'—toujours la même chose.

COURT OFFICIAL Her Majesty may ask you questions. You will avoid, as far as possible, asking any questions in return. For instance, you must not say 'Does your Majesty also paint?' If Her Majesty wishes, she will inform you of the fact herself. If Her Majesty discusses Art with you—as she may do—do not insist too much upon your own opinion; allow Her Majesty to have the last word, and to have it early, in any matter on which you find that you differ.

CONSTANT Mais oui, Monsieur, parfaitement!

COURT OFFICIAL If anything Her Majesty says embarrasses you—I mean, if you feel embarrassed in stating your own view, then it will be always safe and correct for you to bow, saying nothing. And Her Majesty will herself change the conversation to some new subject.

CONSTANT That will be so? Ah!

COURT OFFICIAL I tell you this, Monsieur Constant, so that you may feel more at ease. Seeing Her Majesty constantly, to us it has become second nature. To those who only attend Court rarely, it is more difficult.

CONSTANT Monsieur, I am extremely obliged.

> (*Another* COURT OFFICIAL *of lower grade now enters and indicates with a half-bow that he is there to know that all is ready, and to make announcement. You see the words 'Her Majesty' formed by his lips, but you do not hear them. He withdraws silently, closing the door.*)

COURT OFFICIAL Her Majesty will be here in a few moments.

CONSTANT Ah, then allow me!

> (*Darting toward the picture, he draws a curtain across it.*)

COURT OFFICIAL But why are you covering the picture, Monsieur?

CONSTANT So that when Her Majesty stand just where she should stand to see it, then I open—so!

COURT OFFICIAL You must not expect Her Majesty to stand where you would wish, Monsieur. She will stand where she herself wishes.

CONSTANT But to see the picture from where it should be seen!

COURT OFFICIAL That Her Majesty will decide for herself, Monsieur.

CONSTANT Ah! Si? That is very English. Yes!

> (*And now the door opens, and two Indian Attendants glide in, and stand motionless on either side. There is a pause; and then—small, short, stout, but with an amazing dignity which is almost grace,* THE QUEEN *enters. She moves forward, halts at a few paces from her visitor (who meanwhile has been repeatedly bowing) and, as the* COURT OFFICIAL *pronounces his name, she bows to him with that marvellous mixture of distance and courtesy which turns her widow's cap into a crown.*)

COURT OFFICIAL Monsieur Benjamin Constant, your Majesty.

THE QUEEN I am very pleased to meet you, Monsieur Constant. You have come only recently from France?

CONSTANT I have had that honour, your Majesty—that pleasure.

THE QUEEN From Paris?

CONSTANT It is from Paris I come, your Majesty.

THE QUEEN It is your first visit to this country?

CONSTANT It is, Madame, it is.

THE QUEEN You live in Paris?

CONSTANT I live always in Paris; I work in Paris, Madame.

THE QUEEN It was very good of you to come, Monsieur. You are going to show me your picture.

CONSTANT Ah, yes! If your Majesty would condescend. Just three steps more away.

THE QUEEN But I always prefer to look at pictures closely, Monsieur, so 'as to see how they are done.

CONSTANT (*resignedly*) Ah, so!

THE QUEEN One has to look closely before one can be sure that they are good.

CONSTANT Ah, but of this picture—a subject so illustrious—I trust that your Majesty shall have no doubt.

> (*He draws the curtain. There is a long pause.* THE QUEEN *looks at the picture with calm, dignified detachment.*)

THE QUEEN We are redder than that, Monsieur.

CONSTANT Ah! but does your Majesty's gracious complexion never vary—a leetle?

THE QUEEN Never as much as that, Monsieur.

CONSTANT Ah, c'est dommage!

THE QUEEN A little more colour, Monsieur, could easily be added.

CONSTANT But then, Madame, what will have to become of my collar-scheme—that is, my picture?

404

THE QUEEN But this is a portrait, Monsieur, of *Me*.

CONSTANT Yes, but of the imagination—all my own. I had no sittings from your Majesty.

THE QUEEN Now that you have seen me, you will be able to correct it.

CONSTANT Oh, but impossible!

> (*The* COURT OFFICIAL *touches his arm, whereat he adds insinuatingly*)

—unless your Majesty should graciously sit to me.

THE QUEEN I have not sat for my portrait, Monsieur, for many years.

CONSTANT But what a deprivation is not that, Madame, to artists, and to the whole world!

THE QUEEN There is something else, Monsieur Constant, which you must correct.

CONSTANT Comment?

THE QUEEN The ribbon of the Garter—the blue; you have made it too light.

CONSTANT But permit me to explain, Madame! The light shining on it—so bright from above—the texture, the silk, the reflection—they do all make it lighter than would look otherwise.

THE QUEEN *It is too light*, Monsieur. I wear the Garter; so I know. Also, though you may not know it, I have practised painting myself. I had two masters to teach me—Sir John Hayter, and Mr. Cope; both excellent artists. They taught me to be true to nature.

CONSTANT They painted your Majesty's portrait, ever?

405

THE QUEEN No. When I was studying with them, I had my portrait painted—in a group with my whole family—by Winterhalter. I will give orders that you shall be shown it before you go. Winterhalter was a great painter, was he not?

CONSTANT Winterhalter? Oh, Winterhalter was everything that the public wished him to be. He had a great name in his day. Now he is dead.

THE QUEEN Yes; more than twelve years ago. I remember sending a wreath to his funeral, and also a letter to his widow. The Prince and I had a great regard for him. There are few artists to-day like him.

CONSTANT Very very few, Madame; or one never hears of them.

THE QUEEN No. ... Your portrait of me has had a great success, Monsieur, I am told?

CONSTANT Un succès fou, Madame. That is the only word for it.

THE QUEEN In Bond Street.

CONSTANT There; yes, Madame.

THE QUEEN Have you other pictures on exhibition as well?

CONSTANT By myself, no, Madame—not in the same room. We are alone together.

THE QUEEN (*after a pause*) You mean, my picture is alone?

CONSTANT (*conscious that he stands corrected*) Yes, I do mean that, your Majesty—that only.

406

THE QUEEN I think it was very clever of you to do it without sittings. I wish I could have given you a sitting— just one. But I never sit now. And I hope, Monsieur, that you will at once make those two corrections: a little more red in the face, and to the ribbon more blue.

CONSTANT The red—oh, yes, Madame—if your Majesty orders it. But the blue—the blue, Madame, that —as the Artist—I must be allowed to—

THE QUEEN Good-bye, Monsieur Constant. It has been a great pleasure to meet you. Thank you very much for bringing the picture. As a picture, I like it. As a portrait, you will now be able, by those alterations, to make it better, I hope. Good-bye.

> (*She offers him her hand. He bends and kisses it. She goes to the door, turns, bows, and retires, followed by her Attendants.*)

CONSTANT (*a little agitated*) Did I right—to kiss?

COURT OFFICIAL I think so.

CONSTANT Did she like the picture enough for me to kiss—you think?

COURT OFFICIAL Oh, I think so, distinctly.

CONSTANT (*with an artist's grievance*) Oh, but she did not understand! She did not understand!

COURT OFFICIAL Her Majesty is accustomed to have her own opinion about things, Monsieur, and not to change it.

CONSTANT Ah! So English!

407

COURT OFFICIAL And now—we have Her Majesty's permission—would you like to see the Winterhalter?

CONSTANT The Winterhalter? No! I know Winterhalter, and all about him, quite well. Eau sucré—that is what he is.

COURT OFFICIAL Eau sacré. Holy water?

CONSTANT Holy? No, I did not say 'holy'; not sacré—sucré: sugar—*and* water!

> (*And then, once more, the* COURT OFFICIAL *of lower grade enters, and this time speaks audibly.*)

SECOND COURT OFFICIAL Her Majesty requests that Monsieur Constant will wait a few moments. Her Majesty has something she wishes to send him.

> (*Having delivered his message, the* COURT OFFICIAL *withdraws, leaving* MONSIEUR CONSTANT *in a twitter of excitement.*)

CONSTANT Ah! but that is—that is—very unexpected! What will it be, you think? Some honour for me? Est-ce possible?

COURT OFFICIAL Perhaps a souvenir, Monsieur. Probably a signed photograph.

CONSTANT (*his hopes dashed*) Oh? . . . Well, so long as it is not a photograph of the Winterhalter, I do not mind. . . . But—redder? How am I to make that a redder face, and not spoil the collar-harmony of my picture?

COURT OFFICIAL Don't, Monsieur. Her Majesty will not see it again.

CONSTANT Ah! Thank you; you are wise, and very kind.

(Again the SECOND COURT OFFICIAL *enters, bearing in his hand a small packet, which he presents to* MONSIEUR CONSTANT.*)*

CONSTANT *(his hopes rising again)* Oh, but this is not a photograph No, it is too small. It is an honour, surely, an order that she send me! *(He opens the packet, while he speaks.)* Hey? What for is this small piece of blue ribbon?

COURT OFFICIAL There is a note pinned to it, I see.

CONSTANT Ah, yes! *(He unpins it, and reads.)* 'You see, Monsieur, I am right.' What this mean?—'You see, Monsieur, I am right'?

COURT OFFICIAL *(after examination)* That is the ribbon of the Garter, Monsieur; the blue about which you and Her Majesty did not quite agree. You are to see, she says, that she was *right*.

CONSTANT Oh! Mais c'est incroyable! She do not understand!

COURT OFFICIAL No, Monsieur, perhaps not. But here we don't say so.

CONSTANT Ah! This is England! I must go back to France! Monsieur, I have to tell you she is no artist. Oh, but a great Queen! A wonderful person! Enfin! . . . This—I may keep?

(He holds up the piece of blue ribbon.)

COURT OFFICIAL Certainly, Monsieur.

CONSTANT *(his reward with him)* Ah! This blue ribbon—for me! Always! Merci!

(*And, with a flourish of satisfaction, he pockets the Souvenir, which will always give point and corroboration to his story whenever he tells it; as he will do frequently, until one day it reaches ears that were waiting for it: and so—finds its place here.*)

Promotion Cometh

Promotion Cometh

20th January 1891

THE QUEEN *and her Visitor are in seated conversation, but the conversation is not intimate. The new Canon's wife has come for inspection; and, much to Her Majesty's surprise and annoyance, the inspection is gradually being shifted to herself. This sort of thing has never happened before: not, at least, since her accession to the throne. But here we are! It is a test of dignity, for the Canon's wife has all the physical advantages! Tall, severe, magisterial, with self-confidence in every line, feature, and gesture; in any other company she would dominate the scene. But here she does not. How on earth that Other, so short, plump, and round-about, manages to do it, Heaven only knows! It is a secret she has made her own for over fifty years, and it will go on, through years of infirmity, to the day of her death. Now, feeling the masterful coils of this boa-constrictor closing round her,* THE QUEEN *tries to make shift of the conversation; and the two Ladies-in-Waiting, seated in respectful attendance in the embrasure of the window, look on and say nothing, except to each other with their eyes. So much freedom of expression Court etiquette allows to them.*

THE QUEEN And I hope you find your house quite comfortable, Mrs. Clayton?

MRS. CLAYTON It will be, your Majesty, as soon as I have had time to make it so.

THE QUEEN Was anything the matter with it? Repairs—drains? The Canon, your husband's predecessor, lived in it to a good old age. He was quite hale and hearty, almost to the last, I believe.

MRS. CLAYTON No bathroom, or housemaid's closet, your Majesty.

THE QUEEN (*in chilled astonishment*) Housemaid's closet!

MRS CLAYTON (*explaining*) For hot-water cans, brooms, and dustpans, your Majesty.

THE QUEEN I never heard of them!

MRS. CLAYTON Indeed? No, Ma'am?

THE QUEEN (*decisively*) We don't have them at Windsor.

MRS. CLAYTON That is a pity, Ma'am.

THE QUEEN Pity? You pity Windsor Castle, Mrs. Clayton!

MRS. CLAYTON (*courageously*) Castles sometimes need renovating, your Majesty.

THE QUEEN Windsor was thoroughly renovated, externally, by King George IV; and internally, by the Prince, my Husband. . . . I will let you see over the Castle, if you like, Mrs. Clayton.

MRS. CLAYTON I shall be most happy, your Majesty. I may be able to suggest some improvements.

THE QUEEN (*incredulously*) Improvements? After what the Prince did himself, I allow nothing to be altered.

MRS. CLAYTON In that case, Ma'am, further suggestions will be useless.

THE QUEEN I am afraid so. You see, Mrs. Clayton, I have recollections. All the things that He did seem to me like yesterday. The Great Exhibition of 'fifty-one. So many new ideas came in then. It was the beginning of a new age; and all his own dear wonderful invention. The world doesn't know, even yet, what it owes to him.

MRS. CLAYTON (*incredulous*) The Prince Consort's invention, your Majesty?

THE QUEEN (*luxuriating sadly in the recollection*) Yes, he started it.

MRS. CLAYTON It didn't get to the Canon's residence, apparently, Ma'am. The kitchen is so dark that my cook can't see to cook without gaslight.

THE QUEEN Indeed? Very sad. . . . Still, you *have* gaslight, I suppose?

MRS. CLAYTON Oh, yes, Ma'am. There *is* gas, of course; not as good as it might be. As soon as the meter is turned on, the whole house reeks of it.

THE QUEEN (*ignoring the complaint*). Then that meets the difficulty. And how do you like Windsor, Mrs. Clayton? . . . the people, I mean?

MRS. CLAYTON There are far too many poor people in Windsor, your Majesty.

THE QUEEN There are.

MRS. CLAYTON Deplorably, shamefully poor.

THE QUEEN Yes, I suppose so.

MRS. CLAYTON I am bound to tell your Majesty that I find they have been much neglected. The parish has not been properly worked, or organised as it should be.

THE QUEEN (*with a touch of ice*) Indeed!

MRS. CLAYTON Just think, Ma'am, there are no Mothers' Meetings. They have never heard of them.

THE QUEEN (*after just thinking*) Nor have I. What do Mothers meet for, Mrs. Clayton?

MRS. CLAYTON I might say—to become civilised, your Majesty. Some I find quite primitive in their notions . . . savages almost . . . certainly not Christian.

THE QUEEN Here in Windsor? Most extraordinary. How can that be possible?

MRS. CLAYTON Anything is possible if left to itself, your Majesty. In this case, it comes from neglect, and lack of education.

THE QUEEN But what is one to do? There are so many of them—far too many, as you say. And social conditions make it so difficult. You can't get rid of ignorance in a day, Mrs. Clayton.

MRS. CLAYTON No; your Majesty, nor in a lifetime, if one does nothing. Indifference, prejudice, class-distinction all help?

THE QUEEN *Help?*

MRS. CLAYTON *Have* helped most certainly to make Windsor what no self-respecting place ought to be.

THE QUEEN (*correctively, for these are wild socialistic notions, which ought not to be expressed*) Would you wish to get rid of class-distinction, Mrs. Clayton?

MRS. CLAYTON I would wish to get rid of anything, Ma'am, which prevents people from recognising their responsibilities. It is what I am hoping to do here—

THE QUEEN Indeed!

MRS. CLAYTON (*continuing*) —as soon as I can find the time for it.

THE QUEEN (*grasping at a straw*) Ah, yes. You have your husband to look after.

MRS. CLAYTON I have, Ma'am. That, of course—

THE QUEEN (*completing the sentence as it should be completed*)—must be your *first* consideration.

MRS. CLAYTON It has always been so, your Majesty. But it is not my last, or only one. I have also my children.

THE QUEEN Ah, yes. You have a large family?

MRS. CLAYTON Only five . . . at present.

THE QUEEN (*deprecating the prospective suggestion*) Dear me! But your husband, the Canon. Is he not—rather delicate?

MRS. CLAYTON Oh, no, your Majesty—quite robust. Not delicate, but difficult. He is a scholar—as perhaps your Majesty knows—and needs quiet and retirement.

THE QUEEN (*with a touch of mischief*) I hope he gets it.

MRS. CLAYTON (*conscious of good management*) He does, Ma'am. I arrange that. During certain hours of the day, I allow him to see nobody. I had to make that rule for him.

THE QUEEN Indeed!

MRS CLAYTON His regular writing hours, I mean, when he is not at home to anyone.

417

THE QUEEN Ah, yes. He is writing history, I believe?

MRS. CLAYTON He is, Ma'am.

THE QUEEN When will it be finished?

MRS. CLAYTON Before he dies, Ma'am, I hope . . . *he* hopes, also. Four volumes have already been published; and there are four more to come.

THE QUEEN Dear me! I should call that an Encyclopædia, not a history.

MRS CLAYTON (*instructively*) History, your Majesty, has become very complicated in these days. Modern research has brought so much more material to light, that it has almost to be rewritten.

THE QUEEN Now, that is rather a pity, when it has been so well done already. Lord Macaulay was a great writer of history, was he not?

MRS. CLAYTON Nobody reads Macaulay now, Ma'am, for facts; only for amusement.

THE QUEEN Dear me! How extraordinary! I used to know Lord Macaulay, Mrs. Clayton. I remember receiving him on his return from India. A most interesting man. In fact, almost all I know about India—the life and habits of the people, I mean, was told me by Lord Macaulay himself—personally!

MRS CLAYTON Indeed, Ma'am. I wonder if it is still true.

THE QUEEN Oh, yes. For he told me that the East never changes, and never will.

MRS. CLAYTON I suppose that is because the missionaries don't do their duty.

418

THE QUEEN Oh, why should you say that, Mrs. Clayton?

MRS. CLAYTON Because, Ma'am, India is larger than Windsor. And when I find how much Windsor—the poor of Windsor—have been neglected, I imagine that India may be in a like state, or worse. I am starting a Mothers' Meeting, your Majesty, and I wondered if, for the opening of the first meeting, your—

THE QUEEN (*intervening, and oh! you should see now the eyes of the Ladies-in-Waiting*) Ah, yes. But you can't have Mothers' Meetings in India, Mrs. Clayton. Purdah makes that impossible.

MRS. CLAYTON I am not proposing to start Mothers' Meetings in India, your Majesty. I was speaking of Windsor; and I wondered—

> (*We almost know what* MRS. CLAYTON *is going to say; and so does* THE QUEEN, *though it is difficult for her to believe it. With an instinct of self-preservation, she rises, and brings the conversation to an end. The Ladies-in-Waiting rise, and* MRS. CLAYTON, *robbed of her prey, has to rise also.*)

THE QUEEN I am so sorry, Mrs. Clayton; but I fear, now, I have an appointment. This has been a most interesting conversation; you have given me much to think about. I believe we are to have the pleasure of hearing the Canon preach on Sunday?

MRS CLAYTON I believe so, your Majesty.

THE QUEEN Has he yet begun writing his sermon?

MRS. CLAYTON I don't know, your Majesty. Sometimes he prefers preaching from notes.

THE QUEEN Oh, I prefer *written* sermons.

MRS. CLAYTON Shall I tell him that is your Majesty's wish?

THE QUEEN (*with a touch of pinprick in her voice*) Oh, no, no! Don't tell him anything. Just let him alone to do as he likes. Good-bye, Mrs. Clayton; and I hope that your house is going to be habitable, when you can find time to attend to it.

MRS. CLAYTON So good of your Majesty to wish it.

> (MRS. CLAYTON *curtsies deeply over the hand graciously offered her.*)

THE QUEEN Good-bye. Lady Grace, will you see Mrs. Clayton safely out, please.

> (MRS. CLAYTON *has made the proper Court passes. At the door she turns again, and, assisted through it by* LADY GRACE, *curtsies herself out. The door shuts. But there is the other Lady-in-Waiting still in attendance.*)

You can go, too, Miss Somers, now. I don't want you. And send Sir Henry Ponsonby to me—immediately.

> (MISS SOMERS *makes her curtsy. Again the door shuts and* THE QUEEN *is alone. Taking up the stick, with which she now walks when troubled by rheumatism, she begins moving about the room; and the sharp tapping of her stick upon the carpet gives an emphasis to what she has now to say to herself.*)

Instant promotion! . . . Instant promotion! . . . Yes . . . yes . . . yes, indeed! . . . Instant . . . *instant* promotion!

420

(SIR HENRY PONSONBY *has entered, and stands, quietly observant. He sees plainly that something is amiss.*)

SIR HENRY Your Majesty wished to see me?

THE QUEEN (*turning sharply*) Sir Henry, will you please make a note that Canon Clayton is to have instant promotion . . . to the first vacancy that offers.

SIR HENRY Vacancy, Ma'am? What sort of vacancy?

THE QUEEN Dean, or Bishop . . . it does not matter which. Whichever comes first. For if that woman stays here, as long as she expects to stay, she will make me go and open her Mothers' Meetings. The women of Windsor, she informs me, are living in a very ignorant and neglected condition. *And I am one of them!*

SIR HENRY (*scandalised, yet amused*) Dear me! Dear me!

THE QUEEN Therefore I say . . . instant promotion! Isn't there a vacant Bishopric or Deanery just now? Any Deanery will do. Surely there is one?

SIR HENRY I saw in *The Times*, Ma'am, this morning, the death of the Bishop of Ballarat.

THE QUEEN Ah! . . . That will do. Where's Ballarat? Not in Scotland, I hope?

SIR HENRY Oh, no! Ballarat is somewhere in the Antipodes, I believe . . . Australia.

THE QUEEN Ah, that will do quite nicely! Will you please tell the Prime Minister not to begin making any appointment till he has seen *me*. You might mention Canon Clayton's name to him, as a preliminary.

SIR HENRY I doubt, Ma'am, whether we shall be able to persuade Canon Clayton to go out to the Colonies.

THE QUEEN Why not?

SIR HENRY It is hardly the kind of life that would suit him—he being so much a scholar, and a writer.

THE QUEEN Well, can't he write there?

SIR HENRY Not without books for reference, Ma'am . . . and a large library, I fear. He must have within reach some such institution as the British Museum.

THE QUEEN Haven't the Colonies got anything of the sort?

SIR HENRY Hardly yet! . . . only a few of them. Not in Ballarat, I'm afraid.

THE QUEEN Dear me! How extraordinary! How ignorant and neglected they must be, then. Surely a suitable place for Mrs. Clayton to go to. Suggest it to her, Sir Henry. See *her* first, and if she agrees . . . that will settle it.

SIR HENRY Well, your Majesty, I haven't much hope; but I will try.

THE QUEEN (*suddenly remembering*) Oh, what about Peterborough, now that Bishop Magee is going to York?

SIR HENRY Ah, Peterborough! Yes, I had forgotten Peterborough.

THE QUEEN Tell the Prime Minister that if he won't take Ballarat, he is to have Peterborough.

SIR HENRY I will do my best to suggest it, Ma'am.

THE QUEEN Don't suggest it, Sir Henry, say I *wish* it.

SIR HENRY Did she . . . Was she . . . very . . . ?

THE QUEEN Sir Henry, I was never so near being put in my place by anyone. Never! What do others think of her?

SIR HENRY Mrs. Clayton has only been here three months, Ma'am; but already she terrifies people.

(THE QUEEN *takes up her knitting.*)

THE QUEEN So I should imagine—unless they stand up to her, as *I* did.

SIR HENRY They found a name for her, which your Majesty might like to hear.

THE QUEEN Well, and what is it?

SIR HENRY They call her, Ma'am, the 'She-bear of Windsor.'

THE QUEEN And a very good name too! She almost got me in her hug to-day. I only just escaped.

(*At this point a* GENTLEMAN-IN-WAITING *enters, and stands drooping for permission to speak.*)

THE QUEEN Yes, what is it?

GENTLEMAN The Bishops, your Majesty, have arrived, and are waiting your Majesty's pleasure.

THE QUEEN Which Bishops?

GENTLEMAN There are six of them, your Majesty. The Bishop of London; the Bishop of—

SIR HENRY Your Majesty will remember that the appointment was made three weeks ago. Your Majesty wished to discuss with them the appointments to the Royal Commission on Church Discipline, which are now under your Majesty's consideration.

423

THE QUEEN Oh, yes, I knew I had some engagement for this afternoon, though I had forgotten what it was. Yes, I shall have a great deal to say to them about *that*! Tell them to come in. And order tea. They were asked to take tea, I believe, were they not?

GENTLEMAN Your Majesty did so command.

THE QUEEN Very well; let them come in at once. And see that tea follows immediately.

(*Exit the* GENTLEMAN-IN-WAITING.)

Sir Henry, I shall want you to stay. I shall have to talk to them seriously; and you must take notes of what any of them say. This lawlessness in the Church is nearly all their fault. They don't put their foot down as they should do. It doesn't happen in Scotland.

SIR HENRY In the Church of Scotland, Ma'am, there are no Bishops' feet to be put down.

THE QUEEN No. And the Church has done better without them. It has remained Protestant. I wish that the Church of England were Presbyterian, too.

SIR HENRY Indeed, Ma'am, that would be an interesting experiment.

THE QUEEN Yes; so much safer. Mr. Gladstone's appointments were sometimes terrible. Lord Salisbury's are almost worse. A ritualist at Lincoln, and Canons who have become Socialists in more places than one can name. What is religion coming to?

SIR HENRY Possibly to disestablishment, Ma'am.

THE QUEEN Yes. And, where, as Head of the Church, shall I be then? He wanted to make Canon Liddon Bishop of Oxford. I put my foot down on that. . . . Yes?

424

(*The* GENTLEMAN-IN-WAITING *re-enters*.)

GENTLEMAN The Lord Bishops, your Majesty, are here.

THE QUEEN Let them come in.

> (*The* GENTLEMAN-IN-WAITING *steps back to the door, and, with a gesture of 'line clear,' stands back to admit the six invited* BISHOPS, *who advance into the room processionally, and bow. Like Noah negotiating the animals into the Ark, he names them as they enter.*)

GENTLEMAN Your Majesty. . . . The Bishop of London; the Bishop of Winchester; the Bishop of Rochester; the Bishop of Salisbury; the Bishop of Ely; the Bishop of Chichester.

> (*Meantime, while its tail is still entering, the* QUEEN *is graciously receiving the head of the procession, which murmurs appropriate response to her greetings.*)

THE QUEEN My dear Bishop of London, how do you do? My dear Bishop of Winchester, so pleased to see you. . . . My dear Bishop of Rochester, I hope dear Mrs. Brown is better? I hear she has been ill.

ROCHESTER I thank your Majesty, much better.

THE QUEEN How do you do, my dear Bishop? You have come up from Salisbury to-day?

SALISBURY Only from London, your Majesty.

THE QUEEN So you had not too long a journey?

SALISBURY Oh, no, your Majesty.

LONDON Winchester and Salisbury are staying with me at Fulham, Ma'am, for the night. We all came down together.

425

THE QUEEN Very pleasant, I'm sure. So it has not been too inconvenient for you?

THE BISHOPS Oh, no, your Majesty.

THE QUEEN My dear Bishop of Ely, how do you do? And you, my dear Bishop of Chichester; it is a long time since I have seen you. I am so glad that you have all been able to come. Sir Henry, please say that we will have tea at once.

> (*A mere gesture from* SIR HENRY *to the* GENTLEMAN-IN-WAITING *is sufficient. Tea enters automatically, already poured out, and supported on trays by liveried Footmen. Cake and bread and butter follow. A Footman brings a separate tray to Her Majesty; but, with a monosyllabic No, she rejects it. She is going to do the talking; and a tea-cup with its etceteras would be a hindrance. On the other hand, that calculated hindrance is now being imposed on the* BISHOPS. *They stand about, holding small saucers, with spoons and bread and butter precariously balanced. With such accompaniments, it is difficult to be sacerdotal, or argumentative. And argument her Majesty does not mean to allow. For a while the servants are a protection from the impending attack;* THE QUEEN *and her six* BISHOPS *talk of the weather and things that do not matter; and* THE QUEEN, *in her regal way, does it embracingly.*)

THE QUEEN I hope you are all having good weather in your dioceses?

(They are; grateful appreciation of the fact flutters over the tea-cups.)

THE BISHOPS *(dispersedly)* Quite excellent, Ma'am . . . during the last week. . . . Very seasonable. . . . Oh, yes. Things are a little late, under God . . . but one mustn't complain.

(The BISHOP OF LONDON, *however—the future Archbishop—puts more personality into his response.)*

LONDON There was a very high tide at Fulham, Ma'am, yesterday.

THE QUEEN Ah, indeed? That sometimes happens, does it not? Fulham is rather a damp place, I'm afraid.

LONDON It is, Ma'am. But Lambeth is worse. Half the Archbishops die of it.

THE QUEEN Dear me, how sad! . . . and how extraordinary! I hope, my Lords, that none of your palaces are damp?

LONDON All of them, your Majesty. Like ourselves, they are old and falling into decay. Slightly insanitary, most of them.

THE QUEEN Dear me!

(There is a pause. The other BISHOPS *have been apprehensively admiring the conversational powers of* BISHOP TEMPLE, *their leader. But now he is finishing his bread and butter, and reaching out his hand for cake, which a Footman stoopingly supplies.)*

THE QUEEN *(to* WINCHESTER*)* I hope, my dear Bishop, that you and the Bishop of Salisbury have had the oppor-

427

tunity, while at Fulham, of talking over with the Bishop of London the matter about which I wrote to him? . . . Tell the servants to go, Sir Henry! . . . It is very important that I should know your views on the subject, and that you should know *mine*. My Lord Bishops, I am referring to the Royal Commission on Church Discipline, which is about to be appointed.

(*The Footmen have departed.*)

LONDON Which *has* been appointed, Ma'am.

THE QUEEN But not yet confirmed by *me*. I wish to see it strengthened.

LONDON Indeed, Ma'am? With permission, I venture to think that it is already large enough.

THE QUEEN So do I. Certain persons have been included who ought not to be there: whose appointment I do not approve.

LONDON Indeed, Ma'am? As I am largely responsible for the clerical nominations, I am anxious to hear your Majesty's objections.

THE QUEEN There are too many of the High Church Party.

LONDON There must be some, Ma'am.

THE QUEEN Why?

LONDON They are representative, Ma'am. They form a very large, and learned, and influential part of the Church Established.

THE QUEEN Yes; and I want it stopped—put an end to, at once.

LONDON Extermination, Ma'am, in these days, is rather difficult.

428

THE QUEEN They ought not to be encouraged; they ought not to be officially recognised at all.

LONDON I'm afraid, Ma'am, that they have historical claims which cannot be entirely ignored.

THE QUEEN I am not talking about history, Dr. Temple; I am talking about *now*.

LONDON So am I, Ma'am.

THE QUEEN Oh? Then, why mention history? What I wish to say is that all this Romish Ritual has got to be put down. . . . I won't have it!

LONDON Nor will I, Madam—for myself; I have no use for it.

THE QUEEN But the Lincoln Judgment *allows* it. Most extraordinary!

LONDON The Lincoln Judgment, Ma'am, for which I am partly responsible—

THE QUEEN (*interposing*) Yes, I *know*.

LONDON (*continuing*)—has greatly disappointed the High Church Party. They find some of its conclusions very difficult to accept. But the Bishop himself has bowed to the Judgment. That is a great point to have achieved.

THE QUEEN Well, if he hadn't, he must have resigned.

LONDON But would he?

THE QUEEN He ought never to have been made a Bishop. I was against it; and, you see, *I was right*.

LONDON He has made a very good Bishop.

THE QUEEN (*scandalised*) A *good* Bishop!

429

LONDON He is very much beloved in his own diocese—indeed it would be a wonder were it otherwise. Dr. King of Lincoln is more of a saint than all the rest of us put together.

THE QUEEN Indeed? I don't claim to be a judge of saints; but are not saints sometimes superstitious?

LONDON They are, Ma'am, they are. That has been one of the great troubles of Church history. But we are getting over it.

THE QUEEN We are not getting over *him*.

LONDON We are not, Ma'am.

THE QUEEN I consider the Lincoln Judgment most deplorable: leaving him on the Bench at all is a great mistake.

LONDON I am afraid, Ma'am, that your disapproval is largely due to history: it being mainly upon history that the Lincoln Judgment was based.

THE QUEEN Indeed? Then no wonder.

LONDON No wonder, as you say, Ma'am.

THE QUEEN History? It reads to *me* as though it were trying to make out that at the Reformation nothing happened.

LONDON Ah, no, Ma'am; it was only trying to make out what *did* happen.

THE QUEEN (*astonished*) Don't you *know*?

LONDON Not as clearly as I would like to know: none of us do.

THE QUEEN Then I don't wonder!

LONDON No, Ma'am; nor do I.

THE QUEEN I am afraid that is our only point of agreement, Dr. Temple. It is very painful to me to have to speak to *Bishops* about how things are going in the Church, of which I am the Head. But, being in that position, I have to speak with authority. And I say, again, that all this flaunting Ritual has got to be put down: I won't have it! It does not happen in Scotland; so why should it happen here?

LONDON Technically speaking, Ma'am, the Scottish Church is heretical: it is not Episcopal.

THE QUEEN I am Head of the Scottish Church, Dr. Temple. Am I heretical?

LONDON I should not like to say, Ma'am. I trust not.

THE QUEEN *I* trust not. But it is not the Church of Scotland, but the Church of England which we are now discussing. Why, with so many Bishops in authority, is there so much disobedience?

> (*To be out of this—a mere temporary expedient, indicative of a weak character—the* BISHOP OF CHICHESTER *tiptoes to the cakestand, and helps himself.*)

ROCHESTER The question is very difficult, Ma'am.

THE QUEEN It is. But the difficulty must be met. It's no use temporising about it. Delay is compromising the Church, and my position as Head of it. . . . Things have got to be altered.

WINCHESTER The question is, Ma'am, how can we get the clergy to obey?

THE QUEEN If they don't, send them to prison!

LONDON We did that to one. It was no good.

431

THE QUEEN No, because he was let out again. If they had imprisoned a dozen—

LONDON Then, I fear, Ma'am, there would have been a large secession to Rome; and an increased circulation of the *Church Times*.

THE QUEEN Well, if they have Romish beliefs, let them go to Rome. Do any of you approve of such practices?

THE BISHOPS (*precipitately*) No. Oh, no. . . . Very regrettable.

LONDON Also, in my opinion, superstitious and foolish. But the law can't do everything, Ma'am. . . . It can't alter a stubborn mind.

THE QUEEN Well, if the law needs strengthening, strengthen it! . . . This has got to be put down! And the law *can* do something, at all events. My Lords, what are *you* going to do about it?

SALISBURY Your Majesty may be assured that we shall all do our best . . . to bring back to the Church the peace and unity which it needs.

THE QUEEN Yes; and drastic discipline is the only thing that will do it. Some of the Bishops have got so in the habit of being disobeyed, that they do nothing . . . nothing whatever!

WINCHESTER What, definitely, would your Majesty wish us to do? The circumstances are often very difficult.

THE QUEEN I wish you all to speak strongly for the strengthening of Church Discipline when the matter comes before your Lordships' House—as it will do presently. That is why I have sent for you to-day.

432

(*The* BISHOP OF CHICHESTER *jolts his tea-spoon, and upsets his cake.*)

Sir Henry, give the Bishop of Chichester another piece of cake. He has dropped his.

CHICHESTER I beg your Majesty's pardon; I did not perceive that I had done so.

(*In a paroxysm of nervousness, he recovers the fallen fragment, and is about to take a bite of it.*)

THE QUEEN Don't eat it! Take another!

CHICHESTER (*in an aside to* SIR HENRY, *who is now offering him the cake-stand*) No more, I thank you. I might repeat my clumsiness. These saucers ... rather small, you know ... for the cake. Relieve me of it. ... Thank you!

(*He gets rid of the cake.*)

THE QUEEN Why is there this difference, I want to know, between England and Scotland? In Scotland we have no trouble, none at all. And *they* manage without Bishops. Why is religion in Scotland so much better, and purer, and more Protestant, than in England?

LONDON That, Ma'am, is a very complicated matter of history. Hardly to be explained over a cup of tea ... not thoroughly and satisfactorily.

THE QUEEN I don't require to have it explained, so long as you get it altered. Have you all had as much tea as you want?

THE BISHOPS Quite, your Majesty. ... Oh, quite.

CHICHESTER (*with his cake still on his mind*) Most refreshing!

WINCHESTER (*ingratiatingly*) And very good tea, too, Ma'am, if I may be allowed to say so.

THE QUEEN Oh, yes. I get all my tea from India. I hope *you* all get *your* tea from India as an encouragement to the Empire. I feel that we should all do so.

LONDON Really, Ma'am, I don't know where my tea comes from. I generally take green tea; and more of it, I am afraid, than is good for me.

THE QUEEN That is a pity. Too much green tea, I have heard, is quite dangerous. Tell Mrs. Temple from me, that she shouldn't allow it.

LONDON Mrs. Temple cannot interfere, Ma'am. I make it myself in my own study.

THE QUEEN What habits! Dear me! How extraordinary! . . . Well, my Lords, I thank you very much for coming. I have told you my mind on the subject; and when the matter comes before the House of Lords, I shall read with interest what you all have to say about it. And now, if any of you would like to go round the gardens and the conservatories before you leave, pray do so.

> (*A murmur of thanks comes from the* BISHOPS. *Their ordeal over, the gardens will be a welcome change, both of scene and subject.*)

Sir Henry, will you please?

> (*And* SIR HENRY *goes to call in the* GENTLEMAN-IN-WAITING, *who will be the Bishops' escort from now until their departure. And now, very graciously,* THE QUEEN *dismisses them back to their dioceses.*)

434

Good-bye, my dear Bishop of London. My dear Bishop of Winchester, good-bye. My dear Bishop of Rochester, remember me to your dear wife; I am so glad she is better. Good-bye, my dear Bishop; you go back to Salisbury to-day?

SALISBURY To-morrow, your Majesty.

THE QUEEN Ah, to-morrow. Good-bye, my dear Bishop.

> (*This is to the* BISHOP OF CHICHESTER. *And now only the* BISHOP OF ELY *is left.*)

THE QUEEN Good-bye, my dear Bishop. I was so sorry to hear to-day of the death of the Bishop of Peterborough.

> (SIR HENRY *is now back at her elbow, and almost inaudibly gives the prompting word.*)

SIR HENRY ... Of Ballarat.

THE QUEEN Of Ballarat, I mean.

ELY (*somewhat astray*) Ah, yes ... indeed, Ma'am.

THE QUEEN You knew him, of course?

ELY Hardly, Ma'am. I believe that I assisted at his consecration.

THE QUEEN A great loss to the Church, out in the Colonies, will it not be?

ELY Indeed, yes, Ma'am. Such a large diocese. Almost the size of England.

THE QUEEN Indeed? I hope his successor will be wisely chosen. A great responsibility.

ELY Yes, indeed, Ma'am.

435

THE QUEEN And there is the vacancy at Peterborough too. In all these cases—positions of such importance—it is so necessary to find just the right person.

ELY I am sure that your Majesty's choice—so far as it rests with your Majesty—can always be relied on.

THE QUEEN Very good of you to say so, my dear Bishop. These vacancies are always a great anxiety to me. Things in the Church, being as they are—and the appointments not always all that I could wish. Good-bye. Sir Henry will go with you, and see that you join the others. Good-bye.

> (*The* BISHOP, *accompanied by* SIR HENRY PONSONBY,
> *bows himself out.* THE QUEEN *is left alone.*)

THE QUEEN Well, I hope that's all settled now. I've told them what I think. . . .

> (*Then an earlier thought strikes her.*)

Ah, yes! That woman! . . . Ballarat . . . or Peterborough. . . . Yes! . . . Instant promotion!

> (*And, in less than a week, one of the two vacancies
> is offered—and is accepted.*)

'A Great Relief'

'A Great Relief'

3rd March 1894

THE QUEEN *sits at a writing-table in her private Apartment at Buckingham Palace. With a brisk and pleased expression, she finishes and signs a letter which she then hands over to* SIR HENRY PONSONBY, *who stands in attendance.*

THE QUEEN Sir Henry, will you see that this letter goes to Lord Rosebery *at once.* And if, later, you could see him yourself, say I should be glad to have his answer to-day—this morning, if possible; before anything gets into the papers.

SIR HENRY I will do my best, Ma'am. Would your Majesty prefer for me to go now? That would be the quickest way.

THE QUEEN No, no. You must wait until I have seen Mr. Gladstone. I might want you again. I always find it so difficult to understand what he really means; and still more so now that he has become so deaf.

SIR HENRY I don't think your Majesty will have any difficulty in understanding him on this occasion.

THE QUEEN Indeed, I hope not. Of course, it is going to be painful; but oh, Sir Henry, such a relief!

439

SIR HENRY Quite so, Ma'am; that, I can fully appreciate.

THE QUEEN Then please see that that letter goes at once.

> (SIR HENRY *goes out with the letter, but immediately returns.*)

SIR HENRY Mr. Gladstone is here, Ma'am.

THE QUEEN I will see him.

SIR HENRY Mrs. Gladstone also, I am told, has come with him.

THE QUEEN Poor thing, poor thing! What a life he has led her, to be sure. Will you say that I will see her—afterwards.

> (SIR HENRY *bows, and goes; and* THE QUEEN *continues her writing. Presently the door opens and a* COURT ATTENDANT *makes announcement.*)

ATTENDANT Mr. Gladstone, your Majesty.

> (MR. GLADSTONE *enters, halts at the threshold, and bows low.* THE QUEEN *rises slowly,* MR. GLADSTONE *advances, and bows again over the hand which she raises toward him.*)

THE QUEEN Good morning, Mr. Gladstone. This was not too early for you, I hope?

GLADSTONE Far from it, your Majesty. For the purpose which brings me here, by your Majesty's gracious permission, the earlier the better—for all parties.

THE QUEEN I was not thinking of *parties*, Mr. Gladstone. But to-day I have much to do, which must be

440

done at once—arrangements that cannot wait. My Government must be carried on by somebody. That was my reason for naming so early an hour.

GLADSTONE I thank your Majesty for so graciously explaining.

THE QUEEN (*seating herself*) I only wished you to know. . . . And now, Mr. Gladstone, I am ready to hear anything that you have to tell me.

GLADSTONE (*left standing*) I have already received your Majesty's gracious permission to make resignation of my office as Prime Minister of your Majesty's Government. And your Majesty has granted me this interview for the express purpose of placing in your Majesty's hands this letter tendering that resignation, as, in humble duty, I now do.

> (*He advances and presents the letter, which she takes and lays on the table at her side.*)

THE QUEEN Thank you. Thank you, Mr. Gladstone. Is there anything further you wish to say?

GLADSTONE (*after a pause*) On this last occasion, Ma'am, I feel myself under a deep obligation to express to your Majesty, my sense of the high honour that your Majesty has conferred on me in permitting me once more to be Prime Minister and Head of your Majesty's Government. That office it has been my honour to hold four times, at your Majesty's command, over a considerable period of years. Circumstances have now made it imperative that I can hold it no more.

THE QUEEN I think you have done right, Mr. Gladstone, your health not being what it was.

441

GLADSTONE The reasons for my resignation, Ma'am, are given in that letter. They are not political, they are personal. The Government which, at your Majesty's command, I formed two years ago, has still, I believe, the confidence of the Country; and in the House of Commons it continues to have a majority. Elsewhere, it is not so fortunate. But so long as it stood for policies approved by the electorate, it would have been my duty, and my earnest endeavour, to remain responsible, under your Majesty's commission, for the carrying of those policies into law. But my physical powers have failed me. My eyesight and my hearing no longer enable me to fulfil adequately the duties which my office requires. I have not consciously delayed, Ma'am, in seeking the relief which has become necessary. The close of the session gave a natural opportunity, of which your Majesty has now graciously permitted me to avail myself.

THE QUEEN Thank you, Mr. Gladstone; you have explained the position very clearly. I quite understand. I am so sorry that you should have any trouble or anxiety about your eyes. Pray have them seen to at once; and do take a good rest. I may say at once that the reasons you have stated are quite sufficient. I accept your resignation.

(MR. GLADSTONE *bows*.)

It has been a long time, has it not, since you first took office?

GLADSTONE About fifty-three years ago, Ma'am, I first had the honour.

THE QUEEN How much has happened since then, has it not? What changes!

442

GLADSTONE We have indeed, Ma'am, seen great changes. In the life of the Nation, as well as in our own.

THE QUEEN Yes,.and changes which have not always been for the better, I fear.

GLADSTONE There have been mistakes, Ma'am, no doubt. We all make them.

THE QUEEN Yes. . . . And then others have to pay for them—unfortunately. . . . I understand, Mr. Gladstone, that you would not be willing to accept a peerage?

GLADSTONE With your Majesty's permission, I would say no.

THE QUEEN I would have been glad to offer it.

GLADSTONE I thank your Majesty for so graciously saying.

THE QUEEN It is the least I could do, in consideration of the many years during which you have held such high office, and so much responsibility. For that reason, had you felt able to accept it, I should have been more than willing.

GLADSTONE Again I thank your Majesty. . . . I . . .

(*He pauses; and before the word comes that he wishes to say,* THE QUEEN *has risen, and is once more speaking.*)

THE QUEEN Good-bye, Mr. Gladstone. Will you, please, remember me very specially to dear Mrs. Gladstone. . . . How is she?

GLADSTONE Mrs. Gladstone is here, Ma'am.

THE QUEEN Ah, yes. Sir Henry told me, I remember.

443

GLADSTONE She asks very specially, if, by gracious permission, she may see your Majesty for a few moments before we leave.

THE QUEEN Certainly. Would she, perhaps, like to see me alone?

GLADSTONE I believe she hoped she might see you alone, Ma'am.

THE QUEEN I shall be very pleased. Will you yourself take a message to her, and ask her to come in? And before you go, I have ordered that there shall be some refreshment for you. Good-bye.

(*She extends her hand. He takes it, bowing low.*)

GLADSTONE With most humble duty, I thank your Majesty.

(*He bows himself out.* THE QUEEN *stands looking after him until the door closes. Then, as she returns to her seat, she speaks.*)

THE QUEEN So that is over—at last!

(*She takes up the letter of resignation, and looks at it. Then she rings a handbell. The door opens; an* ATTENDANT *appears.*)

THE QUEEN Tell Sir Henry to come.

(SIR HENRY *is apparently there in waiting. He enters.*)

Sir Henry, this is Mr. Gladstone's letter of resignation. See that it is put safely away.

(SIR HENRY *takes it, and moves to go. The door opens, the* ATTENDANT *announces.*)

ATTENDANT Mrs. Gladstone, your Majesty.

444

(THE QUEEN *rises, and the expression of her face is now quite different from that with which she met, a short while ago, the entry of her great Minister; her liking for the wife being almost as great as her dislike for the husband.*)

THE QUEEN Dear Mrs. Gladstone, I am so pleased to see you.

(MRS. GLADSTONE *curtsies, while* THE QUEEN *holds her hand with hardly any Court formality at all.*)

MRS. GLADSTONE How good of your Majesty to say so. I hoped you would forgive me. I felt I had to come—this last time.

THE QUEEN Oh, yes, of course, I understand. And do, please, sit down. This must be a very trying time for you.

MRS. GLADSTONE (*restraining her tears*) Oh, not for me! It's for him! To have him give up before—before—he has been able to finish what he so hoped, and lived for.

THE QUEEN But how much better, both for him, and for you. It was really the only thing to do. And you must see now that he takes a complete rest. You won't let him touch politics again, will you? Now, promise!

MRS. GLADSTONE (*speaking with difficulty*) Oh, your Majesty! It was to see you . . . so very specially to-day . . . that I came. I wanted . . . to say something.

THE QUEEN Yes?

MRS. GLADSTONE But so difficult!

THE QUEEN I am sure, dear Mrs. Gladstone, anything you wish to say, I shall be willing to hear.

445

MRS. GLADSTONE It is something, which *I* can say, but which he could not; but which I felt you ought to know. I am the only one who can tell you. So I have come. . . .

(*She is crying now; but she controls her voice.*)

It has always been, Ma'am, a great trouble to him—a great grief, that you could not approve of his policy.

THE QUEEN (*stiffening a little*) But his policy was his own choice, Mrs. Gladstone.

MRS. GLADSTONE Yes.

THE QUEEN When I told him—as I often did—how wrong and mistaken it all was, he would not believe me. I did my best. But he would go his own way.

MRS. GLADSTONE Of course, Ma'am, he could not do otherwise, feeling so sure that he was right.

THE QUEEN Whatever his feelings were, Mrs. Gladstone, he did not consult *mine*. If he had any himself, I do not know. But for any pain it may have caused him, *I* am not responsible.

MRS. GLADSTONE But you see, Ma'am, his difficulty. Trying for so many years to mend a great wrong; returning to office for that reason alone; and then—so many hindrances, disappointments, defeats, failures. It was difficult for him to be patient.

THE QUEEN I do not think patience has ever been your husband's strong point, Mrs. Gladstone. He could never stand contradiction. But he has often contradicted *me*.

446

MRS. GLADSTONE Oh, your Majesty, he has his faults, I know. Sometimes he is difficult. But—I have always believed in him, so absolutely! And with his great mind! ... I know that he always meant well!

THE QUEEN I have never blamed *you*, Mrs. Gladstone, for agreeing with your husband. That is always a wife's duty—if possible.

MRS. GLADSTONE We have never quarrelled, Ma'am; never had any difference. Not once. Not once!

THE QUEEN Then I am sure, my dear Mrs. Gladstone, that *you* have nothing with which to reproach yourself. But you had not to meet him over politics, as I had. It has been very unfortunate, of course, and not as I wished. Twenty years ago he told me that he intended to retire from political life; and I advised him to do so. How much happier he would have been had he taken my advice then. All that has happened since has made things so difficult.

MRS. GLADSTONE Oh, yes; but believe me, Ma'am, his devotion to your Majesty, and the Crown, were very great. That *never* altered.

THE QUEEN His political activities have sometimes made that difficult to believe.

MRS. GLADSTONE But I do ask your Majesty to believe it! I do! I do! It is only that I have come to say. Indeed, indeed, Ma'am, his devotion to your Majesty was, and remains still, very great.

THE QUEEN Since you say so, Mrs. Gladstone, I accept your word for it.

MRS. GLADSTONE Will you let me tell him *that*? That you *do* believe?

447

THE QUEEN If it is any comfort for you to tell him so—or for him to hear it—you may tell him that I *do*.

MRS. GLADSTONE Oh, I am so grateful, so grateful, that you will let me tell him that. And that you *do* really believe it.

THE QUEEN Then go now, and tell him at once; for he is waiting.

(*She rises.*)

Good-bye! We shan't often meet again, I suppose? But it has always been a pleasure for me to see you. And I would like you to know that I shall always remember and think of you as a friend. Good-bye, dear Mrs. Gladstone.

(*Speechless,* MRS. GLADSTONE *receives the kiss* THE QUEEN *bestows upon her, curtsies deeply, kisses her hand, and goes.* THE QUEEN *rings, and the Attendant enters for orders.*)

THE QUEEN Send Sir Henry to me at once.

(SIR HENRY *enters after only a moment or two.*)

THE QUEEN Ah, there you are, Sir Henry. Have you been with Mr. Gladstone.

SIR HENRY No, Ma'am; I was waiting, in case your Majesty required me.

THE QUEEN Have you any news yet from Lord Rosebery?

SIR HENRY I have just received a message to say that his answer will be here in a few hours. He indicates, Ma'am, that it may be 'Yes.'

THE QUEEN It could hardly be otherwise. I would not have had anyone else. Had he declined I should have insisted on a dissolution.

SIR HENRY How did you find Mr. Gladstone, Ma'am?

THE QUEEN Very deaf; but able to talk as much as ever. . . . Poor Mrs. Gladstone! For her I am very sorry. Dear, nice creature! What a fate!

Painful Necessity

'Painful Necessity'

1898

THE QUEEN *is seated in one of the Royal Apartments at Windsor. A door opens: a Gentleman enters, and announces,* 'LORD KITCHENER OF KHARTOUM, *your Majesty.' And as this most recent and distinguished recipient of the Royal Favour enters,* THE QUEEN *does him the great honour of rising, and the further honour of presenting him with her hand, over which he jerks a bow.*

THE QUEEN Lord Kitchener, we are very pleased to meet you.

KITCHENER I thank your Majesty for the great honour. Also for the title which your Majesty has now conferred on me.

THE QUEEN You have *quite* deserved it, Lord Kitchener: far more than others I could name, to whom—on the advice of my Ministers—I am obliged to give titles, and marks of distinction, for things which have *not* pleased me.

KITCHENER Which means, I hope, that your Majesty is pleased with *me*?

THE QUEEN Very pleased, Lord Kitchener! I don't think anyone else could have done better.

KITCHENER If your Majesty is satisfied, so am I.

THE QUEEN More than satisfied. You have not only upheld the honour of your Country, you have restored to it what it had *lost*. . . . Well, we won't talk politics; but there was a great deal in the Egyptian policy of my Ministers which I could *not* approve. That is all over, thanks to *you*! And I hope we shall always *keep* Egypt— for the benefit of its native population, as well as for our own.

KITCHENER I hope so, Ma'am: I think so. A little taste of possession goes a long way—settles it, makes it become a habit. After we've been in Egypt fifteen years, it's getting difficult to make a real Englishman believe that it's not just as much ours as India, or any of the other Colonies.

THE QUEEN Well, Lord Kitchener, you call that 'habit.' I call it experience, and the 'political instinct' for which the British race has always been famous. And (the Suez Canal being the way to India) so necessary. If we lost *that*, we might lose India, too.

KITCHENER We might, Ma'am.

THE QUEEN I don't mind telling you, Lord Kitchener, that there is every prospect of my sending you back to India, before long. *I* wish it; and my Ministers are beginning to agree that it will be the best thing possible for India, and for everybody concerned.

KITCHENER I shall always be at your Majesty's orders: a soldier's first duty.

THE QUEEN Yes; and you are a *real* soldier, Lord Kitchener: you don't merely *look* one. (*At this compliment,*

454

Lord Kitchener jerks a bow.) . . . May I have your photograph?

KITCHENER Most honoured, your Majesty.

THE QUEEN Will you send it me—signed? A large and full-length one, please; because you are so tall—as a soldier ought to be.

KITCHENER To that, Ma'am, there are some good exceptions.

THE QUEEN Oh, yes; Lord Roberts is quite a little man, isn't he? But a thorough soldier. I always like meeting him—so loyal, and genuine, and such a good Christian.

KITCHENER He's a very good fellow, Ma'am. He has no jealousy; and that—in the higher ranks—is a rare quality.

THE QUEEN Very satisfactory. Then I hope you and he get on well together. . . . Now do, please, sit down, Lord Kitchener; because there is something rather serious I want to talk to you about. . . . (*With a bow, he seats himself.*) I am quite sure you did it for the best, and thought it necessary; and, of course, as far as *he* was concerned, just what he deserved, and a very good punishment, too! But I don't like it! . . . I mean this digging up of the Mahdi, and the destruction of his tomb. One doesn't like doing that to dead people—if it can be avoided. The Archbishop of Canterbury spoke to me about it, directly it was done. *He* didn't quite like it, either.

KITCHENER No, Ma'am, I daresay not. The Church has often to think and speak one way—for the sake of appearances—while the Army and the Politicians—for getting the thing done—have to think, speak, and act another way.

THE QUEEN (*doubtfully*) Yes; I suppose so. . . . Still— to a dead body—was it necessary?

KITCHENER As he had cut off Gordon's head, Ma'am, we had to cut off *his*—as an example.

(THE QUEEN *had not thought of this.*)

THE QUEEN Yes; *that* I can understand. . . .

KITCHENER And after all, Ma'am, in this Country we've done the same.

THE QUEEN Oh, but surely not!

KITCHENER Yes, Ma'am; we dug up Oliver Cromwell —tarred and feathered him, and hung him up at Westminster, as a warning to others.

THE QUEEN (*approvingly*) Ah, yes; but then, he'd killed his *King*!

KITCHENER Yes, Ma'am; but we also took up Admiral Blake out of Westminster Abbey, and treated him much the same; though he himself had had no hand in killing the King. It was just a form of government which had to be put down, in such a way that it should never come up again. And that was the shortest and cheapest way to it.

THE QUEEN In this case, it has caused more comment than I like.

KITCHENER Yes, Ma'am; from ignorant people.

THE QUEEN But some of them very highly placed, and of excellent character.

KITCHENER Yes, Ma'am; but high place, and excellence do not preclude ignorance—especially when dealing with the customs and superstitions of the East. The Mahdi almost founded a new religion—or, anyway, revived the fanaticism of an old one; and his Tomb would have become the centre of it. Mohammedanism wouldn't be nearly so strong and fanatical as it is, Ma'am, if it hadn't Mohammed's Tomb, and the pilgrimages to it, year in, year out, to keep it going. It would have been just the same had we left the Mahdi where his followers had buried him in triumph—a triumph which, for them, meant a triumph over Christianity, Ma'am.

THE QUEEN Yes; well, of course, that *had* to be prevented somehow. You cut off his head, you say? And what did you do with it?

KITCHENER Made it into an ink-pot, Ma'am.

THE QUEEN (*judicially*) I don't quite like that, Lord Kitchener.

KITCHENER You would, Ma'am, if you saw it. It looks very handsome mounted in silver.

THE QUEEN I mean, I'm rather sorry you should put it to such a use: rather gruesome, and a little—unkind.

KITCHENER It wasn't ever my duty to be kind to *him*, Ma'am. It makes an interesting souvenir for my study; and in helping me to write my official reports, is more usefully and honourably employed than it ever was in the lifetime of its late owner. I thought, Ma'am, I was doing him rather an honour.

THE QUEEN No, Lord Kitchener, please put it away!

KITCHENER I will, Ma'am, I will. . . . Your Majesty would not like to have it for the Windsor Museum?

THE QUEEN No, Lord Kitchener, I think not. Very kind of you to offer it.

457

KITCHENER It would have been a great honour for *him*, Ma'am.

THE QUEEN Yes: but I shouldn't like my Mohammedan subjects to know. It might give them a wrong impression. They might be hurt.

KITCHENER They might, Ma'am; I don't know. We should only be doing to him what the Roman Church has done all down the ages to its own Saints and Martyrs.

THE QUEEN The same thing? How do you mean, Lord Kitchener?

KITCHENER By cutting them up into small pieces, Ma'am, and packing them off, here, there, and everywhere, to be venerated.

THE QUEEN Yes; but to be *venerated*.

KITCHENER The breaking open of tombs, and the dismemberment of their occupants happens in both cases, Ma'am; but for different reasons. The Roman Church does it to encourage superstition; we've done it to put it down; and we've done it very successfully. That, Ma'am, by itself, I think, sufficiently justified the doing of it.

THE QUEEN (*still a little dubious*) Yes, I suppose it does, then. Though I wish it had not been necessary. It didn't seem quite Christian.

KITCHENER Christianity is rather thrown away, Ma'am, in dealing with false prophets, and people of that sort. It was a bloody tyranny, and it had to be put down. The Soudan is now under decent government: in a few years' time, at the present rate of progress, it will be self-supporting, and may even bring us in revenue.

458

THE QUEEN Very satisfactory. And is there any prospect of the natives becoming Christian, now that they see what Christianity really means?

KITCHENER The missionaries would say yes, Ma'am. They always do, in order to justify the expenditure of their missions, and their large families, for which they get a capitation grant. . . . I don't know. Gordon (who knew more about it than most people) said that if the Bishops would only allow polygamy among the natives, Christianity could sweep up the whole of North Africa.

THE QUEEN (*scandalised*) Gordon! General Gordon said that? And he such a good Christian! No, Lord Kitchener, that could never be allowed. Christian morals and principles must not be tampered with, however advantageous the results might seem. It would not be Christianity at all! it would be a reversion to paganism.

KITCHENER Only to the Old Testament, Ma'am.

THE QUEEN Ah! but the Old Testament tells us that polygamy was never a success. David, and Solomon, and even Abraham were examples of that.

KITCHENER Well, Ma'am, on those matters,—being myself a bachelor—I am not an authority.

THE QUEEN Aren't you ever going to marry, Lord Kitchener?

KITCHENER I hope not, Ma'am; not, at any rate, till I have retired from active service.

THE QUEEN But won't that be too late?

KITCHENER Marriage takes up too much time, Ma'am, for a man of my profession.

459

THE QUEEN But are not most of the officers of my Army married, Lord Kitchener?

KITCHENER Yes, Ma'am, and in my estimation none the better for it. When on active service, it makes them mope, and spend a lot of time writing to their wives things that aren't true.

THE QUEEN Not true?

KITCHENER Nobody writes the truth, Ma'am—about War, in letters to his women at home. It couldn't be done.

THE QUEEN Well, of course, women don't *have* to know all the truth; so why should they? The details are too unpleasant.

KITCHENER The whole thing's too unpleasant, Ma'am: except what appears in the papers. That has to be done—to make War popular.

THE QUEEN Yes, I suppose so: a painful necessity; but it has to be. My Empire couldn't get on without occasional wars, I'm afraid; though I wish it could.

KITCHENER Nobody wishes that, Ma'am, more than the married men in the Army. That's why I prefer them unmarried.

THE QUEEN Oh, I see. Well, Lord Kitchener, you have interested me very much: and you have also set my mind at rest on a matter that was rather troubling me. I shall write, and tell the Archbishop all that you have said: and I am sure that he will now agree, and see how necessary it was. . . . (*She rises, and again offers him her hand.*) Good-bye, Lord Kitchener; I am so glad to have met you. And you will be sure to send me that photograph, to which I am looking forward, and shall always greatly value.

KITCHENER I will, Ma'am; indeed, I will.

(*And with no more grace of movement than of mind,*
LORD KITCHENER *bows himself stiffly out.*
THE QUEEN *watches him go, then settles back*
comfortably into her seat—tired, but quite
pleased.)

THE QUEEN What a *nice* man!

Happy and Glorious

Happy and Glorious

20th June 1897

From that 'great relief,' confirmed by the voice of the electorate two years later, THE QUEEN *passes serenely on to the culminating triumph of her reign. The Diamond Jubilee provides material for a tableau rather than a play; and it is as a tableau that we have here presented to us this gathering together, at Buckingham Palace, of more than fifty of the Queen's direct descendants, together with representatives of all the crowned heads of a Europe still at peace.*

The Triumphal Procession is over, and the large upper chamber becomes filled with Royalty. Bonnets, costumes, uniforms mingle in a moving clash of colours; Orders sparkle, sword-chains clink, spurs jingle. Their owners step delicately, bowing their way from group to group; and—some now encountering for the first time—high form and ceremony are still the rule. But here and there Members of the Royal Family, meeting each other, exchange remarks of a familiar character, though sometimes in a foreign accent. And as all (except an Official or two) who thus mix and converse are Royal Highnesses —if nothing more—there is no need to trouble about names. Nobody to-day, except THE QUEEN *herself (and perhaps the Heir-Apparent) is individually important.*

465

So, not as individuals but in the group, we listen to their ROYAL HIGHNESSES *chatting among themselves over the events of the day, filling up time till the Chief Character makes her appearance.*

ROYAL HIGHNESSES Well! So that's over! . . . How beautifully everything went! . . . Excellently! . . . Very well indeed! . . . Nothing could have been better! . . . I hope Mamma enjoyed it as much as we did. . . . Oh, I'm sure she did. . . . What crowds! What cheering! And what perfect order! . . . Yes, the English are a wonderful people. . . . Have you seen Mamma, since she got back? . . . Yes, I have just been with her. . . . How has she borne it? . . . Oh, she's all right. She will be up in a minute. They are getting her into her chair.

AN IMPERIAL HIGHNESS My dear Uncle Bertie, congratulations! What a glorious landmark in the annals of your great Nation!

HIS ROYAL HIGHNESS Thank you. Yes, very satisfactory, I think. I am so glad that you were able to be present.

AN IMPERIAL HIGHNESS Ach! I would not have missed it for anything!

HIS ROYAL HIGHNESS (*to an* OFFICIAL) Sir Arthur, will you please to give orders for the window to be ready?

> (SIR ARTHUR *bows, and goes to give the order. Presently two Footmen enter, and undo the bolts of the centre window. A Court Official enters, comes to His Royal Highness, bows, and makes a communication.*)

466

HIS ROYAL HIGHNESS (*to* HIS IMPERIAL HIGHNESS) Excuse me for one moment.

SIR ARTHUR (*to the Footmen*) Do not go; remain.

> (*They stand to attention on either side of the window. And now, from the corridor outside, comes an approaching sound—a mingling of voices, footsteps, and a low rolling of wheels; and* THE QUEEN *enters, seated in her wheeled chair, accompanied by her two Sons. The assembled Family and the Royal Guests, with the formality befitting a great occasion, bow low upon her entrance. The word 'Congratulations' emerges from the general hum of voices. Then expressions of affection take the place of ceremony.*)

A ROYAL PRINCESS Mamma, dear, how are you?

THE QUEEN Very tired, my dear; but oh, so happy! . . . To think now that it is all over! . . . So glad that I had the strength for it!

PRINCESS And the courage, Mamma, dear!

ANOTHER PRINCESS You were quite wonderful, Mamma!

THE QUEEN Yes, so the Doctor tells me. He has just felt my pulse and taken my temperature. And he says that he could not have believed it possible. Oh, I'm—I'm so thankful!

HIS ROYAL HIGHNESS So is everybody. And now, Mamma, I think you had better take a glass of wine. It will do you good.

THE QUEEN Thank you.

HIS ROYAL HIGHNESS And may we also drink to your good health, Mamma?

THE QUEEN Certainly; why, yes, certainly! Please, all of you!

> (*In the background Attendants have already begun serving wine into glasses. A glass is brought to* THE QUEEN.)

THE QUEEN What is it?

HIS ROYAL HIGHNESS Champagne, Mamma.

THE QUEEN No, no; I will have sherry. (*So sherry is brought.*) How long has it taken?

PRINCESS Nearly three hours, Mamma.

THE QUEEN Oh, dear me! And it seems like yesterday and to-morrow—almost! . . . Three hours!

HIS ROYAL HIGHNESS Your Imperial and Royal Highnesses, I have great pleasure in asking you to drink to the health of Her Majesty, the Queen. May she continue long, in health and prosperity, to enjoy the love of her Children and her people.

> (*The health is drunk with decorous enthusiasm.* THE QUEEN *sits bowing her acknowledgments to all the assembled Family, with tears and smiles.*)

THE QUEEN Thank you! Oh, thank you!

PRINCESS Won't you go and rest now, Mamma?

THE QUEEN Not yet. . . . That cheering that I hear means that my dear people are expecting to see me again. I must try not to disappoint them.

PRINCESS It would be nice if you could, Mamma. You think you can?

468

THE QUEEN Yes, but I can't get up. I must go as I am.
Have the windows opened.

> (*The windows are opened by the Footmen; the
> cheering swells.*)

THE QUEEN Yes, but over the balustrade, they will not
be able to see me. I must be raised. Tell them to bring
in the sliding dais.

HIS ROYAL HIGHNESS It is already there in position,
Mamma.

THE QUEEN Really! How thoughtful!

> (*And so, when the window is opened, the sliding dais
> is let down from without into the window-
> frame. While this is being done with quiet
> efficiency by the well-trained Footmen, the
> QUEEN continues speaking.*)

Then, now, will you, Bertie, and some of the others
go out, and let them know that I am coming? Not too
many, just a few.

> (*So six members of the Royal Family go out on to the
> balcony, and the cheering grows louder.* THE
> QUEEN, *seeing that the dais is now in position,
> makes a gesture of command, and the chair,
> slowly propelled, mounts the ramp prepared
> for it, and passes into the balcony. Immediately
> the cheering becomes tremendous, and would go
> on without abatement for much longer than
> exhausted old human nature can allow.* THE
> QUEEN *gives the signal for retirement; the
> chair is withdrawn, and backs into its former
> central position; and the Royal Family retire,*

469

bowing, from the public gaze. The dais is lifted, the window is closed again.)

THE QUEEN It's very gratifying, very, to find—after all these years—that they do appreciate all that I have tried to do for them—for their good, and for this great Country of ours. We have been so near together to-day—they and I: all my dear people of England, and Scotland—*and* Ireland, and the dear Colonies, and India. From all round the world I have had messages. Such loyalty—such devotion! Most extraordinary! Tell Mr. Chamberlain how very much I approve of all the arrangements he made for the proper representation of all parts of my Empire in the Procession. Everything so perfectly in order. Most gratifying! . . . Well, I must go now and rest, or I shall not be able to take my place at dinner to-night, and that would never do! . . . So happy! . . . As we were coming back—you were in front, Bertie, so perhaps you didn't see—it was just by Hyde Park Corner, there was a great crowd there; and a lot of rough men—of course it ought not to have happened, but it didn't matter—broke right through the lines of the police and troops guarding the route; and they ran alongside the carriage, shouting and cheering me. And I heard them say: 'Go it, Old Girl! You've done it well! You've done it well!' Of course, very unsuitable—the words; but so gratifying! And oh, I hope it's true! I hope it's true! . . . Hark! They are still cheering. . . . Albert! Ah! if only you could have been here!

(And, having said her say, the great, wonderful, little old Lady gives the signal to her Attendants, and is wheeled slowly away.)

DIEU ET MON DROIT

171·